Words of Life 2010

Words of Life 2010

Daily Reflections for Your Spirit

Edited by Caryl Green

NOVALIS

© 2010 Novalis Publishing Inc.

Cover design: Audrey Wells
Cover illustration: Sue Todd
Layout: Audrey Wells

Published by Novalis
10 Lower Spadina Avenue, Suite 400
Toronto, Ontario, Canada
M5V 2Z2
www.novalis.ca

Library and Archives Canada Cataloguing in Publication
Words of life 2010 daily reflections for your spirit / edited by Caryl Green.

ISBN 978-2-89646-170-7

    1. Bible–Meditations. 2. Spiritual life–Christianity–Meditations.
3. Devotional calendars. I. Green, Caryl

Printed in Canada.

We acknowledge the financial support of the Government of Canada through
the Book Publishing Industry Development Program (BPIDP) for our publishing
activities.

Since its launch in 1998 as a monthly magazine, *Words of Life* has provided readers with passages drawn from Scripture, along with reflections and prayers for each day. This book is based upon those reflections and on the Scripture readings for Year C.

The reflections in *Words of Life* draw their inspiration from Scripture *and* from everyday life experiences. The stories in *Words of Life* describe situations when authors have chosen to live according to God's word, in matters both large and small. That choice influenced not only their own lives, but also the lives of family members, friends and colleagues, and the wider community.

I would like thank everyone who contributed to this publication – authors, editors, proofreaders, photographers and designers. A special thanks goes to the authors who have shared so generously of themselves. (A list of authors appears at the end of this book.)

Words of Life offers us a still point in our busy lives to be with God's word. I hope you will be able to take a few moments each day with *Words of Life* – to be aware of God's presence in your life, and to know the deep peace and joy that God's love offers.

Caryl Green

Editor

S o they hurried off and found Mary and Joseph and saw the baby lying in the manger. When the shepherds saw him, they told them what the angel had said about the child. All who heard it were amazed at what the shepherds said. Mary remembered all these things and thought deeply about them. The shepherds went back, singing praises to God for all they had heard and seen; it had been just as the angel had told them.

A week later, when the time came for the baby to be circumcised, he was named Jesus, the name that the angel had given him before he had been conceived.

Luke 2: 16-21

"…singing praises to God…"

Emotional moments

Our daughter went with five other families to Ethiopia, to adopt an orphan. At the foster home, the staff joked, "If you can identify your child, you can have her!" Tentatively, each mother-to-be reached for one of the babies sleeping on a big rug. They looked so tiny, so vulnerable lying there.

Sharon had never seen little Katherine before. But as she picked her up, as each mother in turn held her baby close, tears began to flow. Glasses fogged up. There was not a dry eye in the room… and probably not in the stable in Bethlehem, either! No wonder the shepherds went out, telling everyone what they had seen. Small babies tend to have that effect, especially in unusual circumstances.

Give me a soft heart, God.
Let it overflow whenever I see kindness, gentleness and love.

Themed by: The Jewish authorities sent some priests and Levites to John to ask him, "Who are you? Are you Elijah?" "No, I am not," John answered. "Are you the Prophet?" they asked. "No," he replied. "Then tell us who you are. We have to take an answer back to those who sent us...."

John answered by quoting the prophet Isaiah: "I am 'the voice of someone shouting in the desert: Make a straight path for the Lord to travel!'" The messengers then asked John, "If you are not the Messiah nor Elijah nor the Prophet, why do you baptize?"

John answered, "I baptize with water, but among you stands the one you do not know. He is coming after me, but I am not good enough even to untie his sandals."

John 1: 19-28

> "Make a straight path for the Lord to travel!"

A city's wilderness

January 2nd already! It seems like yesterday that we held our annual Christmas Tree party early in December. Every year we ask our guests for donations of food for St. Francis' Table, a restaurant serving the poor in Parkdale. Collecting for The Table – our friends bring things like canned spaghetti, apple juice and tuna fish – is one of the highlights of Christmas for me.

Parkdale is an area of rooming houses and welfare hotels, hungry kids and new immigrants. Someone with the voice of John the Baptist could shout about the injustices of life in the desert wilderness of Parkdale. I do my small part to make a straight path for the Lord to travel: taking donations of canned spaghetti, apple juice and tuna fish to The Table.

**Lord, may my actions speak for me:
making the rough places smooth, wherever they can.**

S ome men who studied the stars came from the East and asked, "Where is the baby born to be the king of the Jews? We saw his star when it came up in the east, and we have come to worship him...."

When King Herod heard about this, he was very upset... and so he called together all the chief priests and the teachers of the Law and asked them, "Where will the Messiah be born?" ... Herod called the visitors from the East to a secret meeting.... Then he sent them to Bethlehem with these instructions: "Go and make a careful search for the child; and when you find him, let me know, so that I too may go and worship him...." They returned to their country by another road, since God had warned them in a dream not to go back to Herod.

Matthew 2: 1-12

> "They returned to their country by another road..."

A different way

What if the visitors from the East had followed Herod's instructions? What if they had returned to Herod, instead of leaving by another route? The decision they made was a rebellious and defiant one. Did those visitors realize the significance of their decision for future generations? Today, we see its consequences: Jesus would not have lived and there would have been no Messiah.

Sometimes my teenagers go against my instructions. As a parent trying to guide them, I find it hard not to criticize their decisions.

I need to be open to the possibility that they can make good choices and that joy can be found in unexpected places. I need to have faith that the Spirit is guiding them in their journey along life's paths.

Lord, help me to accept that I don't always know best, and that the Spirit moves where it wills.

"The people who live in darkness will see a great light. On those who live in the dark land of death the light will shine." From that time Jesus began to preach his message: "Turn away from your sins, because the kingdom of heaven is near!"

Jesus went all over Galilee, teaching in the synagogues, preaching the Good News about the kingdom, and healing people who had all kinds of disease and sickness. The news about him spread through the whole country of Syria, so that people brought to him all those who were sick, suffering from all kinds .of diseases and disorders: people with demons, and epileptics, and paralytics – and Jesus healed them all. *Matthew 4: 12-17, 23-25*

> "The people who live in darkness
> will see a great light."

God's healing touch

It would be easy to focus on a God who was active in another time. But God is present among us today – not to oversee and observe, but rather to seek us out. God is in relationship with us *now*: actively calling and inviting us to respond. How do I hear God's word today? Where do I experience God's presence in my life?

Today's scripture notes that people responded to the presence of Jesus by bringing him those who were sick, suffering and stressed. The darkness of their pain was released through his caring touch. How I yearn to feel that healing touch, that loving embrace. To hear his voice telling me that I am accepted, loved. To know myself healed, made whole. To live again.

**O God, I open myself to the wonder of your presence.
Touch me, heal me, renew me.**

J esus' disciples came to him and said, "It is already very late.... Send the people away to the nearby farms and villages... in order to buy themselves something to eat."

"You yourselves give them something to eat," Jesus answered. They asked, "Do you want us to go and spend two hundred silver coins on bread in order to feed them?" So Jesus asked them, "How much bread do you have...?" They told him, "Five loaves and also two fish."

Jesus took the five loaves and the two fish, looked up to heaven, and gave thanks to God. He broke the loaves and gave them to his disciples to distribute. He also divided the two fish among them all. Everyone ate and had enough. Then the disciples took up twelve baskets full of what was left of the bread and the fish.

Mark 6: 34-44

"How much bread do you have?"

More than enough

Once my class of special education students was reading a book about a poor, single mother who was asked to take an orphaned child into her home of four children. I asked my class to consider how she could do this. Could she have enough love left over for another child?

One of the students was genuinely surprised by my question and answered without hesitation: "The more children you have, the more love you have. It's like the more love you need to give, the more you have to give."

How like the apostles I'd been, trying to measure love in amounts. My student knew about the magical power of need: how God provides love in abundance – if we're open to receiving it.

Lord, when I feel empty,
help me to trust in your abundant love.

Jesus made his disciples get into the boat and go ahead of him.... When evening came, the boat was in the middle of the lake, while Jesus was alone on land. He saw that his disciples were straining at the oars; so sometime between three and six o'clock in the morning, he came to them, walking on the water. He was going to pass them by, but they saw him walking on the water. "It's a ghost!" they thought, and screamed. They were all terrified when they saw him.

Jesus spoke to them at once, "Courage!" he said. "It is I. Don't be afraid!" Then he got into the boat with them, and the wind died down.

Mark 6: 45-52

"Courage. It is I. Don't be afraid!"

Calm amidst the storm

While his disciples battle the waves, Jesus walks over the water to check on them. When the disciples cringe, thinking he is a ghost, Jesus admonishes them to be brave.

Yet at times, fear is a reasonable reaction. While some may fear bees, heights or flying, often our fears are based on painful experiences. I fear water because of an ice accident that almost killed me when I was twelve.

As spectacular as this storm-defying and water-walking Jesus may be, one of the important lessons is his ability to take my fears in hand and give me reason to trust in him. Jesus stands with me in my fear and invites me to embrace the God who knows me – even my fears – and loves me totally.

Lord, you know my fears. Be with me and help me to live through my fears with courage and strength.

Teach the king to judge with your righteousness, O God;
share with him your own justice,
so that he will rule over your people with justice
and govern the oppressed with righteousness....
He rescues them from oppression and violence;
their lives are precious to him.
Long live the king!
May he be given gold from Sheba;
may prayers be said for him at all times;
may God's blessings be on him always....
May the king's name never be forgotten;
may his fame last as long as the sun.
May all nations ask God to bless them
as he has blessed the king.

Psalm 72: 1-2, 14-17

> "...share with him your own justice..."

Faith and politics

As a citizen of the United States, I have disagreed with many of my nation's policies. I've written to newspapers and government representatives, put signs in my yard, and marched in the streets. I've even participated in acts of civil disobedience and served time in jail. I do these things as a citizen; this is part of democracy.

But I also do these things as a Christian. Not that I want my country to become Christian; it is, and should be, a place for persons of any faith. But I do long for justice. And I believe, as did the Jewish theologian, Abraham Joshua Heschel, that protest can be a prayer asking God to teach our leaders to govern with justice.

God, help me be a citizen who both prays and works for justice.

Once Jesus was in a town where there was a man who was suffering from a dreaded skin disease. When he saw Jesus, he threw himself down and begged him, "Sir, if you want to, you can make me clean!"

Jesus reached out and touched him. "I do want to," he answered. "Be clean!" At once the disease left the man. Jesus ordered him, "Don't tell anyone, but go straight to the priest and let him examine you; then to prove to everyone that you are cured, offer the sacrifice as Moses ordered." But the news about Jesus spread all the more widely,

and crowds of people came to hear him and be healed from their diseases. But he would go away to lonely places, where he prayed.
Luke 5: 12-16

"Jesus would go away to lonely places, where he prayed…"

Finding the time

So much work, so little time! Jesus had sermons to preach, sins to forgive, countless desperate people to heal – people like the man afflicted with a dreaded skin disease. How could Jesus find time for anything else? And yet that's just what he did. Again and again Jesus went away to lonely places to pray.

I know that when responsibilities engulf my whole life, I lose my grip, make bad decisions and work less effectively.

It takes an effort to change my life in order to make time for reflection. I know I can set my alarm earlier, use my trip to work, or get away for a brief walk during the day. With planning and persistence, I can find time in my busy life for prayer.

Lord, teach me to be attentive to you in scripture, silence and prayer.

S ome of John's disciples told him, "Teacher, you remember the man who was with you on the east side of the Jordan, the one you spoke about? Well, he is baptizing now, and everyone is going to him!"

John answered, "No one can have anything unless God gives it. You yourselves are my witnesses that I said, 'I am not the Messiah, but I have been sent ahead of him.' The bridegroom is the one to whom the bride belongs; but the bridegroom's friend, who stands by and listens, is glad when he hears the bridegroom's voice. This is how my own happiness is made complete. He must become more important while I become less important." *John 3: 22-30*

> "...while I become less important."

True humility

John the Baptist was an amazing man of humility. Many times over the course of my life, I have found myself threatened by the successes of other people. Somehow it disturbed me to see them do well. I wanted to scream, "Look at me, too!" or worse yet, to quietly criticize what they did as, "Well, it was good, but..." I lived in fear there would be no attention left for me.

John lives differently. He has heard and understood Jesus' message. He knows the source of all gifts is God alone. John recognizes the bridegroom's voice, and simply rejoices in it. What's more, it brings him complete happiness!

Can you believe it? Room for everyone's gifts, and happiness for all! Competition is made bankrupt by the gospel!

God, increase my faith in your generosity.
Let me recognize and rejoice in the gifts of others.

People's hopes began to rise, and they began to wonder whether John perhaps might be the Messiah. So John said to all of them, "I baptize you with water, but someone is coming who is much greater than I am. I am not good enough even to untie his sandals. He will baptize you with the Holy Spirit and fire."

After all the people had been baptized, Jesus also was baptized. While he was praying, heaven was opened and the Holy Spirit came down upon him in bodily form like a dove. And a voice came from heaven, "You are my own dear Son. I am pleased with you."

Luke 3: 15-16, 21-22

"You are my own dear Son. I am pleased with you."

All children of God

Whenever I hear these words spoken by John the Baptist I shiver a little. Look at John: the virtuous one who followed an austere lifestyle and preached a powerful message of repentance. But comparing himself to Jesus, he thinks only of his unworthiness. Where does that leave the rest of us?

Yet "after all the people had been baptized," Jesus then steps forward to be baptized. Does Jesus let himself be baptized because he identifies with us, ordinary humans that we are? Jesus was no stranger to hunger, thirst, pain and sorrow, just as we are.

Perhaps he also wants us to identify with him as he stands there in the waters of the Jordan. We, like Jesus, are all children of a God who loves us dearly.

**God, help me hear your voice saying,
"You are my own dear child, and I am pleased with you."**

J esus went to Galilee and preached the Good News from God. "The right time has come," he said, "and the kingdom of God is near! Turn away from your sins and believe the Good News!"

As Jesus walked along the shore of Lake Galilee, he saw two fishermen, Simon and his brother Andrew, catching fish with a net. Jesus said to them, "Come with me, and I will teach you to catch people." At once they left their nets and went with him.

He went a little farther on and saw two other brothers, James and John, the sons of Zebedee. They were in their boat getting their nets ready. As soon as Jesus saw them, he called them; they left their father Zebedee in the boat with the hired men and went with Jesus.

Mark 1: 14-20

> "At once they left their nets and went with him."

Committed to...

It sounds so simple. Jesus says, "Follow me," and the disciples do it, leaving everything behind. Including, apparently, at least one wife – because Mark later tells us about Simon Peter's mother-in-law – and possibly some children. Certainly James and John left their father Zebedee holding his fishing nets, wondering where he could find some reliable new employees.

I think I may have heard Jesus call me several times. But each time I had a wife and kids, a job, a mortgage…. I had commitments. What kind of person would I be if I walked out on my family, my church responsibilities, my Scout group, the career into which I'd already invested so many years?

Maybe life was less complicated back then. Or maybe the disciples just had more nerve than I do.

I hear many voices calling me, Lord.
Help me discern which one is yours, and respond to your call.

J esus went to the synagogue and began to teach. The people were amazed at the way he taught, for he wasn't like the teachers of the Law; instead, he taught with authority.

Just then a man with an evil spirit came into the synagogue and screamed, "What do you want with us, Jesus of Nazareth? Are you here to destroy us? I know who you are – you are God's holy messenger!"

Jesus ordered the spirit, "Be quiet, and come out of the man!" The evil spirit shook the man hard, gave a loud scream, and came out of him. The people were all so amazed that they started saying to one another, "What is this? Is it some kind of new teaching? This man has authority to give orders to the evil spirits, and they obey him!"

Mark 1:21-28

"You are God's holy messenger!"

True authority

Often I see authority in a negative way, as a threat to my freedom. I don't want another person or office to have power over me.

Yet the authority that Jesus displayed was one that people experienced in a positive way. They were amazed because it was a life-giving power such as they had not previously seen or experienced. It set people free from whatever demons held them captive or in pain. People found themselves released and renewed to live as God intended them to live: with a sense of sacredness, of dignity and of purpose.

Am I willing to accept Jesus' authority in my life? Can I allow his values to shape my life and lead me to freedom?

God, my demons hold me captive.
Give me the courage to ask for release, for healing, for freedom.

" I love you just as the Father loves me; remain in my love. If you obey my commands, you will remain in my love…. My commandment is this: love one another, just as I love you. The greatest love you can have for your friends is to give your life for them…. I do not call you servants any longer, because servants do not know what their master is doing. Instead, I call you friends, because I have told you everything I heard from my Father. You did not choose me; I chose you and appointed you to go and bear much fruit, the kind of fruit that endures. And so the Father will give you whatever you ask of him in my name. This, then, is what I command you: love one another."

John 15: 9-17

"The greatest love you can have for your friends…"

The gift of life

When I was in my early twenties I hit a rough patch. I felt depressed, unhappy and lost. I've never felt so bad. A man I knew, but with whom I wasn't especially close, called me one evening. He said he'd been thinking about me and wondering how I was. "Not too good," I said, "but thanks for calling."

He called again the next day with the same message… and the day after that, and the day after that. In fact, he called every day for weeks. Some days his phone call was the only thing that kept me going.

I remember his kindness with gratitude. I know that sometimes giving your life for a friend can mean a simple gift of a few minutes or few words.

Lord, I received life when I needed it. Help me to recognize when others need me to be a life-giver, too.

A man suffering from a dreaded skin disease came to Jesus, knelt down, and begged him for help. "If you want to," he said, "you can make me clean." Jesus was filled with pity, and reached out and touched him. "I do want to," he answered. "Be clean!" At once the disease left the man, and he was clean. Then Jesus spoke sternly to him and sent him away at once, after saying to him, "Listen, don't tell anyone about this. But go straight to the priest and let him examine you...." But the man went away and began to spread the news everywhere.

Mark 1: 40-45

"If you want to, you can make me clean."

Ready to help

A close friend of mine has a problem with gambling. She has borrowed money from everyone; she's even admitted to stealing from the company where she works. She's tried counselling a few times, but hasn't been able to stay with it. Sometimes she feels worthless and defeated.

But there is nothing within the human spirit that God cannot help fix. Regardless of who we are, where we've been, or what we've done, God stands with open arms, ready to assist.

In today's passage, Jesus not only assures the man that he is willing to help, but immediately frees him from his ailment. Whatever prevents me from leading a fulfilled life can be overcome when I ask for – and allow myself to receive – God's help.

**God, help me to turn to you
when I want to 'clean up' the messes in my life.**

J esus was preaching the message to the people when four men arrived, carrying a paralyzed man to Jesus. Because of the crowd, however, they could not get the man to him. So they made a hole in the roof right above the place where Jesus was. When they had made an opening, they let the man down, lying on his mat. Seeing how much faith they had, Jesus said to the paralyzed man, "My son, your sins are forgiven."

Some teachers of the Law thought to themselves, "This is blasphemy! God is the only one who can forgive sins!" Jesus knew what they were thinking, so he said, "Is it easier to say to this paralyzed man, 'Your sins are forgiven,' or to say, 'Get up, pick up your mat, and walk'? I will prove to you, then, that the Son of Man has authority on earth to forgive sins." So he said to the paralyzed man, "I tell you, get up, pick up your mat, and go home!" The man got up, picked up his mat, and hurried away.   *Mark 2: 1-12*

> "...four men arrived, carrying a paralyzed man..."

Faithful friends

I know this story is really about faith, forgiveness and authority. But what I can't get out of my head is the power of friendship. I'm impressed by the determination of the four stretcher carriers. First, they struggled through the crowd with the heavy stretcher. When that proved impossible, they didn't give up. Instead, they climbed onto the roof – with the stretcher – cut a hole, and lowered their friend down right in front of Jesus.

That paralyzed man was truly blessed. His sins were forgiven and his paralysis cured. But the blessing he already had should not be forgotten: four good friends.

**Lord, friendship requires loyalty, persistence and effort.
Help me learn to be a good friend.**

As Jesus walked along, he saw a tax collector, Levi, sitting in his office. Jesus said to him, "Follow me." Levi got up and followed him.

Later on Jesus was having a meal in Levi's house. A large number of tax collectors and other outcasts were following Jesus, and many of them joined him and his disciples at the table. Some teachers of the Law, who were Pharisees, saw that Jesus was eating with these outcasts and tax collectors, so they asked his disciples, "Why does he eat with such people?" Jesus heard them and answered, "People who are well do not need a doctor, but only those who are sick. I have not come to call respectable people, but outcasts." *Mark 2: 13-17*

"People who are well do not need a doctor…"

In need of help

As a teacher, I have always enjoyed those gifted students for whom learning comes naturally, whose papers are polished, who offer insights that pleasantly surprise me. They are 'the respectable' ones for me. And they are few, indeed.

But Jesus suggests that my other students – those who seem hopelessly lost in the material – are the ones who really need my teaching, and who *are* worthy of my efforts.

Jesus' ministry is different from mine and yours: not many of us are full-time evangelists. But his message is clear: I should not avoid dealing with difficult people. Rather, I am called to see them as he does – as people whose loneliness I can dispel, whose pain I can ease, whose brokenness I can mend.

God, help me to see you in the difficult people I meet today.

There was a wedding in the town of Cana in Galilee. Jesus' mother was there, and Jesus and his disciples had also been invited to the wedding. When the wine had given out, Jesus' mother said to him, "They are out of wine."

"You must not tell me what to do," Jesus replied. "My time has not yet come."

Jesus' mother then told the servants, "Do whatever he tells you...."

Jesus said to the servants, "Fill these jars with water.... Now draw some water out and take it to the man in charge of the feast." They took him the water, which now had turned into wine, and he tasted it.... He called the bridegroom and said, "Everyone else serves the best wine first, and after the guests have drunk a lot, he serves the ordinary wine. But you have kept the best wine until now!"

John 2: 1-12

> "Do whatever he tells you…"

A mother's wisdom

A fascinating detail in today's reading, the story of Jesus' first miracle, is the way in which Mary seems to 'push' him towards it. Jesus even rebukes her, saying, "You must not tell me what to do." But Mary seems to know his time has come.

From the beginning, Mary knew who Jesus was. She always knew his calling.

All young adults have to break the ties with their mother. But, at the same time, all know that their mother is the one who knows them best.

Devotion to Mary is a celebration of the wise mother – the one who knows us better than we know ourselves. The one who often encourages us and leads us to become our best selves.

Thank you, God, for wise mothers!

S ome people asked Jesus, "Why is it that the disciples of John the Baptist and the disciples of the Pharisees fast, but yours do not?"

Jesus answered, "Do you expect the guests at a wedding party to go without food? Of course not! As long as the bridegroom is with them, they will not do that. But the day will come when the bridegroom will be taken away from them, and then they will fast.

"No one uses a piece of new cloth to patch up an old coat, because the new patch will shrink and tear off some of the old cloth, making an even bigger hole. Nor does anyone pour new wine into used wineskins, because the wine will burst the skins, and both the wine and the skins will be ruined. Instead, new wine must be poured into fresh wineskins."

Mark 2: 18-22

"...new wine must be poured into fresh wineskins."

New beginnings

After almost two decades of estrangement, I am in the process of reconciling with a family member. We've had some good professional help, but the going is rough. There is so much anger; so many years have been lost. At times it is difficult to be together in the same room.

Despite the difficulties, we forge ahead. It is a tender time. Jesus' words lead me to reflect on what 'starting again' really means. What old wineskins might poison our attempts to drink from the same cup? What old patterns and angers could sabotage this process?

It is hard to look forward when the past is so painful. I don't know whether we will be able to work anything out. But, believing in the possibility of a new beginning is a good place to start.

Lord, I believe it is possible to begin again.
Be with me when I lose faith.

Jesus was walking through some wheat fields on a Sabbath. As his disciples walked along with him, they began to pick the heads of wheat. So the Pharisees said to Jesus, "Look, it is against our Law for your disciples to do that on the Sabbath!"

Jesus answered, "Have you never read what David did that time when he needed something to eat? He and his men were hungry, so he went into the house of God and ate the bread offered to God.... According to our Law only the priests may eat this bread – but David ate it and even gave it to his men." And Jesus concluded, "The Sabbath was made for the good of human beings; they were not made for the Sabbath. So the Son of Man is Lord even of the Sabbath."

Mark 2: 23-28

> "Look, it is against our Law…"

Courage to change

I'm glad I wasn't wandering through that cornfield! Jesus had been talking about conversion and making a new start, and that kind of talk threatens me. I wouldn't have taken Jesus on directly but, feeling threatened by his message, I probably would have resorted to 'nitpicking.'

I have a number of ways of avoiding change: deny what I am hearing, delay and maybe forget the message, or discover some little chink in the messenger's behaviour and try to deflect the message.

None of them work very well, and I spend a lot of time and energy avoiding what I know is the right thing to do. When challenged to change my behaviour, 'nitpicking' simply leaves me unprotected, vulnerable and afraid.

**God, help me to realize that you only want the best for me.
Keep me from getting held back by fear.**

There was a man who had a paralyzed hand…. Some people were there who wanted to accuse Jesus of doing wrong; so they watched him closely to see whether he would cure the man on the Sabbath. Jesus said to the man, "Come up here to the front." Then he asked the people, "What does our Law allow us to do on the Sabbath? To help or to harm? To save someone's life or to destroy it?"

But they did not say a thing. Jesus was angry as he looked around at them, but at the same time he felt sorry for them, because they were so stubborn and wrong. Then he said to the man, "Stretch out your hand." He stretched it out, and it became well again. So the Pharisees… made plans to kill Jesus.

Mark 3: 1-6

> "…at the same time he felt sorry for them."

Out of compassion

Did Jesus struggle with this situation? It would have been so easy to respond in anger… so hard to live by his rule of love.

I have been in similar situations: when I am forced to confront those difficult situations in my work or personal life – structures that are unjust, relationships that are unhealthy. My anger is good since it prompts me to action. However, I'm reminded that Jesus responded, not from his anger but out of compassion.

How difficult it is to pause to listen to that quiet voice within. After all, isn't my anger justified? I need to be reminded that I am not alone: God is acting in me and through me to address the situation.

God, help me to find the courage to fight injustice.
Give me the wisdom to act out of love, and not anger.

A large crowd followed Jesus.... All these people came to Jesus because they had heard of the things he was doing.

Jesus told his disciples to get a boat ready for him, so that the people would not crush him. He had healed many people, and all the sick kept pushing their way to him in order to touch him. And whenever the people who had evil spirits in them saw him, they would fall down before him and scream, "You are the Son of God!" Jesus sternly ordered the evil spirits not to tell anyone who he was.

Mark 3: 7-12

> "All the sick kept pushing their way to him."

A brief respite

Working in what's called a 'helping profession,' I often have the experience of people pressing around me, demanding that I meet their needs. Sometimes I feel overwhelmed, almost suffocated, by their demands for attention.

When the crowd was pressing around Jesus, to touch him and be healed, he had an innovative solution. He got into a boat where he could still teach them, but have some distance.

What are the creative solutions in my life, the 'boats' that allow me some distance and prevent me from being consumed by others' needs? Perhaps it's a few minutes of prayer, a humorous comment that helps me see the situation in a fresh perspective, a chat with someone who loves and affirms me.

**Jesus, when I'm feeling overwhelmed,
help me to find creative solutions to the problems I face.**

Jesus went up a hill and called to himself the men he wanted. They came to him, and he chose twelve, whom he named apostles. "I have chosen you to be with me," he told them. "I will also send you out to preach, and you will have authority to drive out demons."

These are the twelve he chose: Simon (Jesus gave him the name Peter); James and his brother John, the sons of Zebedee (Jesus gave them the name Boanerges, which means "Men of Thunder"); Andrew, Philip, Bartholomew, Matthew, Thomas, James son of Alphaeus, Thaddaeus, Simon the Patriot, and Judas Iscariot, who betrayed Jesus.

Mark 3: 13-19

"I have chosen you to be with me."

A team approach

Have you ever been involved in an organization where one person does all the work and nobody else is given a chance to contribute? Eventually the group morale nose-dives and the group breaks apart.

Jesus gave the twelve apostles key roles in his mission. In spite of their obvious faults and weakness, Jesus trusted they would each bring something valuable to the work they were doing together. Still, what a temptation it must have been to say, "Here, let me do it!"

When dealing with my children, my fellow volunteers or colleagues at work, I try to value the talents they have to contribute and let them know they are needed. I want to share decisions and power the way Jesus did with the disciples.

Lord, keep me focused on the need to work together.

Then Jesus went home. Again such a large crowd gathered that Jesus and his disciples had no time to eat. When his family heard about it, they set out to take charge of him, because people were saying, "He's gone mad!"

Mark 3: 20-21

> "…people were saying, 'He's gone mad!'"

In good company

"You've got to be nuts!" they said. "You're going to give up your career to do what? Study theology! You're crazy. You'll never make any money at that! Are you mad?" And yes, even family members were well represented among the critics.

But among the ex-chartered accountants, ex-biologists and ex-business people in my class, I came to know that I wasn't really crazy. I just had different priorities.

A bit of madness can be a good thing, now and then. If you stop today and give your change to a street person, there may be a voice behind you saying "Are you mad?" And maybe you are… but celebrate that madness! You're in the company of Jesus.

**God, free me to go about your work
without worrying about the opinions of others.**

hrist is like a single body, which has many parts; it is still one body, even though it is made up of different parts. In the same way, all of us, whether Jews or Gentiles, whether slaves or free, have been baptized into the one body by the same Spirit, and we have all been given the one Spirit to drink. For the body itself is not made up of only one part, but of many parts....

All of you are Christ's body, and each one is a part of it. In the church God has put all in place.... They are not all apostles or prophets or teachers. Not everyone has the power to work miracles or to heal diseases or to speak in strange tongues or to explain what is said. Set your hearts, then, on the more important gifts.

1 Corinthians 12:12-14, 27-31

> "All of you are Christ's body..."

Acting together

Not long ago members of our community met with school trustees, trying to save our local school from closing. People of all ages, from elderly to newborns, showed up to give their support.

A videotape was shown of one parent interviewing a community leader about the school's arts program. Other parents presented demographics and renovation costs. The daycare workers spoke about the early education program. Our city councillor and a Community Association representative attended. Capable, caring people presented photographs, statistics and eloquent pleas.

In the end, our school may close because of financial concerns that go beyond our neighbourhood. That decision can't take away from how many concerned and talented people make up our community. Acting together, we are Christ's body, and each one is a necessary part of it.

**God, help me to work with others,
affirming and respecting their gifts.**

s Saul was coming near the city of Damascus, suddenly a light from the sky flashed around him. He fell to the ground and heard a voice saying to him, "Saul, Saul! Why do you persecute me?"

"Who are you, Lord?" he asked.

"I am Jesus, whom you persecute," the voice said...." Saul got up from the ground and opened his eyes, but could not see a thing....

Ananias entered the house where Saul was, and placed his hands on him. "Brother Saul," he said, "the Lord has sent me – Jesus himself, who appeared to you on the road as you were coming here. He sent me so that you might see again and be filled with the Holy Spirit." At once something like fish scales fell from Saul's eyes, and he was able to see again.

Acts 9: 1-22

"Something like fish scales fell from Saul's eyes...."

Eyes wide open

I live a quiet life. So unlike Saul, I haven't spent time running around arresting Christians or threatening them with murder. But I do understand him, at least a little.

After all – son of God, rising from the dead, eternal life – it all sounds pretty wacky. Rather than kill the inexplicable, however, my response is to dismiss it – in a polite, non-confrontational way, of course.

Saul, lucky fellow, receives a beam of light, a voice from heaven, and temporary blindness. That certainly gets your attention.

I, in keeping with my quieter doubts and gentler rejection, get only a nagging sense that maybe there's more to this than meets the eye. That, absurdly, maybe it's me who's wacky.

Lord, my eyes are open, but I do not see. Take away the scales.

Some teachers of the Law were saying, "He has Beelzebul in him! It is the chief of the demons who gives him the power to drive them out."

So Jesus called them to him and spoke to them in parables: "How can Satan drive out Satan? If a country divides itself into groups which fight each other, that country will fall apart. If a family divides itself into groups which fight each other, that family will fall apart. So if Satan's kingdom divides into groups, it cannot last, but will fall apart and come to an end."

"No one can break into a strong man's house and take away his belongings unless he first ties up the strong man; then he can plunder his house."

Mark 3: 22-30

"If a family divides itself…"

Family bonds

In one bedroom, a nine-year-old girl watches reruns on her TV. Upstairs her teenaged sister listens to 'her' music. Their mother is heading off to the fitness club; their father eats his supper while watching a news report about runaways. A normal family: pulled in so many directions.

How easy it is to lose touch with those who share our lives. In pursuing our own dreams, we risk that we will wake up one day in a house of strangers.

How can I participate in the public sphere without losing sight of the centrality of 'family'? Outside influences demand so much and pull us in so many directions. How can I keep my family as my focus and continue to remain open to the demands of others in their need?

**Dear God, give me the strength and wisdom
to keep my house together.**

"Once there was a man who went out to sow grain. As he scattered the seed in the field, some of it fell along the path, and the birds came and ate it up. Some of it fell on rocky ground, where there was little soil. The seeds soon sprouted, because the soil wasn't deep. Then, when the sun came up, it burned the young plants; and because the roots had not grown deep enough, the plants soon dried up. Some of the seed fell among thorn bushes, which grew up and choked the plants, and they didn't bear grain. But some seeds fell in good soil, and the plants sprouted, grew, and bore grain: some had thirty grains, others sixty, and others one hundred." Jesus concluded, "Listen, then, if you have ears!"

Mark 4: 1-10

"But some seeds fell in good soil…"

Open to God's Word

Recently I took a course to learn some pain-management skills. It was called "Mindfulness Training," and is based on the teachings of a Buddhist, Thich Nhat Hanh.

While I understood the message quite readily, putting it into practice was something entirely different. It involved stopping my mind from jumping from worry to pain to distraction, and so on.

The leaders assessed me both before and after the course, and compared my two sets of responses. While my level of pain had not changed, my attitude toward it had. I'm learning to listen more closely to God's voice within me. I'm trying not to let the worries of life crowd in and distract me from hearing God's Word.

**God, may I be fertile ground for your Word,
bearing much fruit.**

Jesus continued, "Does anyone ever bring in a lamp and put it under a bowl or under the bed? Isn't it put on the lamp stand? Whatever is hidden away will be brought out into the open, and whatever is covered up will be uncovered. Listen, then, if you have ears!"

He also said to them, "Pay attention to what you hear! The same rules you use to judge others will be used by God to judge you – but with even greater severity. Those who have something will be given more, and those who have nothing will have taken away from them even the little they have."

Mark 4: 21-25

> "Pay attention to what you hear!"

Listen!

The 'sounds of silence' seem to lose out to modern technology: from cell phones to beepers, we are rarely beyond the reach of someone calling out to us.

Jesus' command to 'listen' is to hear but on a different level. As with today's technology, we need to be 'tuned in' in order not to miss the message or scramble the message we send to others.

And what is the message? As members of God's kingdom, we influence others by the way we live and by the way we treat others. We are all bearers of light – carrying within us the potential to influence our world.

As I listen in the silence of my heart, I begin to focus on how I affect others, what message I am sending them. What do I communicate?

God, help me to be aware of what I 'speak' today, by the way I live and by what I say.

"The kingdom of God is like this. A man scatters seed in his field. He sleeps at night, is up and about during the day, and all the while the seeds are sprouting and growing. Yet he does not know how it happens. The soil itself makes the plants grow and bear fruit.... When the grain is ripe, the man starts cutting it with his sickle, because harvest time has come.

"What shall we say the kingdom of God is like? ... A man takes a mustard seed, the smallest seed in the world, and plants it in the ground. After a while it grows up and becomes the biggest of all plants. It puts out such large branches that the birds come and make their nests in its shade."

Mark 4: 26-34

> "What shall we say the kingdom of God is like?"

God of surprises

Jesus' question is a compelling one: "What shall we say the kingdom of God is like?" Jesus' answer, however, leaves his listeners struggling with yet more questions!

These days I find myself searching for answers about God, about life. When I want to pin God down, to be able to define and describe God, Jesus invites me to *experience* God in my daily life.

In our culture of day-timers, planners and never-ending schedules, there is little room for God to surprise us or for us to discover God's plans for us. But God won't be pinned down; neither will God's kingdom. My challenge is to find the seeds of God's presence – which are planted here and now – and to grow with them.

Lord, plant your seeds of discovery and wonder within me today.

Jesus said, "Let us go across to the other side of the lake." So the disciples got into the boat in which Jesus was already sitting.... Suddenly a strong wind blew up, and the waves began to spill over into the boat, so that it was about to fill with water. Jesus was in the back of the boat, sleeping with his head on a pillow. The disciples woke him up and said, "Teacher, don't you care that we are about to die?"

Jesus stood up and commanded the wind, "Be quiet!" and he said to the waves, "Be still!" The wind died down, and there was a great calm. Then Jesus said, "Why are you frightened? Do you still have no faith?"

Mark 4: 35-41

"Why are you frightened?"

Within the storm

Picture the scene: a storm is raging all around; the waves reach higher and higher. As they go down between the swells, the disciples cannot see over them. It is dark, black. The men are small, insignificant before the forces arrayed against them.

How often I feel small, and the storm within me so out of control. It is hard to have faith – that I have been given the strength to cope. Faith that I, like Jesus, can tell the waves: "Be still." I have had to face so many storms: growing up and will I fit in? What will I do with my life? And now: A mortgage, sick children, work… so many fears.

"Why are you frightened? Do you still have no faith?" Let it go. You'll be fine. I am here.

**Dear God, you give me strength to weather the storms.
Help me trust that you are there with me.**

Jesus said, "You will quote this proverb to me, 'Doctor, heal yourself....' Prophets are never welcomed in their hometown. Listen to me: it is true that there were many widows in Israel during the time of Elijah, when there was no rain for three and a half years and a severe famine spread throughout the whole land. Yet Elijah was not sent to anyone in Israel, but only to a widow living in Zarephath in the territory of Sidon. And there were many people suffering from a dreaded skin disease who lived in Israel during the time of the prophet Elisha; yet not one of them was healed, but only Naaman the Syrian."

When the people in the synagogue heard this, they were filled with anger.

Luke 4: 21-30

> "Prophets are never welcomed in their hometown."

Thirsting for God

Defying the religious norms of his day, Jesus repeatedly took up the cause of the downtrodden. Doing so shocked and angered his neighbours.

Today's text reminds me of a time when one of numerous street people who lived in my area disturbed the 'dignity' of our parish's service. He approached the table, with the rest of us, to share the cup of wine. Later, some murmured that the only reason he did this was to satisfy his alcohol addiction.

For whatever reason, Jesus drew this person to him, and satisfied his thirst. Should I be shocked? Am I not one of the downtrodden, thirsting for Jesus' life-giving word? Am I not one who needs my peace disturbed, so that Christ's peace can be mine?

**Lord, open my heart to welcome your good news,
especially in surprising ways.**

A man had an evil spirit in him and lived among the tombs. Nobody could keep him tied with chains any more.... Day and night he wandered among the tombs and through the hills, screaming and cutting himself with stones.

He was some distance away when he saw Jesus; so he ran, fell on his knees before him, and screamed in a loud voice, "Jesus, Son of the Most High God! What do you want with me? For God's sake, I beg you, don't punish me!" (He said this because Jesus was saying, "Evil spirit, come out of this man!")

So Jesus asked him, "What is your name!" The man answered, "My name is 'Mob' – there are so many of us!" And he kept begging Jesus not to send the evil spirits out of that region.

Mark 5: 1-20

> "A man had an evil spirit in him…"

Self-destructive times

From time to time, the various evil spirits living within me seem to arrange for a special general meeting. When I'm over-tired, I can become easily depressed and hypercritical. That's when I have another glass or two to take away the edge. That's when I become more distant, disconnected and remote. That's also the time when I…. Well, I think you get the picture.

Fortunately, unlike this violently self-destructive man in today's reading, I am not in continual misery. But I know what it is to feel overwhelmed by forces beyond my control. That's when I try to connect to the sustaining power of the love of the Lord, to help deal with my weaknesses and failings.

**God, when I fall into the darkness,
may your sustaining light show me a way out.**

A t that time there was a man named Simeon living in Jerusalem. He was a good, God-fearing man and was waiting for Israel to be saved. The Holy Spirit was with him and had assured him that he would not die before he had seen the Lord's promised Messiah. Led by the Spirit, Simeon went into the Temple. When the parents brought the child Jesus into the Temple to do for him what the Law required, Simeon took the child in his arms and gave thanks to God: "Now, Lord, you have kept your promise, and you may let your servant go in peace. With my own eyes I have seen your salvation, which you have prepared in the presence of all peoples: A light to reveal your will to the Gentiles and bring glory to your people Israel."

Luke 2: 22-40

"Simeon took the child in his arms..."

God's gift

On his last birthday, our oldest son legally became an adult. The future stretches before him, filled with endless, dazzling possibilities. His head is full of plans, and his heart is full of hope about what lies ahead.

But when he was born – a mere blink of an eye ago – there was no public acclaim. No holy man proclaimed his importance to a waiting world. No prophet thanked God for his birth and told everyone about him.

God speaks to the hearts of parents. We knew this boy was important to the world. Our job, like Mary and Joseph's, was to do all we could to ensure that he would grow strong and receive God's blessings. Then he'd be ready to walk confidently into that unknown future.

**Lord, give my son, and others like him,
the help they need to step into the world.**

Jesus went back to his hometown, followed by his disciples. On the Sabbath he began to teach in the synagogue. Many people were there; and when they heard him, they were all amazed. "Where did he get all this?" they asked. "What wisdom is this that has been given him? How does he perform miracles? Isn't he the carpenter, the son of Mary, and the brother of James, Joseph, Judas and Simon? Aren't his sisters living here?" And so they rejected him.

Jesus said to them, "Prophets are respected everywhere except in their own hometown and by their relatives and their family."

He was not able to perform any miracles there, except that he placed his hands on a few sick people and healed them. He was greatly surprised, because the people did not have faith.   *Mark 6: 1-6*

"Where did he get all this?"

Ridiculed, rejected

I remember Brendan, a classmate when I was growing up in the U.K. Recently arrived from Ireland, he was the typical bumpkin (or so we thought). He spoke 'funny,' had no sense of humour, and worse, was brilliant. How could someone apparently so inept disturb our well-established and comfortable lives? But he did.

To add insult to injury, he won a scholarship and was identified by the staff as a rare bright hope: a candidate for university. I made his life miserable through my jealousy because he threatened the smallness of my world by looking beyond it.

Remarkably, he never caved in to or even acknowledged this miserable and shameful behaviour. Wherever you may be, Brendan, I apologize for all of it.

**Dear God, may I find the grace not to be threatened
by differences.**

H e called the twelve disciples together and sent them out two by two. He gave them authority over the evil spirits and ordered them, "Don't take anything with you on the trip except a walking stick – no bread, no beggar's bag, no money in your pockets. Wear sandals, but don't carry an extra shirt." He also told them, "Wherever you are welcomed, stay in the same house until you leave that place. If you come to a town where people do not welcome you or will not listen to you, leave it and shake the dust off your feet. That will be a warning to them!"

So they went out... and they drove out many demons, and rubbed olive oil on many sick people and healed them.

Mark 6: 7-13

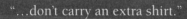

"...don't carry an extra shirt."

Too much baggage

Jesus told his followers to travel lightly on the trip of life. Hmmm... I have four drawers full of clothes: one for socks and underwear, one for shirts, one for trousers, and one for sweaters, pyjamas and the shirts and trousers that won't fit into the other drawers! Then there's the closet that holds more shirts and trousers, ties and jackets.

And when spring comes, all the sweaters, heavy shirts and trousers are put away and replaced by t-shirts and shorts. And that's only clothes! I have many, many other *things*, too.

Maybe that's why life's journey sometimes feels like one heavy step after another. How can I see where I'm going – bent over almost to the ground – under the weight of so much baggage?

Jesus, help me reduce my burden, so that I can travel lightly.

Herodias held a grudge against John and wanted to kill him…. Finally Herodias got her chance…. On Herod's birthday… the daughter of Herodias came in and danced, and pleased Herod and his guests. So the king said to the girl, "What would you like to have? I will give you anything you want…." So the girl asked her mother, "What shall I ask for?"

"The head of John the Baptist," she answered. The girl hurried back at once to the king and demanded, "I want you to give me the head of John the Baptist on a plate!"

This made the king very sad, but he could not refuse her because of the vows he had made in front of all his guests. So he sent off a guard at once with orders to bring John's head. The guard left, went to the prison, and cut John's head off; then he brought it on a plate.

Mark 6: 14-29

> "He sent off a guard… with orders."

Open to others' pain

I have a friend who is a prison guard. He experiences what many of us do at work: those times when we see things we don't think are quite right but are powerless to change. Those times when we lose sleep, wondering if we will have to put our job on the line over a certain issue. Do we harden ourselves so we can live with injustice?

What did the guard in today's reading feel? Was he so jaded and hardened he didn't feel anything?

At times, I see it in my young friend – the hardening. I see it in my colleagues, and in myself. And this is what scares me – the calluses that make us immune to others' suffering. Could this guard really have said 'No'? Would I have? I hope he shed some tears.

Dear God, help me to make difficult choices
that reflect your justice, your love.

The Lord appeared to Solomon in a dream and asked him, "What would you like me to give you?" Solomon answered, "O Lord God, you have let me succeed my father as king, even though I am very young and don't know how to rule.... So give me the wisdom I need to rule your people with justice and to know the difference between good and evil...."

The Lord was pleased that Solomon had asked for this, and so he said to him, "I will give you more wisdom and understanding than anyone has ever had before or will ever have again. I will also give you what you have not asked for: all your life you will have wealth and honour, more than that of any other king... and I will give you a long life."

1 Kings 3: 4-13

> "So give me the wisdom I need..."

Wisdom and understanding

When I turn to God to ask for help, wisdom is not often at the top of my list. Help to find the cars keys seems to be my most urgent request these days!

It's rare for me to stop and think about what I truly need. I tend to ask God for help either in the middle of a crisis or at the end of a long day when clear thinking and a sense of the bigger picture are well beyond my grasp.

Perhaps Solomon's wisdom lay in his ability to reflect on what he truly needed. He knew that it was important to consider the larger community and his place in it. How might my requests change if I do the same?

God, may I recognize my need for wisdom more often.

thank you, Lord, with all my heart;
I sing praise to you before the gods....
You answered me when I called to you;
with your strength you strengthened me....
Even though you are so high above,
you care for the lowly,
and the proud cannot hide from you....
You will do everything you have promised;
Lord, your love is eternal.
Complete the work that you have begun.

Psalm 138: 1-8

> "...you care for the lowly..."

God's presence

An acquaintance of mine works with people who have been abused. My friend's elderly mother helps at the food bank every week. A neighbour raises money for poor children so they can go to summer camp.

I tend to read the newspaper and ask, "Where is God in the murder of this young girl? Where is God in the earthquake that hit this developing country? Where is God in the actions of that corrupt government?"

Now I notice how God is working through the people who help the victims, the poor, the isolated, the sick. I recognize God helping those who suffer through the people around them. And I know that I, too, must let God work through me.

**Lord, let me be your hands and your feet
when I meet people who need your help.**

T hey crossed the lake and came to land at Gennesaret, where they tied up the boat. As they left the boat, people recognized Jesus at once. So they ran throughout the whole region; and wherever they heard he was they brought to him the sick lying on their mats. And everywhere Jesus went, to villages, towns, or farms, people would take their sick to the marketplaces and beg him to let the sick at least touch the edge of his cloak. And all who touched it were made well.

Mark 6: 53-56

> "...all who touched it were made well."

A healing touch

"Why did you become a teacher?" I asked her. She was one of those special ones.
"I dreamed I'd make a difference. That I'd make my students' lives better, and I'd be doing something that meant something. I wanted them all to have good lives."

I guess that's what she and I have in common. I, too, want to help make people better. In my dreams, I heal others with a word, with a smile, like Jesus did.

But life's not like that, is it? I struggle along, often not knowing what to say. Wishing I had a magic word that would make people's pain go away. But I don't. I can only do what I can do. Perhaps dreams, as they say, are the better part of us.

Jesus, you healed with a touch. Help my touch heal others, and help me to accept the limits of that healing.

The Pharisees and the teachers of the Law asked, "Why is it that your disciples do not follow the teaching handed down by our ancestors…?" Jesus answered, "How right Isaiah was! You are hypocrites, just as he wrote: 'These people, says God, honour me with their words, but their heart is really far away from me.'"

Jesus continued, "You have a clever way of rejecting God's law in order to uphold your own teaching. For Moses commanded, 'Respect your father and your mother….' But you teach that if people have something they could use to help their father or mother, but say, 'This is Corban' (which means, it belongs to God), they are excused from helping their father or mother. In this way the teaching you pass on to others cancels out the word of God."

Mark 7: 1-13

> "…but their heart is really far away from me."

God in the questions

Some days I really sympathize with the Pharisees and their penchant for the rules. As an elementary school teacher, I seem to spend a lot of time enforcing school rules that have a million and one exceptions. My students are always eager to point out the contradictions they see – and it drives me crazy!

Often the more I try to pin things down with rules, the more ridiculous they become. My students' constant questioning reminds me that God isn't found in the rules. God is found in my willingness to be surprised!

Sure, a set of foolproof rules would be handy. But if I had a big rulebook, I'd miss out on the chance to discover God – as I wrestle with the questions.

God, remind me to look for you beyond the rules.

The queen of Sheba travelled to Jerusalem.... When she and Solomon met, she asked him all the questions that she could think of. He answered them all; there was nothing too difficult for him to explain....

The queen of Sheba said, "What I heard in my own country about you and your wisdom is true! But I couldn't believe it until I had come and seen it all for myself. But I didn't hear even half of it; your wisdom and wealth are much greater than what I was told.... Praise the Lord your God! He has shown how pleased he is with you by making you king of Israel. Because his love for Israel is eternal, he has made you their king so that you can maintain law and justice."

1 Kings 10: 1-10

"...she asked him all the questions that she could think of."

Asking questions

As a journalist, I've learned to hold back my own reaction to a person's comments, and instead to ask another question based on what they had just said. Once in a while the person ends up telling me things that are very important to them but that they have never been able to fully articulate before, because no one has ever taken the time to listen. Those are moments of privilege for both of us.

The Queen of Sheba had learned one of the great arts of conversation: she knew how to listen. She didn't keep interrupting Solomon with her own opinion; she just kept asking, probing, hungry to understand.

How often do I genuinely learn from others' insights, or delight in their accomplishments, without constantly imposing my own?

**Lord, give me the generosity of spirit to listen,
and then listen some more.**

A woman, whose daughter had an evil spirit in her, heard about Jesus and came to him at once and fell at his feet. The woman was a Gentile, born in the region of Phoenicia in Syria. She begged Jesus to drive the demon out of her daughter. But Jesus answered, "Let us first feed the children. It isn't right to take the children's food and throw it to the dogs."

"Sir," she answered, "even the dogs under the table eat the children's leftovers!"

Jesus said to her, "Because of that answer, go back home, where you will find that the demon has gone out of your daughter!"

She went home and found her child lying on the bed; the demon had indeed gone out of her.   *Mark 7: 24-30*

"Because of that answer, go back home…"

Desperate times

My friend was choking from asthma. The pharmacist at the drug store refused to re-fill her prescription until I had her doctor's approval. However, the doctor was away at a cottage, and his wife wanted to protect the one weekend he'd had off all summer.

I begged and cajoled; I lost all sense of propriety. Eventually, with her voice dripping sarcasm, the doctor's wife gave me his number. I succeeded in getting the medication for my friend, and within a few minutes she was breathing normally.

That exchange with the doctor's wife stayed in my mind all weekend. I could not help but think that both the Phoenician woman and I had succeeded because of our bold, maybe even rude, persistence. Desperate measures for desperate times!

**God, help me to accept that desperation
can push me to lose my sense of reserve.**

Some people brought [Jesus] a man who was deaf and could hardly speak, and they begged Jesus to place his hands on him. So Jesus took him off alone, away from the crowd, put his fingers in the man's ears, spat, and touched the man's tongue. Then Jesus looked up to heaven, gave a deep groan, and said to the man, "*Ephphatha*," which means, "Open up!"

At once the man was able to hear, his speech impediment was removed, and he began to talk without any trouble. Then Jesus ordered the people not to speak of it to anyone; but the more he ordered them not to, the more they told it. And all who heard were completely amazed. "How well he does everything.... He even causes the deaf to hear and the dumb to speak!"   *Mark 7: 31-37*

> "He even causes the deaf to hear and the dumb to speak!"

Straight from the heart

The deaf hear and the dumb speak! Yet how often I witness the opposite: when co-workers, managers and employees, spouses, parents and children are deaf to one another's voices. When they cannot say what they truly feel.

And how often I feel that I am not heard or that I cannot say what I feel. Sometimes it seems so hopeless, so impossible to know what to do, where to turn.

Why are we 'deaf'? Why are we unable to speak? Is it our lack of faith that it's possible – if we keep trying – to really hear and really speak?

I take hope from this story. If I keep trying I *will* learn to speak from within; I will learn to listen with my heart. My act of faith is to stay and try.

**May my ears be opened to others
and may my voice speak what is truly inside of me.**

J esus said, "I feel sorry for these people, because they have been with me for three days and now have nothing to eat. If I send them home without feeding them, they will faint as they go...."

His disciples asked him, "Where in this desert can anyone find enough food to feed all these people?"

"How much bread do you have?" Jesus asked. "Seven loaves," they answered. Jesus took the seven loaves, gave thanks to God, broke them, and gave them to his disciples to distribute to the crowd; and the disciples did so. They also had a few small fish. Jesus gave thanks for these and told the disciples to distribute them too. Everybody ate and had enough. Then the disciples took up seven baskets full of pieces left over.

Mark 8: 1-10

"Where in this desert can anyone find enough food...?"

Expect the unexpected

One reason I like the disciples is because they are rarely wise; instead, they are often ordinary and dull, just like me. You would think that after spending months and years with Jesus, they would have learned to look for the unexpected, to delight in witnessing God's grace in action. But here they are again, seeing only what is right in front of their noses.

I don't judge them harshly because I see myself in their plodding focus on the obvious. I, too, see the 'facts' right in front of me. How can anyone solve widespread poverty? Environmental degradation? Economic injustice? It's all too much. It can't be done.

I can see Jesus smiling at them while ignoring their negative words, just as he smiles at me while ignoring mine: "Well, what have you got? Let's begin there."

Lord, help me to see life through your eyes, and to respond.

J esus said, "Happy are you poor; the kingdom of God is yours! Happy are you who are hungry now; you will be filled! Happy are you who weep now; you will laugh! Happy are you when people hate you, reject you, insult you, and say that you are evil, all because of the Son of Man! Be glad when that happens and dance for joy, because a great reward is kept for you in heaven...

"But how terrible for you who are rich now; you have had your easy life! How terrible for you who are full now; you will go hungry! How terrible for you who laugh now; you will mourn and weep! How terrible when all people speak well of you; their ancestors said the very same things about the false prophets."

Luke 6: 17, 20-26

> "Happy are you who weep now..."

A God who cares

How I wish that Jesus were kidding when he said these things! I keep trying to read them in a way that makes them easier to accept.

I don't like the thought of rejection, insults and slander. I don't like mourning and weeping, being poor or hungry. And yet, these are the experiences I am called to live. Experiences of lingering unemployment, grief over the loss of a loved one, or pain at being maligned ... these carve out my internal capacity for joy, happiness and peace.

Such moments do prepare me to receive the kingdom. And oddly enough, they also contain the kingdom, as I experience an intimately caring God right by my side.

**God, grant me the courage to believe
that your presence transforms pain into new life.**

Some Pharisees came to Jesus and started to argue with him. They wanted to trap him, so they asked him to perform a miracle to show that God approved of him. But Jesus gave a deep groan and said, "Why do the people of this day ask for a miracle? No, I tell you! No such proof will be given to these people!" He left them, got back into the boat, and started across to the other side of the lake.

Mark 8: 11-13

"No such proof will be given to these people!"

Allowing for miracles

The message Rose received during her childhood was, "You are useless, a burden to us." She became self-destructive and developed an eating disorder. As an adolescent, Rose moved to a home where people said to her, "You're beautiful. I want to get to know you." Gradually, growing in trust and openness, she revealed the treasure of love hidden in her heart. Today she is quite radiant. A miracle happened for Rose.

Jesus performed miracles for many people. "Your faith has saved you," he often said. The Pharisees, however, sought only to discredit Jesus, to tear him down. They made it impossible for miracles to happen.

Through my words and actions, do I build people up or tear them down? Do I invite God's healing power or block it?

**Lord, may I have the faith in myself, and in others,
that will allow you to work wonders in our lives.**

The disciples had forgotten to bring enough bread with them in the boat. "Take care," Jesus warned them, "and be on your guard against the yeast of the Pharisees and the yeast of Herod."

They started discussing among themselves: "He says this because we don't have any bread."

Jesus asked them, "Why are you discussing about not having any bread? You have eyes – can't you see? You have ears – can't you hear? Don't you remember when I broke the five loaves for the five thousand people? How many baskets full of leftover pieces did you take up?" "Twelve," they answered. "And when I broke the seven loaves for the four thousand people," asked Jesus, "how many baskets full of leftover pieces did you take up?" "Seven," they answered. "And you still don't understand?"

Mark 8: 14-21

> "And you still don't understand?"

Open to believing

I'm quite sure that, had I been there in that boat, I'd be just as confused as the disciples. I'd worry about doing something that might embarrass the 'boss' in front of all those people. Or I'd try to figure out who was really to blame. My selfish concerns about protecting my precious self-image would prevent me from grasping what was really happening.

The disciples had heard it all and, still, they didn't catch on. I recognize this pattern because I, too, tend to focus on details at the expense of the big picture.

God's grandeur is all around me – not just in special places or moments – but everywhere, every fleeting moment. I must learn to look with my eyes, my mind and my heart truly open.

God, let me always be open to your presence.
Be patient with me when I fail to see you.

Here we are, then, speaking for Christ, as though God himself were making his appeal through us. We plead on Christ's behalf: let God change you from enemies into his friends! Christ was without sin, but for our sake God made him share our sin in order that in union with him we might share the righteousness of God.

In our work together with God, then, we beg you who have received God's grace not to let it be wasted. Hear what God says: "When the time came for me to show you favour, I heard you; when the day arrived for me to save you, I helped you."

2 Corinthians 5: 20 – 6: 2

"Here we are, then, speaking for Christ..."

In Christ's name

Several years before he died, my father gave me power of attorney. Not until later did I realize what an enormous act of trust that was. Because a power of attorney gave me the same authority that he had – over his property, his bank accounts, his business affairs. I could act in his name.

The third great commandment says, "Thou shalt not take the name of the Lord in vain." My father trusted me not to take his name in vain.

Jesus, too, gave his disciples a kind of power of attorney. "Even the demons obeyed us," they exulted, "when we gave them a command in your name." That, too, took enormous trust on Jesus' part. Now we, like Paul, are trusted to speak in his name.

God, may I always speak in your name faithfully and lovingly.

" Today I am giving you a choice between good and evil, between life and death. If you obey the commands of the Lord your God, if you love him, obey him, and keep all his laws, then you will prosper and become a nation of many people. The Lord your God will bless you in the land that you are about to occupy. But if you disobey and refuse to listen, and are led away to worship other gods, you will be destroyed – I warn you here and now.... I am now giving you the choice between life and death, between God's blessing and God's curse, and I call heaven and earth to witness the choice you make. Choose life. Love the Lord your God, obey him and be faithful to him."

Deuteronomy 30: 15-20

"Choose life."

A fundamental lesson

At times I tell my students, "Okay, listen up, because this will be on the test." While lots of material will be on the test, sometimes I want them to recognize that this particular point is fundamentally important; that confusion over it will lead to greater problems elsewhere; and that it's probably trickier to grasp than it appears, so they need to give it their full attention.

God does something similar here, telling Israel (and me), "Look, this is going to be on the test, and you can't afford to get it wrong. And even though I'm going to tell you the right answer ahead of time, it's still going to take all of your attention to figure it out, day to day. So, listen carefully: Choose life!" Did you catch that?

God, life offers me so many choices.
Help me to make a clear choice for life today.

The people ask, "Why should we fast if the Lord never notices? Why should we go without food if he pays no attention?"

The Lord says to them, "The truth is that at the same time you fast, you pursue your own interests and oppress your workers. Your fasting makes you violent, and you quarrel and fight. Do you think this kind of fasting will make me listen to your prayers? The kind of fasting I want is this: Remove the chains of oppression and the yoke of injustice, and let the oppressed go free. Share your food with the hungry and open your homes to the homeless poor. Give clothes to those who have nothing to wear, and do not refuse to help your own relatives. Then my favour will shine on you like the morning sun."

Isaiah 58: 1-9

> "Share your food with the hungry…"

Practical results

I watched the meetings of the Earth Summit one year in Johannesburg. With fine words and noble sentiments, speaker after speaker endorsed sustainable development and caring for the poorest nations while protecting the environment. But no one offered to sacrifice his or her own affluence to let it happen.

I remember Jean Vanier saying, 30 years before, "It's not what you have in your refrigerator that matters, but who is allowed to get a meal from it."

It's a small sacrifice for me to reduce my spending, or to eat less. I might even benefit from it! But unless my self-discipline feeds someone else, unless the clothes I give up keep someone else warm, it's all smoke and mirrors.

Noble sentiments need practical outcomes.

**Lord, I don't want to give up anything I have;
but unless I do, we'll all have nothing.**

After this, Jesus went out and saw a tax collector named Levi, sitting in his office. Jesus said to him, "Follow me." Levi got up, left everything, and followed him. Then Levi had a big feast in his house for Jesus, and among the guests were a large number of tax collectors and other people. Some Pharisees and some teachers of the Law who belonged to their group complained to Jesus' disciples. "Why do you eat and drink with tax collectors and other outcasts?" they asked. Jesus answered them, "People who are well do not need a doctor, but only those who are sick. I have not come to call respectable people to repent, but outcasts."

Luke 5: 27-32

"Levi got up and left everything…"

Following through

What an extraordinary story! Jesus comes up to the tax official sitting in his office and says, "Follow me." And the tax collector gets up, leaves his lucrative position of power and sets off with Jesus.

Sometimes the big, difficult decisions come easily to me: I respond in a moment of grace. Impulsively I reach out to someone who has been my enemy, or speak against an abuse of power in my workplace. I make the decision to walk away from an unhealthy friendship.

It's following through that's difficult: holding firm when I've made the first step. Levi probably had second thoughts when he realized how poor and vulnerable Jesus was. What made Levi an apostle was that he persevered with his daring deed.

Teach me, Lord, to follow my good and generous impulses when you call me to act.

J esus was led by the Spirit into the desert, where he was tempted by the Devil for forty days. In all that time he ate nothing.... The Devil said, "If you are God's Son, order this stone to turn into bread." Jesus answered, "The scripture says, 'Human beings cannot live on bread alone.'"

Then the Devil showed him all the kingdoms of the world. "I will give you all this power and wealth... if you worship me." Jesus answered, "The scripture says, 'Worship the Lord your God and serve only him!'"

Then the Devil took him to Jerusalem... "If you are God's Son, throw yourself down from here. For the scripture says, 'God will order his angels to take good care of you....'" Jesus answered, "The scripture says, 'Do not put the Lord your God to the test.'"

Luke 4: 1-13

> "...where he was tempted by the Devil..."

Temptation

I don't always handle hunger and pride well. At times I find myself hungering for security that will calm my fears, for authority that will make me feel important, for physical gratification that will leave me feeling lonelier and more isolated than before.

I know it's wishful thinking: if I had a bit more security, if my authority was never challenged, if my popularity were greater... then life would unfold more smoothly, and then I would be happy.

I'm always amazed (and reassured!) that the temptations Jesus faced in the desert are the very ones I face every day in my home, in my office and in my community.

God, help me to be aware that temptation is nothing new, and that others have lived through it.

who am an elder myself, appeal to the church elders among you. I am a witness of Christ's sufferings, and I will share in the glory that , will be revealed. I appeal to you to be shepherds of the flock that God gave you and to take care of it willingly, as God wants you to, and not unwillingly. Do your work, not for mere pay, but from a real desire to serve. Do not try to rule over those who have been put in your care, but be examples to the flock. And when the Chief Shepherd appears, you will receive the glorious crown which will never lose its brightness.

I Peter 5: 1-4

> "...but from a real desire to serve."

God in the details

I once worked for a manager who must have read today's passage... and who lived it. And, believe it or not, he managed a huge government department where data were kept, computer programs written, and, somewhere down the line, cheques were mailed out.

The manager exhorted us to always remember, "You are serving the people of Canada. Think of the person who's going to receive that cheque." In the midst of the minutiae of the job, he always had that as his ultimate value. It helped give meaning to those tedious afternoons.

These days I'm challenged to not let the minute-to-minute stresses make my days a survival contest. Today's reading reminds me that each of my actions affects someone else, for better or for worse.

God, give me the strength to follow your ways.

"When you pray, do not use a lot of meaningless words. Your Father already knows what you need before you ask him. This, then, is how you should pray: 'Our Father in heaven: May your holy name be honoured; may your Kingdom come; may your will be done on earth as it is in heaven. Give us today the food we need. Forgive us the wrongs we have done, as we forgive the wrongs that others have done to us. Do not bring us to hard testing, but keep us safe from the Evil One.'

"If you forgive others the wrongs they have done to you, your Father in heaven will also forgive you. But if you do not forgive others, then your Father will not forgive the wrongs you have done."

Matthew 6: 7-15

> "Forgive others the wrongs they have done."

Forgiving myself

How do I know that I have been forgiven? Do I wait until I die or do I experience God's forgiveness here and now? I think of the times when I've held on to my anger, to the wrongs that were done to me. I see how that anger remained inside, working away, hurting myself more than the 'transgressor.'

A country song goes, "A heart stained in anger grows weak and grows bitter. You become your own prisoner…." If I judge harshly, I judge not only others, but myself also.

So God's forgiveness begins here, with forgiving myself. When I forgive others, I experience in a real way that I, too, am forgivable. In the words of William Shakespeare, "The quality of mercy is twice blessed."

Dear God, help me to forgive.
May I not remain a prisoner of my anger.

"How evil are the people of this day! They ask for a miracle, but none will be given them except the miracle of Jonah. In the same way that the prophet Jonah was a sign for the people of Nineveh, so the Son of Man will be a sign for the people of this day. On the Judgment Day the Queen of Sheba will stand up and accuse the people of today, because she travelled all the way from her country to listen to King Solomon's wise teaching; and there is something here, I tell you, greater than Solomon. On the Judgment Day the people of Nineveh will stand up and accuse you, because they turned from their sins when they heard Jonah preach; and I assure you that there is something here greater than Jonah!"

Luke 11: 29-32

> "They ask for a miracle…"

Wanted: a miracle

I have to admit it: there are times when I want to see a miracle, too. Not just your whiff-of-the-holy, stretching-the-bounds-of-coincidence moment. No, I want a Grade-A, breaks-the-laws-of-physics, overwhelms-human-intelligence, crushes-our-understanding-of-life, removes-all-doubt, public event.

Then the questions that won't go away will be answered. The fear that sometimes visits me late at night will disappear. My timid eyes, that don't want to look over the edge of the abyss, will see solid ground below.

But that isn't God's way. God doesn't grab me by the shoulders and shout in my ear. No, God speaks to me quietly – in ways that I easily miss, if I'm not listening carefully.

**Lord, may I hear your voice in the silence,
and know your presence in the emptiness.**

"**A**sk, and you will receive; seek, and you will find; knock, and the door will be opened to you.... Would any of you who are fathers give your son a stone when he asks for bread? Or would you give him a snake when he asks for a fish? As bad as you are, you know how to give good things to your children. How much more, then, will your Father in heaven give good things to those who ask him!

"Do for others what you want them to do for you: this is the meaning of the Law of Moses and of the teachings of the prophets."

Matthew 7: 7-12

"Do for others..."

Ask, and you'll receive

I struggle with today's reading: "Ask, and you will receive." I can't forget the pictures. Pictures of horror: people fed into gas chambers, or killed in massacres, famines and floods. Did they ask for help? Did they get help? Is there a greater plan for them? One I can't understand? So I struggle, and I come to this: "Do for others what you want them to do for you."

Another picture comes to mind: my father, in 1957. He's taking his last buck out of his tattered wallet, and he's giving it to me. His last buck, and he's giving it to me.

"Ask and you will receive...." I still don't understand that. "Do for others...." Maybe it's up to me to make it come true.

Lord, when I am asked,
let me give completely and without hesitation.

"If you are angry with your brother you will be brought to trial, if you call your brother 'You good-for-nothing!' you will be brought before the Council.... So if you are about to offer your gift to God at the altar and there you remember that your brother has something against you, leave your gift there in front of the altar, go at once and make peace with your brother, and then come back and offer your gift to God.

"If someone brings a lawsuit against you and takes you to court, settle the dispute while there is time, before you get to court. Once you are there, you will be turned over to the judge, who will hand you over to the police, and you will be put in jail."

Matthew 5: 20-26

> "...go at once and make peace with your brother..."

Saying sorry

I worked in a school for children with behavioural problems. Throughout the day, disputes would arise: "I want that, too!" "He hit me first!" The clinical worker would intervene by asking, "Would our school be fun if children hit and fought all the time?" His approach was not, "Do this. Do that," but rather, "When someone hits me, I feel sad and angry. When they say they are sorry, I feel happy again."

How different am I from those young children? I want to have my way; I struggle to say, "I'm sorry"; I find it hard to accept an apology when it's offered, to let go of my grudge.

Some days that worker looked so exhausted. I imagine Jesus did too, trying to get through to the disciples, and me.

Lord, help me change my actions, and my heart.

"**Y**ou have heard that it was said, 'Love your friends, hate your enemies.' But now I tell you: love your enemies and pray for those who persecute you, so that you may become the children of your Father in heaven. For he makes his sun to shine on bad and good people alike, and gives rain to those who do good and to those who do evil. Why should God reward you if you love only the people who love you? Even the tax collectors do that! And if you speak only to your friends, have you done anything out of the ordinary? Even the pagans do that! You must be perfect – just as your Father in heaven is perfect."

Matthew 5: 43-48

"...have you done anything out of the ordinary?"

Jealousy

My mother was a wise woman. When I was young, she used to warn me never to compare myself to others. There would always be someone better off and someone worse off than myself, she'd say, and making those distinctions would only cause trouble.

The older I get, the more truth I see in her words. Jealousy is one of those sins we acknowledge, but don't really talk about. While I can admit that I lack love for a certain person, I have a hard time admitting that I am jealous of them.

But what, more than jealousy, can undermine my ability to love others? What, if not jealousy, makes me second-guess a God who rewards those I think less than worthy?

Dear Lord, heal my heart
so I can love with the purity and intensity you desire.

Pay attention to those who follow the right example that we have set for you. I have told you this many times before, and now I repeat it with tears: there are many whose lives make them enemies of Christ's death on the cross....

My friends, how dear you are to me, and how I miss you! How happy you make me, and how proud I am of you!

Euodia and Syntyche, please, I beg you, try to agree as sisters in the Lord. And you too, my faithful partner, I want you to help these women; for they have worked hard with me to spread the gospel, together with Clement and all my other fellow workers, whose names are in God's book of the living.   *Philippians 3: 17 – 4: 4*

> "...try to agree as sisters in the Lord."

Beyond differences

Paul speaks to the whole community, then turns his attention to two women who are not getting along... going so far as to address them by name!

Paul expresses wonderful spiritual thoughts on what the coming of Christ will mean to all of us. But he is also concerned about the disagreement between Euodia and Syntyche and he begs them to reconcile.

These two women seem to be leaders in the church. Did they hold differing ideas, differing models of leadership? How did their disagreement affect the community? Whatever their conflict, division in the church seems nothing new, does it?

Paul reminds Euodia and Syntyche – and me – that imitating Christ means seeking reconciliation and wholeness.

> **God, when I am at odds with another person,**
> **let me seek reconciliation in your name.**

prayed to the Lord my God and confessed the sins of my people. I said, "Lord God, you are great, and we honour you. You are faithful to your covenant and show constant love to those who love you and do what you command.

"We have sinned, we have been evil, we have done wrong…. We have not listened to your servants the prophets, who spoke in your name to our kings, our rulers, our ancestors, and our whole nation. You, Lord, always do what is right, but we have always brought disgrace on ourselves…. You are merciful and forgiving, although we have rebelled against you. We did not listen to you, O Lord our God, when you told us to live according to the laws which you gave us through your servants the prophets."

Daniel 9: 3-10

> "…and confessed the sins of my people."

Society's sin

Daniel confessed "the sins of his people." What sins of my people would I confess today? I know I couldn't get away with the hypocrisy of confessing another person's personal sins. Of course, I am tempted to do that, and that in itself is a sin.

Daniel had something else in mind. He was talking about social sin. I don't know what sin he was confessing but there are still many to choose from today. Sins like letting millions in Africa die of AIDS and famine – because, in our wealth, we find we are not wealthy enough. Sins like preferring tax cuts to offering health care to the poor and a living wage to immigrants. Our list may be longer than Daniel's.

**Lord, your prophets confessed their collective sins.
Help me to recognize ours.**

"The teachers of the Law and the Pharisees are the authorized interpreters of Moses' Law. So you must obey and follow everything they tell you to do; do not, however, imitate their actions, because they don't practise what they preach. They tie onto people's backs loads that are heavy and hard to carry yet they aren't willing even to lift a finger to help them carry those loads…. They love to be greeted with respect in the marketplaces and to have people call them 'Teacher.' You must not be called 'Teacher,' because you are all equal and have only one Teacher…. The greatest one among you must be your servant. Whoever makes himself great will be humbled, and whoever humbles himself will be made great."

Matthew 23: 1-12

"Whoever humbles himself will be made great."

Beyond my fears

I admit it – the stories about the Pharisees make me feel so *good*. How misguided they were, I think to myself. They couldn't see the forest for the trees!

But if I'm honest, I must acknowledge that sometimes I act like a Pharisee: when I think I'm better than others. When I don't practise what I preach. When I get so focused on following the rules that I can't leave room for a better way.

If I could let go…. If I could be less rigid…. If I could accept that I'm OK – with my strengths and weaknesses – and don't need to pretend that I'm better than I really am…. Maybe then I'd get somewhere. Maybe then I'd see the forest in the middle of all those trees.

**Jesus, help me see beyond my fears and doubts
so I can be open to your presence.**

The wife of Zebedee came to Jesus, bowed before him, and asked him for a favour. "What do you want?" Jesus asked. She answered, "Promise me that these two sons of mine will sit at your right and your left when you are King." "You don't know what you are asking for," Jesus answered. "Can you drink the cup of suffering that I am about to drink?" "We can," they answered.

Jesus said, "If one of you wants to be great, you must be the servant of the rest; and if one of you wants to be first, you must be the slave of the others – like the Son of Man, who did not come to be served, but to serve and to give his life to redeem many people."

Matthew 20: 17-28

"You don't know what you are asking for…"

Chosen to serve

I can imagine Jesus shaking his head, perhaps muttering to himself, when the Zebedee boys get their mother to ask Jesus for a favour. Some favour: that her sons hold the balance of power in Jesus' kingdom!

In his response, Jesus reminds them (and me) of the conditions of God's kingdom: to be first is to serve. God's kingdom is not that of Rome or Herod or *People* magazine, where fame is sought and gloried in. In another wonderful reversal of the conventional, Jesus throws his lot with those disregarded by society.

At times my head needs a shaking up to see as Jesus sees and to be as Jesus is. What a strange kingdom! But what a compassionate God!

**Lord, make me your servant of peace,
rather than giving me my 'piece' of the kingdom.**

"There was once a rich man and a poor man named Lazarus…. Lazarus died and was carried by the angels to sit beside Abraham in heaven. The rich man died and was buried, and in Hades. He called out, 'Father Abraham! Take pity on me; send Lazarus to dip his finger in some water and cool off my tongue, because I am in great pain in this fire!' But Abraham said, 'Remember that in your lifetime you were given all the good things, while Lazarus got all the bad things. Now he is enjoying himself here, while you are in pain…. There is a deep pit lying between us, so that those who want to cross over from here to you cannot do so.'"

Luke 16: 19 – 17: 3

"…a poor man named Lazarus…"

Rich and poor

Leaving the grocery store, I hear the old man singing and playing his guitar. He is standing by the curb with his dog next to him. He is blind. He has been working this site for years. I don't know his name. Behind him are four newspaper boxes. Their front pages carry the pictures of the rich and the mighty. I know their names.

How often do I pass by the old guy as I put my money in the box to get a newspaper? He can't see me. Perhaps this fact alleviates some of my guilt.

However, when my young son is with me, he insists on putting money in the old man's guitar case. Obviously he sees, and hears… more than I do.

God of the named and the nameless,
help me live up to the name, 'Christian.'

J acob loved Joseph more than all his other sons, because he had been born to him when he was old. He made a long robe with full sleeves for him. When his brothers saw that their father loved Joseph more than he loved them, they hated their brother....

Joseph's brothers plotted against him and decided to kill him. They said to one another, "Come on now, let's kill him and throw his body into one of the dry wells...."

Reuben heard them and tried to save Joseph. "Let's not kill him," he said. "Just throw him into this well in the wilderness, but don't hurt him...." When Joseph came up to his brothers, they ripped off his long robe with full sleeves. Then they took him and threw him into the well.

Genesis 37: 3-4, 12-13, 17-28

> "...and threw him into the well."

Sibling rivalry

I've thrown my brother down many a well over the years, though never intentionally. Last summer, as we sat out on the deck, my mother told me something I didn't want to hear. "Your brother has always felt that he has lived under your shadow." My immediate response was to dismiss such a preposterous idea. But she persisted. "He always looked up to you and somehow felt that he could never live up to the standards you set."

"But he's running the company's division, doing an executive MBA, has two kids, has built an extension on his house all by himself, and is a marathon cyclist!"

Then I realized how I, too, have kept a list of accomplishments that I can serve up as resentments whenever necessary.

Dear God, let me learn to celebrate – rather than count – the differences between myself and others.

72

"There was once a man who had two sons…. [The older son] called one of the servants: 'What's going on?' 'Your brother has come back home, and your father has killed the prize calf….' The older brother was so angry…. 'Look, all these years I have worked for you like a slave, and I have never disobeyed your orders. What have you given me? Not even a goat for me to have a feast with my friends! But this son of yours wasted all your property on prostitutes, and when he comes back home, you kill the prize calf for him!' 'My son,' the father answered, 'you are always here with me, and everything I have is yours. But we had to celebrate, because your brother was dead, but now he is alive; he was lost, but now he has been found.'"

Luke 15: 11-32

> "There was once a man who had two sons…"

Lost and found

Sometimes I'm a little like the prodigal son, or rather, prodigal daughter. I squander an evening reading gossip magazines and watching trash TV; I waste money on useless beauty creams; instead of eating sensible, healthy meals, I binge on cookies and chocolate bars.

Sometimes, I'm more like the elder brother (in my case, elder sister). I work diligently at my job, save money prudently, and try to live responsibly. I virtuously donate time, talents and treasure to my community.

Because of this contrast between the light and dark sides of my heart, I love the parable of the prodigal son. What profound insight into human nature: the inconstant blend of prudent and wasteful, virtuous and sinful, dead and alive that makes up human life!

Lord, help me to celebrate how I am sometimes lost, sometimes found, but always loved by you.

One day while Moses was taking care of the sheep… he came to Sinai, the holy mountain. There the angel of the Lord appeared to him as a flame coming from the middle of a bush. Moses saw that the bush was on fire but that it was not burning up. "This is strange," he thought. "Why isn't the bush burning up? I will go closer and see."

The Lord called to Moses from the middle of the bush and said, "Moses! Moses!" He answered, "Yes, here I am."

God said, "Do not come any closer. Take off your sandals, because you are standing on holy ground. I am the God of your ancestors, the God of Abraham, Isaac, and Jacob."

Exodus 3: 1-8, 13-15

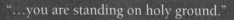

"…you are standing on holy ground."

Holy ground

These days I find myself "standing on holy ground" in seemingly ordinary places. When I take my car to the local garage and the owner takes a few moments out of his busy schedule to inquire about my family, my work… I know that God cares.

When I go to the pool for my noon-time swim, and I hear some of the 'regulars' discussing a friend who has been hospitalized; he has no family in the area so they arrange to visit him… I know that God draws near to those in need.

When I drop in at my friend's restaurant and she's busy in the kitchen: we talk – amidst the pots and the pans – about family challenges and concerns, often sharing a hug or a few tears… I know that I am standing in God's presence.

Dear God, open my eyes to recognize your presence in the seemingly ordinary people and places in my life.

Naaman, the commander of the Syrian army, was a great soldier, but he suffered from a dreaded skin disease. In one of their raids against Israel, the Syrians had carried off a little Israelite girl, who became a servant of Naaman's wife. One day she said to her mistress, "I wish that my master could go to the prophet who lives in Samaria! He would cure him of his disease." ... So Naaman went with his horses and chariot and stopped at the entrance to Elisha's house. Elisha sent a servant out to tell him to go and wash himself seven times in the Jordan River, and he would be completely cured of his disease.... So Naaman went down to the Jordan, dipped himself in it seven times, as Elisha had instructed, and he was completely cured.

2 Kings 5: 1-15

> "...and he was completely cured."

A simple request

How was it that Naaman found healing and an experience of God? First, he was desperate, suffering from a disease with no known cure. Second, he paid attention to a servant girl and took her advice to heart. In venturing forth to visit a prophet in neighbouring Israel, he let go of his national pride. And by listening again to a servant he was able to let go of the heroic and follow the simple way asked for by Elisha. In short, he learned humility.

In my own life, too, it is often only when I am in a desperate situation, when my pride comes crumbling down, that I can hear and trust in those ordinary people in my life who are right beside me.

**Lord, may I have the humility
to receive the wisdom of the people in my life.**

Peter came to Jesus and asked, "Lord, if my brother keeps on sinning against me, how many times do I have to forgive him? Seven times?"

"No, not seven times," answered Jesus, "but seventy times seven, because the Kingdom of heaven is like this. Once there was a king who decided to check on his servants' accounts...."

"The king said to the servant, 'I forgave you the whole amount you owed me, just because you asked me to. You should have had mercy on your fellow servant, just as I had mercy on you.' The king was very angry, and he sent the servant to jail to be punished...." Jesus concluded, "That is how my Father in heaven will treat every one of you unless you forgive your brother from your heart."

Matthew 18: 21-35

"...forgive your brother from your heart."

Straight from the heart

Have you ever watched a couple of preschoolers at play? Reports of injustice happen regularly. "He hurt me!" cries the one who grabbed a toy out of the other's hand first. "She pretended to shoot me!" yells the one who wouldn't take turns. Although this behaviour drives me crazy, I know what they mean.

It feels good to blame someone else when I make a mistake, but God has no patience with that kind of behaviour. God has forgiven me thousands of times. Why should I balk when it is my turn to forgive?

Taking the first step towards reconciliation can be painful, but not as painful as harbouring my bitterness and resentment. Offering forgiveness – even if the other has not apologized – is worth the cost.

Lord, beginning today,
let me forgive just one person from my heart.

"Do not think that I have come to do away with the Law of Moses and the teachings of the prophets. I have not come to do away with them, but to make their teachings come true. Remember that as long as heaven and earth last, not the least point nor the smallest detail of the Law will be done away with – not until the end of all things. So then, whoever disobeys even the least important of the commandments and teaches others to do the same, will be least in the kingdom of heaven. On the other hand, whoever obeys the Law and teaches others to do the same, will be great in the kingdom of heaven."

Matthew 5: 17-19

"Whoever obeys the Law…"

The law of love

At work, I'm sometimes harsh with people who disagree with me. The other day, I got into an argument. I righteously placed myself on what I took to be the 'higher moral ground.' Later I realized that my attitude of superiority had not only compromised the position I was defending, but it had also distanced me from God's love.

Jesus teaches us to love one another. Each time my pride or arrogance causes me to break this commandment, I also teach others to do the same. I become least in the kingdom.

I need to accept Jesus' invitation to love with a humble, unencumbered heart. If my behaviour helps others to do the same, I can hope to find a warm welcome in the kingdom of God.

Jesus, teach me to follow your teaching with a humble heart.

O thers wanted to trap Jesus, so they asked him to perform a miracle to show that God approved of him. But Jesus knew what they were thinking, so he said to them, "Any country that divides itself into groups which fight each other will not last very long; a family divided against itself falls apart. So if Satan's kingdom has groups fighting each other, how can it last? You say that I drive out demons because Beelzebul gives me the power to do so. If this is how I drive them out, how do your followers drive them out? Your own followers prove that you are wrong! No, it is rather by means of God's power that I drive out demons, and this proves that the kingdom of God has already come to you."

Luke 11:14-23

> "A family divided against itself falls apart."

Healing the division

How many of us experience 'a divided family': divisions between siblings; between partners; between in-laws; between parents and children! Whatever the cause of the division, if left to fester, it takes on a life of its own. Feelings are hurt. Communications break down. Relationships falter. A family falls apart and all suffer.

But if things are turned around; if our differences are seen in light of our common goal; if "the kingdom of God has already come to you," then we cannot remain divided. We are united in God's love. With this truth in mind – truly central in our minds and hearts – we have the power to overcome the divisions that tear us apart.

Can I allow myself to be absorbed into God rather than being so self-absorbed?

**God, give me the courage
to go beyond the misunderstandings that I experience.**

A teacher of the Law came to [Jesus] with a question: "Which commandment is the most important of all?" Jesus replied, "The most important one is this: 'Love the Lord your God with all your heart, with all your soul, with all your mind, and with all your strength.' The second most important commandment is this: 'Love your neighbour as you love yourself.' There is no other commandment more important than these two."

The teacher of the Law said, "It is true, as you say… you must love God with all your heart and with all your mind and with all your strength; and you must love your neighbour as you love yourself. It is more important to obey these two commandments than to offer on the altar animals and other sacrifices to God."

Mark 12: 28-34

> "…you must love your neighbour as you love yourself."

One rule

Not long ago, a friend of mine joined Overeaters Anonymous. Her guiding principle has become HALT: she doesn't eat when she's Hungry, Angry, Lonely or Tired. Living with an eating disorder means she is no longer in touch with her true hunger. Rules are required to guide and regulate her eating habits.

What about my own life? I know that when I fill myself with fast food or junk food I lose the taste for truly good and healthy food. Similarly, when I opt for 'instant intimacy' and shallow relationships, I lose the hunger for true and healthy love.

When faced with a decision, instead of looking to many rules, I need to stop and ask: Is my choice based on the greatest rule of all, God's law of love?

Lord, keep my heart hungry for the love that makes me whole, free and alive!

The people say, "Let's return to the Lord…. In two or three days he will revive us, and we will live in his presence. Let us try to know the Lord. He will come to us as surely as the day dawns, as surely as the spring rains fall upon the earth."

But the Lord says, "Israel and Judah, what am I going to do with you? Your love for me disappears as quickly as morning mist…. That is why I have sent my prophets to you with my message of judgment and destruction. What I want from you is plain and clear: I want your constant love, not your animal sacrifices. I would rather have my people know me than burn offerings to me."

Hosea 5: 15 – 6: 6

"I would rather have my people know me…"

Time for God

After months of giving to others at work and at home, I was exhausted. It was a relief to paddle the canoe on that quiet, summer evening. The sun glowed red as it slowly dropped toward the horizon, and a warm breeze blew softly around me. A family of loons called hauntingly to one another, their voices echoing in the surrounding hills.

I relaxed amid this peacefulness, tensions and responsibilities slipping away. I felt the stirrings of peace, and my soul lifted ever so slightly.

For the first time in many months, I noticed the beauty of my surroundings, and I was filled with gratitude. I recognized God's generosity and abundance – both in the world around me and in my own life. I sat for a long time in silence, loving the moment and its Creator.

Gracious God, forgive me when I choose the busyness of activity over time with you.

"The older son asked, 'What's going on?' 'Your brother has come back home,' the servant answered.... The older brother was so angry that he would not go into the house... [and said] to his father, 'Look, all these years I have worked for you like a slave, and I have never disobeyed your orders. What have you given me? Not even a goat for me to have a feast with my friends! But this son of yours wasted all your property on prostitutes, and when he comes back home, you kill the prize calf for him!' 'My son,' the father answered, 'you are always here with me, and everything I have is yours. But we had to celebrate and be happy, because your brother was dead, but now he is alive; he was lost, but now he has been found.'"

Luke 15: 1-3, 11-32

> "...he was lost, but now he has been found."

Today's needs

How to avoid the cliché? Loving father, and sad but wiser prodigal... everybody's happy. And the older brother: do I chastise him, or sympathize with him? After all, he's justified in feeling as he does.

Many students where I teach have failed before, through their own fault. If I took a hard line, "Rules are rules," I'd be right; I'd be justified. And they'd fail again.

But this parable shouts, "Don't look at what's justified; look at what's needed!" And don't think, "I forgive because I'm virtuous and I overlook your transgressions." Rather, "When I see what you need, right now, I've already forgotten your transgressions!"

Yes, my students will have to learn; but if I see with my heart, I'll see their struggle first, and then help them learn the rules.

**Dear Lord, help me put the past to rest
and not dwell on past transgressions.**

Agovernment official went to Jesus and asked him to go to Capernaum and heal his son, who was about to die. Jesus said to him, "None of you will ever believe unless you see miracles and wonders."

"Sir," replied the official, "come with me before my child dies." Jesus said to him, "Go; your son will live!"

The man believed Jesus' words and went. On his way home his servants met him with the news, "Your boy is going to live!" He asked them what time it was when his son got better, and they answered, "It was one o'clock yesterday afternoon when the fever left him." Then the father remembered that it was at that very hour when Jesus had told him, "Your son will live." So he and all his family believed.

John 4: 43-54

> "…unless you see miracles and wonders."

Accepting to believe

As a writer, I'm fascinated by John's techniques. Most writers would simply describe a miracle. John invites readers to choose which of two miracles they will believe.

After criticizing people for demanding 'miracles and wonders,' Jesus provides two of them. He heals an official's son, a full day's walk away.

Of course, some people might argue that the boy would have recovered anyway. I've had malaria myself. When the fever breaks, I can feel it leave. Suddenly, I'm cool again, and clear-headed. Like the official's slaves, I can name the exact time.

So, John asks, which miracle will you believe? That Jesus healed someone at a distance? Or that Jesus somehow knew at a distance exactly when the fever would break?

**Lord, I keep looking for rational explanations;
perhaps I should be more willing just to accept.**

Near the Sheep Gate in Jerusalem there is a pool with five porches. Sick people were lying on the porches – the blind, the lame, and the paralyzed. A man was there who had been sick for thirty-eight years. Jesus knew that the man had been sick for a long time; so he asked him, "Do you want to get well?"

The man answered, "Sir, I don't have anyone to put me in the pool when the water is stirred up; while I am trying to get in, somebody else gets there first." Jesus said, "Get up, pick up your mat, and walk." Immediately the man got well; he picked up his mat and started walking.

John 5: 1-16

"Do you want to get well?"

A helping hand

Oh, the poignant details in these stories! Take the story of the lame man healed on the Sabbath. Bad enough to be paralyzed for thirty-eight years, but to lose the chance for a miracle because "somebody else gets there first" – how pathetic!

There aren't many 'healing pools' on the streets of downtown Toronto, but I see plenty of people who can't keep up with life here. People who can't read enough to fill out their tax returns; people who aren't strong enough to walk up the subway stairs when the escalator is out of order; those who aren't educated enough to land the good technical jobs, the only ones advertized these days in the classified ads. Will anyone give them a helping hand?

**When I'm strong enough to walk on my own,
Lord, teach me to help those who aren't.**

They began to persecute Jesus, because he had done this healing on a Sabbath. Jesus answered them, "My Father is always working, and I too must work." This saying made the Jewish authorities all the more determined to kill him; not only had he broken the Sabbath law, but he had said that God was his own Father and in this way had made himself equal with God.

Jesus answered them, "I tell you the truth: the Son can do nothing on his own; he does only what he sees his Father doing.... For the Father loves the Son and shows him all that he himself is doing.... Just as the Father raises the dead and gives them life, in the same way the Son gives life to those he wants to."

John 5: 16-30

> "...had made himself equal with God."

True intimacy

When I invite my friend and his wife to dinner, I'm always impressed by his answer. He says that he'll first speak with his wife and then reply to my invitation as soon as possible.

What is it that so impresses me in my friend's attitude? I'm struck by his mindfulness – of his wife, whose opinion he considers in all his decisions, and by his devotion to this relationship that gives shape and purpose to his life.

In today's reading, I hear the same profound mindfulness – in the reverence and respect with which Jesus speaks of God. And in that deeply intimate relationship between Jesus and his father – that gives shape and purpose to Jesus' life.

Oh, to be the object of such affection!

God, encourage me to be mindful of you
and of others in my decision-making.

"John was like a lamp, burning and shining, and you were willing for a while to enjoy his light. But I have a witness on my behalf which is even greater than the witness that John gave: what I do, that is, the deeds my Father gave me to do, these speak on my behalf and show that the Father has sent me....

"I am not looking for human praise. But I know... that you have no love for God in your hearts.... Do not think, however, that I am the one who will accuse you. Moses, in whom you have put your hope, is the very one who will accuse you. If you had really believed Moses, you would have believed me.... But since you do not believe what he wrote, how can you believe what I say?"

John 5: 31-47

> "If you had really believed Moses…"

Secure in God's love

The Pharisees were complacent in their dependence on the law that they'd received from Moses. Observing the 'letter of the law' ensured their salvation, or so they thought! Jesus challenges them to go beyond this dependency – to get to know God and to place their hopes for salvation in him.

How often do I place my hopes for the future in a pension plan, a bigger house, a promotion, or my plans for my children? After all, that's how society defines success, isn't it?

How difficult it is to place my hope in the one who offers me only the security of God's love. Jesus challenges me to focus on what really matters in life: to make honesty more important than advancement, generosity more important than comfort.

Lord, free me from the need for guarantees.
Let me find my true security in you.

The Lord said to Nathan, "Go and tell my servant David that I say to him, 'You are not the one to build a temple for me to live in.... When you die and are buried with your ancestors, I will make one of your sons king and will keep his kingdom strong. He will be the one to build a temple for me, and I will make sure that his dynasty continues forever. I will be his father, and he will be my son. When he does wrong, I will punish him as a father punishes his son.... You will always have descendants, and I will make your kingdom last forever. Your dynasty will never end.'"

2 Samuel 7: 4-5, 12-16

"You are not the one to build a temple for me..."

A legacy that lasts

Nathan reminds me of a boss I once had. We learned never to act immediately on his decisions. "Wait a day," his associate regularly cautioned us. "By tomorrow he'll have had second thoughts."

David wanted to build a house for God. Nathan said 'Yes.' Overnight, he had second thoughts. The next day, he told David 'No.' But God turned that 'No' into a glorious 'Yes.' Playing with meanings of 'house,' God told David, "I don't want to live in the house of David (a building). I want to live in the house of David (a lineage)."

A generation later, Solomon did what David was not allowed to do. Is it just coincidence that David's empire broke down soon after? Did the temple become a prison, allowing the people to isolate God from daily life?

Lord, I dream of doing great things for you.
Make me content with doing little things well.

S ome of the people said, "This man is really the Prophet!" Others said, "He is the Messiah!" But others said, "The Messiah will not come from Galilee! The scripture says that the Messiah will be a descendant of King David and will be born in Bethlehem, the town where David lived." So there was a division in the crowd because of Jesus....

One of the Pharisees there was Nicodemus, the man who had gone to see Jesus before. He said, "According to our Law we cannot condemn people before hearing them and finding out what they have done."

"Well," they answered, "are you also from Galilee? Study the Scriptures and you will learn that no prophet ever comes from Galilee."

John 7: 40-53

> "...no prophet ever comes from Galilee."

A modern day prophet

He had no business saying or doing the things he did – he had no authority! His background was inadequate, to say the least. The people he collected around himself were hardly upper crust folks either. No wonder he stirred up so much trouble. Maybe he didn't cause riots, but he certainly fuelled unreasonable expectations for some people. I don't know who he thought he was, but the bottom line was this: God didn't work through Black persons. Everyone knew that.

Next month marks the 42nd anniversary of the assassination of Martin Luther King, Jr. He is one of only a handful of twentieth-century persons who might legitimately be called a messiah: a person anointed and chosen by God to be a liberating force in history.

God, help me see you wherever love liberates,
rather than where I expect to find you.

The teachers of the Law and the Pharisees brought in a woman who had been caught committing adultery. "Teacher, in our Law Moses commanded that such a woman must be stoned to death. What do you say?" They said this to trap Jesus. But he bent over and wrote on the ground with his finger....

He said, "Whichever one of you has committed no sin may throw the first stone at her." Then he bent over again and wrote on the ground. When they heard this, they all left, one by one, the older ones first. Jesus said to [the woman], "Where are they? Is there no one left to condemn you?" "No one, sir," she answered. "Well, then, I do not condemn you either. Go, but do not sin again."

John 8: 1-11

> "I do not condemn you either."

Do not judge

One day, as I walked my son across the schoolyard, one boy spat on another's shoes. He retaliated by shoving the first hard onto the pavement. They both saw me at the same time, and knew they were caught in the act. They watched and waited. So did the gathering crowd.

I quietly sent for the teacher. As I handed them over, I described the situation and indicated that neither had behaved appropriately. This was not my territory in which to render judgment. But, as I walked away, I offered a silent prayer for that teacher and for those students. And for all of us who, at times, find ourselves in the position of judge. How we need the wisdom and guidance of the One who is free to judge perfectly!

Lord, free me from the desire to cast stones of condemnation. Teach me to offer mercy, justice and truth.

The Lord is my shepherd;
I have everything I need.
He lets me rest in fields of green grass
and leads me to quiet pools of fresh water….
He guides me in the right paths,
as he has promised….
You prepare a banquet for me,
where all my enemies can see me;
you welcome me as an honoured guest
and fill my cup to the brim.
I know that your goodness and love
will be with me all my life;
and your house will be my home
as long as I live.   *Psalm 23: 1-6*

"I have everything I need."

A guiding hand

I always worry about whether I've made the right choices – about how to raise the kids, career moves, where to live…. The list goes on.

When I look back at our old photo albums and see the smiling faces, I realize that things were good – even when they did not go the way I planned.

At mid-life, I look back and begin to see a pattern. I realize that the Lord has been my shepherd, even though I didn't realize it at the time. And things that I thought were problems, even disasters, led me to places I would not otherwise have gone. In fact, my life is richer and more interesting when I step back and let God show me the way.

Dear God, give me the humility to let go
and accept your guiding hand in my life.

"Who are you?" Jesus answered, "What I have told you from the very beginning…. The one who sent me is truthful, and I tell the world only what I have heard from him."

They did not understand that Jesus was talking to them about the Father. So he said, "When you lift up the Son of Man, you will know that 'I Am Who I Am'; then you will know that I do nothing on my own authority; but I say only what the Father has instructed me to say. And he who sent me is with me; he has not left me alone, because I always do what pleases him." Many who heard Jesus say these things believed in him.

John 8: 21-30

"When you lift up the Son of Man, you will know…"

Who are you?

Jesus has the uncanny ability of going to the heart of the matter. Today's reading presents us with an important question: who are you, Jesus? Instead of consoling, Jesus' response unsettles and even confronts.

Jesus' pithy response is to declare his identity as 'I Am Who I Am.' What does this mean? The gospels illustrate *who* he is by *what* he does. Jesus heals and enables people crushed by disease; he frees from inner prisons; he feeds the body and spirit. Jesus is God in the flesh – touching and holding us.

In revealing "he who is," Jesus reveals who we are: mysterious, changing and growing into the fullness of life at Easter. But first, "I Am Who I Am" hangs on a cross and is laid in a tomb. Then…

Lord, I am challenged to discover you anew.
Surprise me with who you are.

Jesus said, "If you obey my teaching, you are really my disciples; you will know the truth, and the truth will set you free."

"We are the descendants of Abraham," they answered, "and we have never been anybody's slaves...."

"If you really were Abraham's children," Jesus replied, "you would do the same things that he did. All I have ever done is to tell you the truth I heard from God, yet you are trying to kill me...."

"God himself is the only Father we have," they answered, "and we are his true children." Jesus said, "If God really were your Father, you would love me, because I came from God and now I am here. I did not come on my own authority, but he sent me."

John 8: 31-42

> "If you obey my teaching..."

True disciples

When our kids were young we read to them constantly. We must have read *The Chronicles of Narnia* by C. S. Lewis at least three times to successive ages of kids.

In the seventh book of the series, *The Last Battle*, a soldier turns up whose religious practice is to worship a diabolical god. Though he worships this false god, all his life he is judged as worthy by the true God: "No service which is vile can be done to me and none which is not vile can be done to him."

Dorothy Day put it another way when she said that atheists she knew, who sacrificed their lives to struggle for peace and serve the poor, were, in truth, lovers of Christ.

Lord, may I refrain from judging others.
You alone know what lies hidden in our hearts.

G od sent the angel Gabriel to a young woman promised in marriage to a man named Joseph. Her name was Mary. The angel said, "Peace be with you! The Lord is with you and has greatly blessed you!" Mary was deeply troubled by the angel's message, and she wondered what his words meant. The angel said, "Don't be afraid, Mary; God has been gracious to you. You will become pregnant and give birth to a son, and you will name him Jesus...." Mary said to the angel, "I am a virgin. How, then, can this be?" The angel answered, "The Holy Spirit will come on you, and God's power will rest upon you...."

"I am the Lord's servant," said Mary; "may it happen to me as you have said."

Luke 1: 26-38

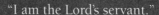

"I am the Lord's servant."

Free to be

Was Mary preoccupied with thoughts of Joseph that day, dreaming perhaps of their approaching marriage? In any event, the appearance of an angel must have caught her totally off guard. This was not in her plan!

While the angel's message troubled her, Mary quickly recovered her balance and responded out of her deepest identity: "I am the Lord's servant." Knowing this, she could be open to the action of the Holy Spirit: "May it happen to me as you have said."

Do I know my own deepest identity? Knowing this, I am free to respond to the Spirit – even when I am thrown off course by the unexpected, and asked to move into the unknown.

Lord, teach me to know, and live, from my deepest truth.

My God is my protection,
and with him I am safe.
He protects me like a shield;
he defends me and keeps me safe….
Praise the Lord!
The danger of death was all around me;
the waves of destruction rolled over me.
The danger of death was around me,
and the grave set its trap for me.
In my trouble I called to the Lord;
I called to my God for help.
In his temple he heard my voice;
he listened to my cry for help.

Psalm 18: 1-6

> "In my trouble I called to the Lord."

Going home to God

For months, as cancer slowly took my mother away, death lapped at me like steady, rolling waves that grew higher every day. It was often a struggle to keep my head above water.

But my mother remained unperturbed. As she weakened physically, her inner strength increased and she grew more and more serene. She accepted with gratitude whatever life offered to her.

I marvelled at this and wondered where she found her strength.

Now I realize that, in her own quiet way, she had called on God. God had been her strong fortress, providing her safety and protection – not from death, which comes to us all, but from the terror of death. She was already safe at home, even before she left us.

Lord, be my protector – not just on my last day, but every day.

Many of the people saw what Jesus did, and they believed in him. But some of them returned to the Pharisees and told them what Jesus had done. So the Pharisees and the chief priests met with the Council and said, "What shall we do? Look at all the miracles this man is performing! If we let him go on in this way, everyone will believe in him, and the Roman authorities will take action and destroy our Temple and our nation!"

One of them, named Caiaphas, who was High Priest that year, said, "What fools you are! Don't you realize that it is better for you to have one man die for the people, instead of having the whole nation destroyed?" From that day on the Jewish authorities made plans to kill Jesus.   *John 11:45-57*

"…the authorities made plans to kill Jesus."

A caring society

How do the authorities make plans to kill someone? Start by advertising locally for 'murderers wanted'? Sounds ridiculous when described this way, but maybe things were different in Jesus' day.

Flash forward to the 21st century. What about our authorities, those whom we elect to govern our world? What does it mean when we turn hundreds of bewildered mental patients out onto the streets without proper community support? How should we describe the policy of abandoning our frail elderly in overcrowded, understaffed nursing homes? What about condemning thousands of poor children to a bleak, hopeless childhood because of cutbacks to the welfare system? Perhaps it's easy enough to "make plans to kill" the human spirit when we make fiscal restraint our most important civic virtue.

**Lord, help me to live your words of life
in a society that denies the needs of people.**

When the hour came, Jesus took his place at the table with the apostles. He said to them, "I have wanted so much to eat this Passover meal with you before I suffer...."

Then Jesus took a cup, gave thanks to God, and said, "Take this and share it among yourselves. I tell you that from now on I will not drink this wine until the kingdom of God comes."

Then he took a piece of bread, gave thanks to God, broke it, and gave it to them, saying, "This is my body, which is given for you. Do this in memory of me." In the same way, he gave them the cup after the supper, saying, "This cup is God's new covenant sealed with my blood, which is poured out for you."

Luke 22: 14 – 23: 56

"...sealed with my blood..."

The new covenant

My mother sold her engagement diamond, and sent the money to the missions. "Mom! You're giving it away?" I asked. "What did Our Lord give?" she replied. Jesus, I want to give like you, but I mean, be realistic.... Sealed with my blood.

I know, but I gave at work. I pay taxes. Besides, I didn't cause the problem.... Sealed with my blood.

But how can I speak up? I'll be the only one. Besides, it won't do any good.... Sealed with my blood.

Forgive her? She never even thinks of my perspective! Why should I...? Sealed with my blood.

C'mon, it's too much; I'm so tired. Yes, my child, and so was I.

Dear Jesus, hear my cry: I need your help to give as you did.

Jesus went to Bethany, the home of Lazarus, the man he had raised from death. They prepared a dinner for him there, which Martha helped serve…. Then Mary took a whole pint of a very expensive perfume made of pure nard, poured it on Jesus' feet, and wiped them with her hair. The sweet smell of the perfume filled the whole house. One of Jesus' disciples, Judas Iscariot – the one who was going to betray him – said, "Why wasn't this perfume sold for three hundred silver coins and the money given to the poor…?" But Jesus said, "Leave her alone! Let her keep what she has for the day of my burial. You will always have poor people with you, but you will not always have me." *John 12: 1-11*

> "The sweet smell of the perfume filled the whole house."

A small, caring gesture

Having invited friends for supper, I was pleased that, just as they arrived, the kitchen aromas had spread to the front hall. My guests joyfully remarked, "Even the air makes us feel welcome!"

Mary's gesture of hospitality changed the atmosphere of the dinner scene and truly touched Jesus. Her action expressed her deep devotion to Jesus, and perhaps it gave him some comfort as he faced the dark days ahead.

It takes so little to make a difference in the lives of others. Often I downplay what I have to share – even if it is only a well-cooked meal for friends. My small investment of time and effort can lift the spirits of others who might be carrying a heavy burden.

**God, it takes so little to make such a difference
in the lives of others. Encourage me!**

J esus declared, "I am telling you the truth: one of you is going to betray me." The disciples looked at one another, completely puzzled about whom he meant. One of the disciples, the one whom Jesus loved, was sitting next to Jesus. Simon Peter motioned to him and said, "Ask him whom he is talking about." So that disciple moved closer to Jesus' side and asked, "Who is it, Lord?"

Jesus answered, "I will dip some bread in the sauce and give it to him; he is the man." So he took a piece of bread, dipped it, and gave it to Judas. As soon as Judas took the bread, Satan entered into him. Jesus said to him, "Hurry and do what you must…." Judas accepted the bread and went out at once.

John 13: 21-38

"…one of you is going to betray me."

Acts of betrayal

Dear Judas, you are deep within me. You cannot bear to accept that the good is here and now. You cannot accept the mystery that occurs right before you. You will not enter into the transformation that is needed. Why? What paralyzes you?

Each of us betrays the deepest reality of our selves. Each of us betrays Jesus and the new life he offers. The form may vary, but the truth remains: our addictions, excesses, worrying, unkind words and many fears all deny the new life made possible through Jesus' suffering, death and resurrection.

I need to look around to ask who will be the next to betray…. I know Judas lives within me. I am the one so dearly in need of God's mercy.

Merciful God, forgive my betrayals and my denials.
Help me turn again to your life-giving love.

The Sovereign Lord has taught me what to say,
so that I can strengthen the weary.
Every morning he makes me eager
to hear what he is going to teach me.
The Lord has given me understanding,
and I have not rebelled or turned away from him.
I bared my back to those who beat me.
I did not stop them when they insulted me....
But their insults cannot hurt me
because the Sovereign Lord gives me help.
I brace myself to endure them.

I know that I will not be disgraced,
for God is near,
and he will prove me innocent.   *Isaiah 50: 4-9*

"The Lord has given me understanding..."

In face of violence

Lately, when I drop my son off at school, I've noticed kids bullying other kids. I watch closely. When necessary, I intervene, because my heart goes out to the ones who are too little, too fragile or too innocent to put a bully in their place.

Bullying doesn't stop when children leave school. I see it happening between my neighbours, within families, in my community, and between countries fighting for land and power.

I find it hard to turn my back on insults and acts of violence directed at me or at those I love. But I know that if I follow Jesus' example of peace, justice and forgiveness, no real harm can come to me.

Jesus, give me the strength and courage to follow your example.

Jesus took off his outer garment, and tied a towel around his waist. Then he poured some water into a washbasin and began to wash the disciples' feet and dry them with the towel. He came to Simon Peter, who said to him, "Never at any time will you wash my feet!"

"If I do not wash your feet," Jesus answered, "you will no longer be my disciple." Simon Peter answered, "Lord, do not wash only my feet, then! Wash my hands and head, too!"

"Do you understand what I have just done to you?" he asked. "I, your Lord and Teacher, have just washed your feet. You, then, should wash one another's feet. I have set an example for you, so that you will do just what I have done for you."

John 13: 1-15

> "You, then, should wash one another's feet…"

Acts of service

One summer we went camping and hiking along two of the most beautiful rivers in our region of Quebec. Being near those rivers was humbling and restorative, and set me thinking about our relationship with nature.

I've often heard people say that environmental problems are due to the Judeo-Christian idea of humans dominating nature. Today's reading shows just what Jesus thinks of domination: he turns the whole idea on its head. Instead of demanding the disciples' submission, he washes their feet, a humble act of service.

Jesus wants me to show the same kind of respect and care toward other human beings, and also toward the whole of creation. Both those rivers washed my feet: how can I wash theirs?

Lord, you have given us so much.
Teach me to honour the earth.

Judas went to the garden, taking with him a group of Roman soldiers and some Temple guards…. Simon Peter, who had a sword, drew it and struck the High Priest's slave, cutting off his right ear…. Then the Roman soldiers with their commanding officer and the Jewish guards arrested Jesus….

Simon Peter and another disciple followed Jesus…. It was cold, so the servants and guards had built a charcoal fire and were standing around it, warming themselves. So Peter stood with them, warming himself…. The others said, "Aren't you also one of the disciples of that man?" But Peter denied it. "No, I am not," he said.

One of the High Priest's slaves spoke up. "Didn't I see you with him in the garden?" he asked. Again Peter said "No" – and at once a rooster crowed.

John 18: 1 – 19: 42

"Peter stood with them, warming himself…"

Loved, and forgiven

Peter puts up a big show of gallantry: cutting off a poor servant's ear, wanting to show how brave he is, trying to defend Jesus. A little later Peter denies he even knows Jesus.

I can just see myself standing there: warming my hands by the fire, even though they aren't cold, trying not to be noticed. How many times have I failed to stand up for Jesus in the face of injustice or lies, because I'm afraid to be labelled? I quietly carry on warming my hands at the fire.

But in spite of this terrible betrayal, Jesus called Peter 'the Rock,' the most solid of his friends! Jesus not only forgave Peter, he entrusted the church to him, and then died for him. He loved him.

**Lord, help me to not despair at my failings;
you have already forgiven them.**

Very early on Sunday morning the women went to the tomb, carrying the spices they had prepared. They found the stone rolled away from the entrance to the tomb, so they went in; but they did not find the body of the Lord Jesus…. Suddenly two men in bright shining clothes stood by them. Full of fear, the women bowed down to the ground, as the men said, "Why are you looking among the dead for one who is alive? He is not here; he has been raised…."

The women returned from the tomb, and told all these things to the eleven disciples and all the rest…. But the apostles thought that what the women said was nonsense, and they did not believe them.
Luke 24: 1-12

> "…thought that what the women said was nonsense…"

Witness of women

The first witnesses to the resurrection were women. On that fact, all four gospels agree. Yet I don't remember ever hearing that taught, in Sunday school or in Sunday sermons. The credit always went to the male disciples, Peter and John.

I guess there was a 'glass ceiling' even then – the invisible barrier that many women perceive blocking them from the senior executive offices that are usually on the top floor.

The women ran back to tell the male disciples, and they thought it was nonsense. Julian of Norwich taught of a God who loves, and her bishop thought it was heresy. Mother Teresa aided the dying, and the medical establishment called it futile. So little has changed.

If I suffer from spiritual tunnel vision, God, help me broaden my perspectives.

Early on Sunday morning, while it was still dark, Mary Magdalene went to the tomb…. While she was still crying, she bent over and looked in the tomb and saw two angels there dressed in white, sitting where the body of Jesus had been….

She turned around and saw Jesus standing there…. She thought he was the gardener, so she said to him, "If you took him away, sir, tell me where you have put him, and I will go and get him." Jesus said to her, "Mary!" She turned toward him and said in Hebrew, "Rabboni!" "Do not hold on to me." Jesus told her, "because I have not yet gone back up to the Father. But go to my brothers and tell them that I am returning to him who is my Father and their Father, my God and their God."

John 20: 1-18

"Jesus said to her, 'Mary!'"

Called by name

Mary loved Jesus so deeply that she went to the cemetery determined to do something. Love called for action. Early in the morning Mary left the other mourners, and followed her heart.

Mary probably didn't know exactly what she planned to do at Jesus' tomb. But when the 'gardener' began asking questions, Mary knew how desperately she wanted to find Jesus.

Pain and anguish can blind me to reality just as they did Mary. Like her, often I can't see Jesus standing before me. I can only pray that he will call me by name and tell me the good news: God's love is stronger than death and, one day, I will experience that love in all its fullness, together with the ones I love.

**God, help me to recognize Jesus in 'gardeners'
and hear when you call me by name.**

They left the tomb in a hurry, afraid and yet filled with joy, and ran to tell his disciples. Suddenly Jesus met them and said, "Peace be with you." They came up to him, took hold of his feet, and worshipped him. "Do not be afraid," Jesus said to them. "Go and tell my brothers to go to Galilee, and there they will see me."

While the women went on their way, some of the soldiers guarding the tomb went back to the city and told the chief priests everything that had happened. The chief priests met with the elders and made their plan; they gave a large sum of money to the soldiers and said, "You are to say that his disciples came during the night and stole his body while you were asleep."

Matthew 28: 8-15

"…afraid and yet filled of joy…"

In the face of grief

Hundreds of candle-lit vigils sprang up spontaneously following the attack on the World Trade Center in New York. My heart broke as I watched friends and relatives standing vigil, clutching pictures of loved ones who were missing. These people gathered – as did the women at the tomb – to be together, to find support and to pray.

Can this experience of unimaginable loss and grief ever turn to joy? I find myself still outside the tomb, still unable to believe in the possibility of resurrection and new life.

I read how the women turned from the tomb and ran to tell the disciples what they knew to be true. I hope that, in time, my feet will turn and run with them, with faith and with joy.

Risen Christ, guide my journey in times of grief.
Help me to believe in your promise of new life.

The Lord loves what is righteous and just;
his constant love fills the earth....
The Lord watches over those who obey him,
those who trust in his constant love.
He saves them from death;
he keeps them alive in times of famine.
We put our hope in the Lord;
he is our protector and our help.
We are glad because of him;
we trust in his holy name.

May your constant love be with us, Lord,
as we put our hope in you.
Psalm 33: 4-5, 18-22

"...he keeps them alive..."

Gift of life

In the aftermath of Hurricane Katrina, the media covered some amazing stories. One woman in her 80s had lost everything. She was interviewed live on camera in a simple housedress. The interviewer enumerated all her losses, trying to convey how much even the lucky ones suffered.

You've lost all your clothes? Yes. And all your belongings? Yes. And your photographs? "Yes," she said, "I had pictures of my family on every wall in my house, and they're all gone."

Then, probably to the surprise of her interviewer, she continued, "I don't need much now, just these clothes to wear. I only want to live." Her losses did not make her bitter or anxious; they made her focus on the greatest gift of all: the gift of life.

**How often I take for granted this beautiful life.
Thank you, Lord.**

Two of Jesus' followers were going to a village named Emmaus, about seven miles from Jerusalem.... As they talked and discussed, Jesus himself drew near and walked along with them; they saw him, but somehow did not recognize him....

As they came near the village, Jesus acted as if he were going farther; but they held him back, saying, "Stay with us; the day is almost over and it is getting dark." So he went in.... He sat down to eat with them, took the bread, and said the blessing; then he broke the bread and gave it to them. Then their eyes were opened and they recognized him, but he disappeared from their sight. They said to each other, "Wasn't it like a fire burning in us when he talked to us on the road and explained the Scriptures to us?"

Luke 24: 13-35

"Their eyes were opened and they recognized him..."

Breaking bread

A small group of us sat in a crowded restaurant. We wanted to say grace, but we didn't want to draw attention to ourselves. No one wanted to make the first move.

At that moment, my friend picked up a bun that the waiter had placed on our table. He held it up, tore it in half, and passed it around. He didn't need to say a word. We all knew exactly the symbolism of his gesture. It became a kind of trademark for our group whenever we gathered.

Whatever Jesus did with the bread, at that inn in Emmaus, it was characteristic enough of him that they recognized his gesture. And in recognizing the gesture, they recognized him.

**Jesus, may all my actions
let others recognize your presence in me.**

The two then explained to [the disciples] what had happened on the road, and how they had recognized the Lord when he broke the bread. While the two were telling them this, suddenly the Lord himself stood among them and said to them, "Peace be with you." They were terrified, thinking that they were seeing a ghost. But he said to them, "Why are you alarmed? Why are these doubts coming up in your minds? Look at my hands and my feet, and see that it is I myself. Feel me…." He said this and showed them his hands and his feet. They still could not believe, they were so full of joy and wonder; so he asked them, "Do you have anything here to eat?" They gave him a piece of cooked fish, which he took and ate.

Luke 24: 35-48

"…suddenly the Lord himself stood among them…"

Standing among us

I remember fish-paste sandwiches, little cakes with a thin topcoat of lemon icing and the clinging aroma of tea, bubbling in a large urn. Clusters of adults, half-whispered conversations in the awkwardness after a funeral. We, the children, were relegated to the sidelines.

One of my aunts would tell a story, recalling the person who had died. Laughing through tears, people would nod, cherishing the details. Someone would start singing, quietly until everyone joined in. Somehow, the tearful sadness in the room would turn warm, as if the person they were mourning had joined them for one more chorus.

It's a bit like the astonished disciples in today's reading: confused by grief, unable to understand what they had seen… until Jesus stood before them once again.

**Jesus, in moments of grief and uncertainty,
keep my mind and heart open to your presence.**

S imon Peter said, "I am going fishing."

"We will come with you," the other disciples told him. So they went out in a boat, but all that night they did not catch a thing. As the sun was rising, Jesus stood at the water's edge, but the disciples did not know that it was Jesus. He asked them, "Young men, haven't you caught anything?"

"Not a thing," they answered. He said, "Throw your net out on the right side of the boat, and you will catch some." So they threw the net out and could not pull it back in, because they had caught so many fish....

When they stepped ashore, they saw a charcoal fire there with fish on it and some bread. Then Jesus said, "Bring some of the fish you have just caught.... Come and eat."

John 21: 1-14

> "Bring some of the fish..."

A fish story

This story always makes me smile. The hapless fishermen, working on their own, don't catch a single fish all night! But when they work *with* Jesus, their nets can barely hold the catch.

So often I work at cross purposes with God – doing things my way, with poor results – rather than trying God's way, with astonishing results.

But that's not the end of the story. Jesus invites the fishermen to bring some of the fish, which he cooks and shares with them to keep them fed and strong.

Can I, too, bring the fruits of my labours to God, so they may be shared with others as nourishment?

Lord, help me to remember that my work is not just for myself, but for those around me.

T he members of the Council were amazed to see how bold Peter and John were and to learn that they were ordinary men of no education…. "What shall we do with these men?" they asked. "Everyone in Jerusalem knows that this extraordinary miracle has been performed by them, and we cannot deny it. But to keep this matter from spreading any further among the people, let us warn these men never again to speak to anyone in the name of Jesus…."

Peter and John answered them, "You yourselves judge which is right in God's sight – to obey you or to obey God. For we cannot stop speaking of what we ourselves have seen and heard." So the Council warned them even more strongly and then set them free.   *Acts 4: 13-21*

"…they were ordinary men of no education."

Expert witnesses

I once worked at a radio station that had an index system of phone numbers of experts who could talk credibly on any given topic. Radio producers believe their listeners like the authoritative charm of articulate experts, especially those with good credentials.

This list proved especially useful in the early hours of the morning when news items tend to be 'bagged.' I remember being overwhelmed by the experts' levels of knowledge about topics that I had never even considered!

But, in today's reading, along come Peter and John, tipping all of that 'expert' logic on its head. No degrees, no credentials of any kind. Just their own lived experience and raw, unbending faith. And they confound those who *think* they know.

**Dear God, help me to see, and to live,
an authentic witness to your love.**

I t was late that Sunday evening, and the disciples were gathered together behind locked doors, because they were afraid of the Jewish authorities. Then Jesus came and stood among them. "Peace be with you," he said. After saying this, he showed them his hands and his side. The disciples were filled with joy at seeing the Lord. Jesus said to them, "As the Father sent me, so I send you." Then he breathed on them and said, "Receive the Holy Spirit. If you forgive people's sins, they are forgiven; if you do not forgive them, they are not forgiven...."

Jesus performed many other miracles that are not written down in this book. But these have been written in order that you may believe that Jesus is the Messiah, and that through your faith in him you may have life.

John 20: 19-31

"Receive the Holy Spirit."

Answering the call

When I was a teenager, I used to wonder what God wanted me to do with my life. It's taken a long time, and a number of false starts, but I've discovered that my strengths, my passions and even my weaknesses show me the way.

Jesus gave his fearful disciples an enormous mission: to go out and change the world. But each of them – hot-headed Peter, quiet John, ambitious James – would fulfill that mission in a unique way, according to his own set of strengths and challenges.

Today, God offers me a mission of my own. My particular temperament and circumstances will help me discern the way I am to change the world around me. How will I answer the call?

**Lord, help me to use all of my personality
to bring your peace to the world.**

One night Nicodemus went to Jesus and said, "Rabbi, we know that you are a teacher sent by God. No one could perform the miracles you are doing unless God were with him." Jesus answered, "I am telling you the truth: no one can see the kingdom of God without being born again."

"How can a grown man be born again?" Nicodemus asked. "He certainly cannot enter his mother's womb and be born a second time!"

"I am telling you the truth," replied Jesus, "that no one can enter the kingdom of God without being born of water and the Spirit. A person is born physically of human parents, but is born spiritually of the Spirit. Do not be surprised because I tell you that you must all be born again."

John 3: 1-8

> "How can a grown man be born again?"

Born again?

I was his teacher in an adult education class. A victim of serious physical abuse when he was a child, he was now full of anger.

You can imagine the rest: repeat offender, semi-literate, cocaine dependent, alcoholic. This guy needed to be born again! And you know what? He truly wanted to be.

But it's not easy when you can barely read, and when you have an addiction, a criminal record and a spirit so battered it can't really believe in anything, even itself.

"How can a grown man be born again?" I still don't know the answer; I really don't. But if I truly believe what I profess to believe, I need to keep looking for it.

**Show me, Lord, how a grown man can be born again.
I need to know.**

The group of believers was one in mind and heart. None of them said that any of their belongings were their own, but they all shared with one another everything they had. With great power the apostles gave witness to the resurrection of the Lord Jesus, and God poured rich blessings on them all. There was no one in the group who was in need. Those who owned fields or houses would sell them, bring the money received from the sale, and turn it over to the apostles; and the money was distributed according to the needs of the people.

Acts 4: 32-37

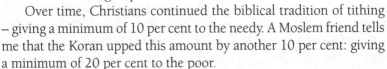

> "...they all shared with one another everything they had."

Caring for the needy

Today's reading tells how the members of the early Christian community shared their belongings with one another. And, because of this practice, "there was no one in the group who was in need."

Over time, Christians continued the biblical tradition of tithing – giving a minimum of 10 per cent to the needy. A Moslem friend tells me that the Koran upped this amount by another 10 per cent: giving a minimum of 20 per cent to the poor.

Today, our country objects to making a contribution to the poor and needy of the world in the amount of seven-tenths of one per cent of the GDP. It seems that seven-tenths of one per cent – as compared to 10 or 20 per cent – is very hard-hearted math in anyone's book.

**Lord, loosen my tight grasp on my belongings,
and help me discover the joy this brings.**

will always thank the Lord;
I will never stop praising him.
I will praise him for what he has done;
may all who are oppressed listen and be glad!
Proclaim with me the Lord's greatness;
let us praise his name together!
I prayed to the Lord, and he answered me;
he freed me from all my fears....
The helpless call to him, and he answers;
he saves them from all their troubles.
His angel guards those who honour the Lord
and rescues them from danger.
Find out for yourself how good the Lord is.
Psalm 34: 1-8

"Find out for yourself how good the Lord is."

Goodness and mystery

When I was a boy, I believed that God's goodness would be shown
by dramatic or miraculous actions. Heavenly choirs would sing as an
angel swooped down and rescued me from some near disaster.

As I got older, my imagination became less literal. God's goodness
would be revealed through good things happening. The righteous would
benefit from their actions. Love would be returned to the loving.

But now I know that the loving are not always loved; the good
suffer; justice is repaid with indifference – God's goodness is seen in
mystery and paradox. God is found at the heart of suffering. In the
moment of bleak emptiness, God is present. How is this so? I don't
know. It just is.

Lord, thank you for revealing yourself to me in so many ways.

They brought the apostles in, made them stand before the Council, and the High Priest questioned them. "We gave you strict orders not to teach in the name of this man," he said; "but see what you have done! You have spread your teaching all over Jerusalem, and you want to make us responsible for his death!"

Peter and the other apostles answered, "We must obey God, not humans. The God of our ancestors raised Jesus from death, after you had killed him by nailing him to a cross. God raised him to his right side as Leader and Saviour, to give the people of Israel the opportunity to repent and have their sins forgiven. We are witnesses to these things – we and the Holy Spirit, who is God's gift to those who obey him."

Acts 5: 27-33

"We must obey God, not humans."

God's view

"What do you see in Thomas?" I asked my twelve-year-old son, regarding his friendship with a classmate who clearly trailed him physically, socially and intellectually. I was humbled by his answer, embarrassed that I had even asked the question.

"When I met Thomas last year, right after we moved here, I noticed a lot of kids teased him because he wasn't as smart or as coordinated as they were, Dad. But Thomas is OK. He's a good kid, and it didn't seem right to me that no one was his friend."

Ben's blossoming mind has decided he doesn't need God. But whether he realizes it or not, my adolescent-atheist son knows well when to obey God's wish, rather than human whim. May I do the same!

God, may I hear your voice among the many voices I hear today.

J esus asked Philip, "Where can we buy enough food to feed all these people?" Philip answered, "For everyone to have even a little, it would take more than two hundred silver coins to buy enough bread."

Another one of his disciples said, "There is a boy here who has five loaves of barley bread and two fish…."

"Make the people sit down," Jesus told them. So all the people sat down. Jesus took the bread, gave thanks to God, and distributed it to the people who were sitting there. He did the same with the fish, and they all had as much as they wanted. When they were all full, he said to his disciples, "Gather the pieces left over…." [They] filled twelve baskets with the pieces left over from the five barley loaves that the people had eaten.

John 6: 1-15

> "Where can we buy enough food…?"

Small beginnings

Feeding five thousand people with five loaves and two fish started with an unnamed boy who chose to give up his own lunch.

Philip had been arguing with Jesus that there wasn't enough food for everyone. "It would take more than two hundred silver coins to buy enough bread." But a boy stepped forward with his loaves and fish, and that was the beginning of the miracle.

Anything I give away seems to be so small in relation to the huge needs in our world. But I give it anyway – in the hope of a miracle. This is just as true in my own family, as it is in the realm of foreign aid.

**Lord, when it comes to miracles,
remind me that I can choose *how* to participate in them.**

When evening came, Jesus' disciples went down to the lake, got into a boat, and went back across the lake toward Capernaum. Night came on, and Jesus still had not come to them. By then a strong wind was blowing and stirring up the water.

The disciples had rowed about three or four miles when they saw Jesus walking on the water, coming near the boat, and they were terrified. "Don't be afraid," Jesus told them, "it is I!" Then they willingly took him into the boat, and immediately the boat reached land at the place they were heading for.

John 6: 16-21

> "...a strong wind was blowing and stirring up the water."

Between two shores

Years ago, five of us had to cross ten miles of lake in a small, open boat. It was windy but the fellow taking us thought it'd be OK. "Besides," he said, "if I waited every time it was rough, I'd never go anywhere." By the time we got to the other side, we were bailing and even he was very glad to have made it.

Life isn't always safe! If I stay on shore, there's no risk, but I'll never get where I need to go. It's that middle, turbulent part that's scary: when I'm between two shores, like the disciples that night.

Maybe miracles don't happen today, but help does come – a phone call, a word of encouragement – and I know that I'm not alone.

**Lord, when life is most stormy,
let me feel your presence coming across the water to help me.**

J esus said to Simon Peter, "Simon, son of John, do you love me more than these others do?" "Yes, Lord," he answered, "you know that I love you."

Jesus said to him, "Take care of my lambs." A second time Jesus said to him, "Simon, son of John, do you love me?" "Yes, Lord," he answered, "you know that I love you."

Jesus said to him, "Take care of my sheep." A third time Jesus said, "Simon, son of John, do you love me?" Peter became sad because Jesus asked him the third time, "Do you love me?" and so he said to him, "Lord, you know everything; you know that I love you!"

Jesus said to him, "Take care of my sheep...." Then Jesus said to him, "Follow me!"   *John 21: 1-19*

> "...you know that I love you."

Love in action

When an elderly gentleman found himself widowed and alone – she welcomed him as an honoured guest at Sunday brunches and holiday celebrations.

When a close friend had an abortion, and she disagreed with her friend's choice – she poured her energy into providing support for other young, pregnant women.

When children showed up at school without food and without adequate winter clothing – she rounded up supplies and organized volunteers to start a Breakfast Club.

When a neighbour was diagnosed with a terminal illness, and his wife needed to be with him at the hospital – she opened her home to their young children, offering them a secure refuge.

She doesn't talk about love much. She doesn't have to – her actions say it all.

Lord, give me the courage to put my words of love into action.

The rulers meet and plot against me,
but I will study your teachings.
Your instructions give me pleasure....
Teach me your ways.
Help me to understand your laws,
and I will meditate on your wonderful teachings.
I am overcome by sorrow;
strengthen me, as you have promised.
Keep me from going the wrong way,
and in your goodness teach me your law.
I have chosen to be obedient;
I have paid attention to your judgments.

Psalm 119: 23-30

"...teach me your ways."

Faced with a choice

We were in a hurry to get to my five-year-old
daughter's music lesson. While I waited for her to do up her seatbelt,
she asked: "Mummy, does God control our hearts and our brains?"

I took a deep breath and launched into a rather laboured explanation of how God created us yet gave us freedom of heart and mind. "Now hurry up, or we'll be late," I said.

"So we can choose to take the path to God or the path to the devil?" she persisted, as she struggled with her belt. "Um, yes," I said, uncertainly.

"Well, I'm going to take the path to God," she declared, and stuck her thumb in her mouth. No psalmist could have announced his resolution more eloquently.

**Lord, give me the heart of a child,
and renew my choice for love, life and others every day.**

They replied, "What miracle will you perform so that we may see it and believe you? What will you do? Our ancestors ate manna in the desert, just as the scripture says, 'He gave them bread from heaven to eat.'"

"I am telling you the truth," Jesus said. "What Moses gave you was not the bread from heaven; it is my Father who gives you the real bread from heaven. For the bread that God gives is he who comes down from heaven and gives life to the world."

"Sir," they asked him, "give us this bread always."

"I am the bread of life," Jesus told them. "Those who come to me will never be hungry; those who believe in me will never be thirsty."

John 6: 30-35

"What miracle will you perform...?"

Seeing the miracle

During introductions in a beginners' art class, a woman informed me she was taking my course as the result of a bet with a friend. Having been involved in sports all her life, she saw herself more as a 'jock' than an artist.

I assured her that making art is a talent possessed by more than a select few; it is a skill anyone can learn. During the program, not only did she master the basic skills, she found that she really liked to draw. "It's a miracle!" she exclaimed, "I didn't know I could do this. It's like I see the whole world differently!"

I think she's right: seeing the world in a new way is a miracle. We simply need the willingness to look.

God, help me to look for, and to see, the miracles in my life.

" I am the bread of life. Those who come to me will never be hungry; those who believe in me will never be thirsty…. Everyone whom my Father gives me will come to me. I will never turn away anyone who comes to me, because I have come down from heaven to do not my own will but the will of him who sent me. And it is the will of him who sent me that I should not lose any of all those he has given me, but that I should raise them all to life on the last day. For what my Father wants is that all who see the Son and believe in him should have eternal life. And I will raise them to life on the last day."

John 6: 35-40

> "I will raise them to life on the last day."

Faith in the promise

He was curled up in the bed next to mine in the hospital, and his large hand easily reached mine. The ebony skin had gone dusty from the dialysis; he was slipping away and he wanted to pray.

"There have been times when I've been hungry and thirsty," he said, "but other times I had to just work at believing. The Father of us all sent Jesus down here and he never told lies, even to the officials. Why should we think he'd lie about something big like this? Jesus, be with me on this last lap. I'm coming home." He went silent, and died a bit later. The nurse pried his fingers open and I cried.

I remember this moment and Jesus' promise: "I will never turn away anyone."

God, death is a reality.
Help me to recall Jesus' presence now and at that moment.

"The prophets wrote, 'Everyone will be taught by God.' Anyone who hears the Father and learns from him comes to me. This does not mean that anyone has seen the Father; he who is from God is the only one who has seen the Father. I am telling you the truth: he who believes has eternal life. I am the bread of life. Your ancestors ate manna in the desert, but they died. But the bread that comes down from heaven is of such a kind that whoever eats it will not die. I am the living bread that came down from heaven. If you eat this bread, you will live forever. The bread that I will give you is my flesh, which I give so that the world may live."

John 6: 44-51

> "...so that the world may live."

Bread for life

Imagine the scene: the people standing around, not knowing what Jesus was talking about. Two thousand years later and, truth be told, I don't think I know. Not really.

These people couldn't know what was to come. Couldn't know how Jesus was to "give his flesh" on the cross. They couldn't know the lengths to which he would go. Couldn't know what it would cost him.

Do I have to go to the same lengths to have everlasting life? How do I "eat his flesh" and continue to live a middle-class life, in a culture that is focused on materialism and self-indulgence? And at what cost?

Two thousand years later and I don't think I know. Not really.

Dear Lord, help me figure out how to live, how truly to live.

A s Saul was coming near the city of Damascus, suddenly a light from the sky flashed around him. He fell to the ground and heard a voice saying to him, "Saul, Saul! Why do you persecute me?" "Who are you, Lord?" he asked. "I am Jesus, whom you persecute," the voice said…. Saul got up from the ground and opened his eyes, but could not see a thing….

Ananias entered the house where Saul was, and placed his hands on him. "Brother Saul," he said, "the Lord has sent me – Jesus himself, who appeared to you on the road as you were coming here. He sent me so that you might see again and be filled with the Holy Spirit." At once something like fish scales fell from Saul's eyes, and he was able to see again.

Acts 9: 1-20

"…and he was able to see again."

With eyes of faith

The light in April has a special quality to it. The sun's strength is increasing, and the days are getting longer. Bare winter branches soften with cascades of fragile buds. I lift my head and marvel at a sky suddenly bursting with new life. Spring calls me to see with new eyes, to look beyond what seems grey and hopeless.

God chose Saul even though he was persecuting Jesus' followers. How often have I been blinded by my assumptions about others? How often have I overlooked the new patterns and possibilities in my relationships?

Whether it's a difficult dynamic with a friend or a challenging interaction with a family member, now is the time for me to take a second look, with new eyes.

God, heal my blindness.
May I look at others through eyes of faith and hope.

"I am telling you the truth: if you do not eat the flesh of the Son of Man and drink his blood, you will not have life in yourselves." Many of his followers heard this and said, "This teaching is too hard." Without being told, Jesus knew that they were grumbling about this, so he said, "Does this make you want to give up? Suppose that you should see the Son of Man go back up to the place where he was before? What gives life is God's Spirit; human power is of no use at all. The words I have spoken to you bring God's life-giving Spirit…. No people can come to me unless the Father makes it possible for them to do so."

John 6: 53, 60-69

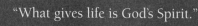

"What gives life is God's Spirit."

Fed by love

No wonder the disciples were troubled! Could Jesus really want to turn them into cannibals? Were they supposed to gnaw on Jesus' bones? I have an advantage: I know about the last supper where Jesus took bread and wine and said, "*This* is my body…. *This* is my blood."

My own trouble is different. I'm often left gnawing on the human shortcomings of those who preside at the table of the Lord – and those who gather around it. Even telling myself that I have failings, too, doesn't help. I keep looking for perfectly wise and loving people.

From now on, I want to focus on something else: on the way God uses ordinary, flawed means – bread, wine, human beings – to lead me to eternal life.

Lord, nourish me with your body and blood, with your word, and with the love of friends and family.

"**M**y sheep listen to my voice; I know them, and they follow me. I give them eternal life, and they shall never die. No one can snatch them away from me. What my Father has given me is greater than everything, and no one can snatch them away from the Father's care. The Father and I are one."

John 10: 27-30

> "No one can snatch them away."

Trust in God

It's not too flattering to be compared to sheep. They're so weak, and, let's face it, so stupid. I once saw sheep, panicked by a storm, running over the rocks along a seaside cliff. Their minds too small to see the danger, many fell to their deaths, running from the noise of the wind.

How often I am like those sheep: running from perceived danger… into real danger! Working incessantly for security or refusing to face up to my alcoholism… and risking the loss of my family.

How much easier to weather life's storms if I recognize that I am weak, too weak to do it alone, and that my vision is limited. And discovering that, if I let go, someone will help me.

Dear God, let me trust in your wisdom and remain calm, resting in your hand.

Jesus said, "I am telling you the truth: ...the one who goes in through the gate is the shepherd of the sheep. The gatekeeper opens the gate for him; the sheep hear his voice as he calls his own sheep by name, and he leads them out. When he has brought them out, he goes ahead of them, and the sheep follow him, because they know his voice....

"I am telling you the truth. I am the gate for the sheep. All others who came before me are thieves and robbers.... Those who come in by me will be saved; they will come in and go out and find pasture. The thief comes only in order to steal, kill and destroy. I have come in order that you might have life – life in all its fullness."

John 10: 1-10

> "...as he calls his own sheep by name..."

Called by name

One of the hardest aspects of being a single parent is having no one with whom to share your worries: when the children get sick, when the car breaks down, when the everyday demands seem too much to carry....

One day, when a friend was visiting, all three of my children needed me – all urgently and all at the same time! My friend gently said, "You take care of the kids. I'll take care of you." Together we managed the crisis, and life went on.

Later, remembering her words, tears welled up from deep within. How I yearn to have someone to whom I can turn when things get rough. I forget that God is there, offering to care for me in times of need.

Lord, thank you for friends who care.
Their support reminds me of your loving presence.

S ome of the believers who were scattered by the persecution that took place when Stephen was killed went as far as Phoenicia, Cyprus, and Antioch, telling the message to Jews only. But other believers, who were from Cyprus and Cyrene, went to Antioch and proclaimed the message to Gentiles also, telling them the Good News about the Lord Jesus. The Lord's power was with them, and a great number of people believed and turned to the Lord.

The news about this reached the church in Jerusalem, so they sent Barnabas to Antioch.... Then Barnabas went to Tarsus to look for Saul. When he found him, he took him to Antioch, and for a whole year the two met with the people of the church and taught a large group. It was at Antioch that the believers were first called Christians. *Acts 11:19-26*

"...and a great number of people believed..."

Unexpected growth

Every winter, we fill our bird feeder with sunflower seeds. Birds are messy eaters: their busy beaks scatter shells – and a few un-cracked seeds – all over our deck and patio. We sweep up what we can to put in the garbage or, being environmentally conscious, in the compost. But every spring, an unplanned crop of sunflowers pops up between the patio stones and in nearby flowerbeds.

The stoning of Stephen launched a wave of persecution that scattered the faithful throughout the eastern Mediterranean. It was supposed to sweep up this new, unsettling Jewish splinter group and dump them in the garbage can of history.

But something unexpected happened. Sunflowers popped up all over. And some of them took a new name – Christian.

God, show me how my painful experiences can turn into the seeds for new growth.

"Whoever believes in me believes not only in me but also in him who sent me. Whoever sees me sees also him who sent me. I have come into the world as light, so that everyone who believes in me should not remain in the darkness.

"If people hear my message and do not obey it, I will not judge them. I came, not to judge the world, but to save it. Those who reject me and do not accept my message have one who will judge them. The words I have spoken will be their judge on the last day!

"This is true, because I have not spoken on my own authority, but the Father who sent me has commanded me what I must say and speak. And I know that his command brings eternal life."

John 12: 44-50

> "Whoever sees me sees also him who sent me."

Finding God

As a teacher, I find it hard to admit that there are some students I just don't like. I'm thinking about one boy in particular. He is a constant mess of coughing and sneezing, with a nose that runs perpetually. He also has some very irritating personality traits.

On a professional level I've tried to meet his needs, but deep down I think I've really failed that boy. I haven't been able to see the face of God when I look into his eyes.

It's easy for me to find God in those students who are easily loveable. And I feel satisfied when I've met their needs. Today's reading challenges me to look a little deeper – to find God in the faces of those students I find hard to like.

**Help me, God, to see your face
in the features of those I'd rather not embrace.**

" I am telling you the truth: no slaves are greater than their master, and no messengers are greater than the one who sent them. Now that you know this truth, how happy you will be if you put it into practice! I am not talking about all of you; I know those I have chosen. But the scripture must come true that says, 'The man who shared my food turned against me.' I tell you this now before it happens, so that when it does happen, you will believe that 'I Am Who I Am.' I am telling you the truth: whoever receives anyone I send receives me also; and whoever receives me receives him who sent me."

John 13: 16-20

> "How happy you will be
> if you put it into practice!"

Joy in serving

Ours is a world of slaves and masters. Do not children from the Third World knot wool into carpets? Do not these same slave-waged carpets pad the cozy floors of the moneyed and privileged? Do not young and unskilled workers juggle three part-time jobs? And ironically, the 'freedom 55' crowd complain about meager returns from mutual funds!

Yet Jesus purposely sought to serve those who were impoverished and enslaved. These followers, who took him at his word, likewise became servants. And what did they receive as their reward? Is that not a smile on the face of Mother Teresa? Is there not serenity in Jean Vanier and his fellow l'Arche members? Joy lives in those who are Jesus' servants.

Lord, your word promises life.
Help me live your good news in all I say and do.

"Do not be worried and upset," Jesus told them. "Believe in God and believe also in me. There are many rooms in my Father's house, and I am going to prepare a place for you. I would not tell you this if it were not so. And after I go and prepare a place for you, I will come back and take you to myself, so that you will be where I am. You know the way that leads to the place where I am going."

Thomas said to him, "Lord, we do not know where you are going; so how can we know the way to get there?" Jesus answered him, "I am the way, the truth, and the life; no one goes to the Father except by me."

John 14: 1-6

> "I am the way, the truth, and the life."

The path to follow

Recently I moved house and had to plan a new garden. When setting it up I saw that I needed to have a good idea where I would build the *paths*. These paths would be used every day – whether they were used to go to the compost or to give me a spot to view and enjoy my whole garden.

"I am the way, the truth, and the life; no one goes to the Father except by me." Where do I want to go? What do I want to attain in my life? If I am aiming towards union with God – both in my lifetime and at the end of my life – Jesus is the path I must follow, one I must *choose* to follow every day.

**Lord, help me in the choices I make today.
Walk with me on this path I am following.**

When the Jews saw the crowds, they were filled with jealousy; they disputed what Paul was saying and insulted him. But Paul and Barnabas spoke out even more boldly: "It was necessary that the word of God should be spoken first to you. But since you reject it... we will leave you and go to the Gentiles. For this is the commandment that the Lord has given us: 'I have made you a light for the Gentiles, so that all the world may be saved.'"

The word of the Lord spread everywhere in that region. But the Jews... started a persecution against Paul and Barnabas and threw them out.... The apostles shook the dust off their feet in protest and went on to Iconium. The believers in Antioch were full of joy and the Holy Spirit.

Acts 13: 44-52

> "The believers... were full of joy."

With peace and joy

As a union activist, Maria often dealt with angry people on both sides of the negotiating table – her fellow union members as well as the employers. Surrounded by hostile forces, she reached out to build bridges rather than to provoke confrontations. While she worked hard to protect vulnerable employees, she also recognized the forces that shaped the bosses' behaviour.

In some ways, her ability to act constructively in the midst of animosity reminds me of the remarkable believers that Paul and Barnabas left behind in Antioch. Filled with the Holy Spirit, they lived with joy, a joy that would spread and touch the lives of others. Like Maria, centering their hearts on the important things made it possible to live happily in the midst of hostility.

Lord, make me aware of your deep and abiding love when others criticize or reject me.

t was now the day before the Passover Festival. Jesus knew that the hour had come for him to leave this world and go to the Father.

After Judas had left, Jesus said, "Now the Son of Man's glory is revealed; now God's glory is revealed through him. And if God's glory is revealed through him, then God will reveal the glory of the Son of Man in himself, and he will do so at once. My children, I shall not be with you very much longer.

"And now I give you a new commandment: love one another. As I have loved you, so you must love one another. If you have love for one another, then everyone will know that you are my disciples."

John 13: 1, 31-35

"As I have loved you, so you just love..."

A witness to love

If I could bring today's reading to my everyday life, I would be a different person: I would be much gentler. And my life would be much simpler for having but one question to ask: "How do I love this person who stands in front of me?" Nothing else would matter.

If I'm really honest with myself, I must admit that I have a subtle way of asking: "How can I get what I want from this person?" or "How can I please this person in order to feel more comfortable with myself?" Not very flattering, but true.

To gaze upon others with gentleness, love and concern would be, well, different. If I changed, perhaps I'd be a better witness to Jesus' good news also!

**God, give me the openness to live your love
in all that I do and say.**

"For a long time I have been with you all; yet you do not know me, Philip? Do you not believe that I am in the Father and the Father is in me? The words that I have spoken to you," Jesus said to his disciples, "do not come from me. The Father, who remains in me, does his own work. Believe me when I say that I am in the Father and the Father is in me. If not, believe because of the things I do. I am telling you the truth: those who believe in me will do what I do – yes, they will do even greater things, because I am going to the Father. And I will do whatever you ask for in my name, so that the Father's glory will be shown through the Son. If you ask me for anything in my name, I will do it."

John 14: 6-14

> "…those who believe in me will do what I do…"

Echoing Jesus

My son has started going to a *dojo*, a traditional martial arts school. Because he is a beginner, many of the exercises he does are incomplete. They train a particular set of muscles or a specific instinctive move. The goal – after months of practice – will be to put the muscles, movements and awareness together so that when the *sensei* (the teacher) says, "Do what I do," Ben will be able to echo the art of the sensei with his own body.

In today's reading, Jesus says that we believe less with our minds than with our whole being. We believe by *doing* as Jesus does – by investing our lives in love.

My goal is to echo the art of Jesus with my own body.

God, make me a willing and eager student of your art.

A ll your creatures, Lord, will praise you,
and all your people will give you thanks.
They will speak of the glory of your royal power
and tell of your might,
so that everyone will know your mighty deeds
and the glorious majesty of your kingdom.
Your rule is eternal,
and you are king forever….
I will always praise the Lord;
let all his creatures praise his holy name forever.

Psalm 145: 10-13, 21

"All your creatures, Lord, will praise you."

All of God's creatures

The geese are coming back. I could hear them last night, at dusk. Soon it will be hummingbirds and, yes, monarch butterflies riding the winds on their delicate wings, all the way from Mexico. How do they know the way? What is the language of their instinct?

"All your creatures, Lord, will praise you."

There is only one of your creatures for whom there is never enough. Only one of your creatures who will kill – not for food or to protect its young, but for greed. Or hate. Or from some twisted notion of who you are.

Yes, yes, I know. The animals have no free will. But I sometimes wonder: who pleases God more – the monarch butterfly, or the inventor of the smart bomb?

Lord, help me praise you with my life.

" I am the real vine, and my Father is the gardener. He breaks off every branch in me that does not bear fruit; and he prunes every branch that does bear fruit, so that it will be clean and bear more fruit. You have been made clean already by the teaching I have given you. Remain united to me, and I will remain united to you. A branch cannot bear fruit by itself; it can do so only if it remains in the vine. In the same way you cannot bear fruit unless you remain in me.

"I am the vine, and you are the branches. Those who remain in me, and I in them, will bear much fruit; for you can do nothing without me."

John 15: 1-8

"…and bear more fruit."

Bearing fruit

I had my heart set on getting the contract, but she literally laughed at my proposal, to which I had devoted many hours of work. I walked away feeling very 'pruned down.'

When I got home, there was a message waiting for me. The refugees – whom our parish set out to sponsor a year and a half ago – were arriving in two weeks' time!

Five years ago a child had been separated from her family when they came under rebel fire and fled in opposite directions. As I phoned this child – now a teenager who lives in our town – my earlier sense of humiliation and loss withered. We wept together with joy and relief at the good news. One branch was cut away; the other bore fruit.

**Lord, help me to stay connected with you,
and to let go of the bits you trim away.**

"I love you just as the Father loves me; remain in my love. If you obey my commands, you will remain in my love, just as I have obeyed my Father's commands and remain in his love.

"I have told you this so that my joy may be in you and that your joy may be complete."

John 15: 9-11

"...remain in my love."

Source of all joy

The expression "remain in my love" is also translated "abide in my love." The word 'abide' evokes images of relaxing, taking life slowly. Today's reading reminds me to slow down, to relax in Jesus' love – to take time to be quiet and to listen.

Often I turn on my computer, my television or my stereo without much thought. In fact, when my heart and mind are longing for nourishment, I make the mistake of trying to fill the void with entertainment. This always leaves me feeling unfulfilled.

Sooner or later I am drawn back to the source that provides me with a deeper joy. Being entertained requires very little response on my part. Abiding in God's love asks more of me and, as a result, sustains me.

Lord, help me to slow down so that I may abide in your love.

"My commandment is this: love one another, just as I love you. The greatest love you can have for your friends is to give your life for them. And you are my friends if you do what I command you. I do not call you servants any longer, because servants do not know what their master is doing. Instead, I call you friends, because I have told you everything I heard from my Father. You did not choose me; I chose you and appointed you to go and bear much fruit, the kind of fruit that endures. And so the Father will give you whatever you ask of him in my name. This, then, is what I command you: love one another."

John 15: 12-17

> "I chose you…"

The chosen ones

My daughter's face lights up like a sunbeam as she tells me the news: her music teacher has asked her to perform a special song at the spring concert. She is bursting with pride. I can see her walking a little taller. Excitement echoes in her voice. She glows with new energy as she goes off to practise with renewed enthusiasm!

I think of my daughter's excitement at being chosen when I consider today's reading. Did the disciples feel the same way when Jesus told them that he had chosen them to continue his work? I imagine standing among them, feeling their excitement.

Jesus' words have echoed across the ages, and even to our day. How is Jesus speaking to me, today?

Jesus, I hear your words and give thanks for your love.

As [Paul and Timothy] went through the towns, they delivered to the believers the rules decided upon by the apostles and elders in Jerusalem, and they told them to obey those rules. So the churches were made stronger in the faith and grew in numbers every day. They travelled through the region of Phrygia and Galatia because the Holy Spirit did not let them preach the message in the province of Asia…. So they travelled right on through Mysia and went to Troas. That night Paul had a vision in which he saw a Macedonian standing and begging him, "Come over to Macedonia and help us!" As soon as Paul had this vision, we got ready to leave for Macedonia, because we decided that God had called us to preach the Good News to the people there.

Acts 16: 1-10

> "That night Paul had a vision…"

Are dreams real?

We, in the scientific West, treat dreams as unreal, a meaningless firing of mental synapses during sleep. The East has a different attitude to dreams and visions.

Paul dreamed of a man inviting him to come to Macedonia. And so he brought Christianity to what we now call Europe.

At one point, when my marriage was in trouble, I dreamed I was single again. I called everyone I knew for a date. They were all busy. I found myself spending Saturday night alone. Again.

I realized I didn't want to spend my life that way. That dream may have happened only in my mind, but it had real effects. It changed my attitude.

I wonder, sometimes, what's real and what isn't.

**You have many ways of speaking to me, God.
Keep me from ignoring any of them.**

"Those who love me will obey my teaching. My Father will love them, and my Father and I will come to them and live with them. Those who do not love me do not obey my teaching....

"Peace is what I leave with you; it is my own peace that I give you. I do not give it as the world does. Do not be worried and upset; do not be afraid. You heard me say to you, 'I am leaving, but I will come back to you.' If you loved me, you would be glad that I am going to the Father; for he is greater than I. I have told you this now before it all happens, so that when it does happen, you will believe."

John 14: 23-29

> "Do not be worried and upset."

True peace

At a recent funeral, as we followed the casket out of the church, we sang, "Since Love is Lord of heaven and earth, how can I keep from singing?" I sang the words with a heavy heart: the tears flowed and the feeling of loss cut deep.

I noticed one woman singing with a smile on her face and her arms raised in praise. How could she be so happy? I wondered. Then I realized that she really and truly believed the words of that song – and was living them.

My own feelings of sorrow and loss kept me from rejoicing that my friend is now with God. Faced with the emptiness that death brings, I struggle to trust the peace that Jesus offers me.

Lord, you promise to wipe away all our worries and fears. Help me to believe that your love is stronger than death.

We left by ship from Troas and sailed straight across to Samothrace, and the next day to Neapolis. From there we went inland to Philippi…. On the Sabbath we went out of the city to the riverside, where we thought there would be a place where Jews gathered for prayer. We sat down and talked to the women who gathered there. One of those who heard us was Lydia from Thyatira, who was a dealer in purple cloth. She was a woman who worshipped God, and the Lord opened her mind to pay attention to what Paul was saying. After she and the people of her house had been baptized, she invited us, "Come and stay in my house if you have decided that I am a true believer in the Lord." And she persuaded us to go.

Acts 16: 11-15

> "…we went out of the city to the riverside…"

By the river

Some of the best moments of my life have been by rivers. So I can understand why Paul and his companions would expect to find a place of prayer by the river. Perhaps Philippi did not have the necessary ten Jewish men for a synagogue. So if people wanted to pray, they would gather at the river.

I don't know what it is about flowing water. It doesn't matter to me whether it's a small brook, burbling happily through grassy banks, or a vast river, sliding silently along, or a mountain torrent, filling the air with spray. As the writer of Psalm 23 says, the running waters restore my soul. Rivers make me think of God – always the same, yet always different.

When I'm happy, my cup overflows. When I'm sad, my eyes do. Thank you, Lord, for your life-giving water.

The officials tore the clothes off Paul and Silas and ordered them to be whipped. After a severe beating, they were thrown into jail, and the jailer was ordered to lock them up tight....

About midnight Paul and Silas were praying and singing hymns to God, and the other prisoners were listening to them. Suddenly there was a violent earthquake, which shook the prison to its foundations. At once all the doors opened, and the chains fell off all the prisoners....

The jailer called for a light, rushed in, and fell trembling at the feet of Paul and Silas. Then he led them out and asked, "Sirs, what must I do to be saved?" They answered, "Believe in the Lord Jesus, and you will be saved."

Acts 16: 22-34

"...they were thrown into jail..."

Standing up for God

When I was a boy, I loved stories of saints and martyrs – especially martyrs. I imagined myself in situations like Paul and Silas'. Like them, I was always heroic, unfazed by beatings or jailings, singing hymns in the face of death. And finally, when God's power was revealed, everyone saw just how mistaken they'd been. I was recognized as the truly holy person I was.

Now I realize life is both easier and harder than that. I am unlikely to be tortured or arrested for my religious beliefs. Unfortunately, I am just as unlikely to see miraculous signs of God's majesty.

Today, evil is subtle and quiet, and perhaps more dangerous for its friendly face. And God, where is God? I sometimes have to ask.

**Lord, help me follow you when all around is darkness,
and my prison chains are gold.**

"I have much more to tell you, but now it would be too much for you to bear. When, however, the Spirit comes, who reveals the truth about God, he will lead you into all the truth. He will not speak on his own authority, but he will speak of what he hears and will tell you of things to come. He will give me glory, because he will take what I say and tell it to you. All that my Father has is mine; that is why I said that the Spirit will take what I give him and tell it to you."

John 16: 12-15

"...will lead you into all the truth."

Knowing and responding

Sometimes it's easy to see the truth, to know what to do. Sometimes it's not so easy: like when a friend asks for answers to an assignment he hasn't done. I know he has problems at home, and last night was a bad night. Yet this is becoming a habit. What should I do?

Sometimes I know what to do... yet? When I was a teenager, a woman who was drunk fell and dropped a large sum of money in the wind. My friend and I collected it for her. She tried to pay us $100 each. I knew what to do, but it was hard to do it.

Perhaps the Spirit guides me to the truth, but will I follow? As the bard says, "Aye, there's the rub."

God, let me have insight to recognize the truth, and the courage to act on it.

"In a little while you will not see me any more, and then a little while later you will see me." Some of his disciples asked among themselves, "What does this mean? He tells us that in a little while we will not see him, and then a little while later we will see him…. What does this 'a little while' mean? We don't know what he is talking about!"

Jesus knew that they wanted to question him, so he said, "I said, 'In a little while you will not see me, and then a little while later you will see me.' Is this what you are asking about among yourselves? I am telling you the truth: you will cry and weep, but the world will be glad; you will be sad, but your sadness will turn into gladness."

John 16: 16-20

> "…a little while later you will see me."

In a little while

She's been there all along, right under my left foot. It's been months since I've seen her, but I knew she'd be back in the spring. I knew that, six to eight inches below the earth's surface, there always was hope for spring beauty. Any day now she'll bloom forth – unmistakably that red tulip I planted three years ago.

Like the tulip, God's Spirit is close to me – right under my skin. I know the Spirit is here even though I can't see her. And whether I wait a day, a month or a lifetime, I know I'll see the Spirit again. I'll recognize her because, just as the tulip can't be mistaken for a daffodil, God's Spirit can't be mistaken when she reveals herself to the beloved.

**Lord, help me to recognize you
when you reveal yourself in my life.**

There was a meeting of the believers, about a hundred and twenty in all, and Peter stood up to speak. "My friends, someone must join us as a witness to the resurrection of the Lord Jesus. He must be one of the men who were in our group during the whole time that the Lord Jesus travelled about with us...."

So they proposed two men: Joseph, who was called Barsabbas, and Matthias. Then they prayed, "Lord, you know the thoughts of everyone, so show us which of these two you have chosen to serve as an apostle in the place of Judas, who left to go to the place where he belongs." Then they drew lots to choose between the two men, and the one chosen was Matthias, who was added to the group of eleven apostles.

Acts 1: 15-17, 20-26

> "Then they drew lots..."

Choose and move on

Sometimes I get paralyzed about a decision. Should I leave a job that's driving me crazy? Do I need to change the way I deal with my spouse? my child? my friend?

When the disciples were faced with a difficult decision, they used their heads to think things through and came up with two candidates. Then they opened their hearts in prayer. But they still didn't have a decision. Finally they did something shocking. They drew lots. They gambled.

When I've gathered all the information I can get; when I've prayed over my decision, and still can't make up my mind, maybe I should follow the disciples' example. Maybe I should say one last prayer, flip a coin, and get on with my life.

Lord, when I have a decision to make,
help me to balance the need for caution with the need for action.

A Jew named Apollos, who had been born in Alexandria, came to Ephesus. He was an eloquent speaker and had a thorough knowledge of the Scriptures. He had been instructed in the Way of the Lord, and with great enthusiasm he proclaimed and taught correctly the facts about Jesus. However, he knew only the baptism of John…. When Priscilla and Aquila heard him, they took him home with them and explained to him more correctly the Way of God. Apollos then decided to go to Achaia, so the believers in Ephesus helped him by writing to the believers in Achaia, urging them to welcome him. When he arrived, he was a great help to those who through God's grace had become believers.

Acts 18: 23-28

> "He had been instructed in the Way of the Lord…"

"Just do it!"

I remember the new brother in our parish. He had grown up poor and tough. And he'd come to religion late in life. He worked with, as he said, "the yout'."

People wanted to get the youth of the parish to attend religion classes. They met to discuss possible strategies. This new brother asked, "Do we always have to teach them something? Can't we just help them?"

As the years passed, I saw him practise what he preached. He never expounded his beliefs or corrected others about theirs. In his second-hand clothes, he *did*: he visited jails, hospitals and rehab programs.

Explaining 'the correct way' is easier than living the great commandments. I wish I knew the Way of the Lord.

**Lord, let me concentrate on how I live,
not on teaching others how they should.**

We have, then, my friends, complete freedom to go into the Most Holy Place by means of the death of Jesus. He opened for us a new way, a living way, through the curtain – that is, through his own body.... So let us come near to God with a sincere heart and a sure faith, with hearts that have been purified from a guilty conscience and with bodies washed with clean water. Let us hold on firmly to the hope we profess, because we can trust God to keep his promise. Let us be concerned for one another, to help one another to show love and to do good. Let us not give up the habit of meeting together... instead, let us encourage one another all the more.

Hebrews 9: 24-28; 10: 19-25

"He opened for us a new way, a living way..."

A living way

She was devastated by the news: the lump in her breast was cancerous. "Why me?" she cried. She had always cared for her body, having trained for and competed in numerous marathons. Now it felt like her body had betrayed her.

As she waited for confirmation of the diagnosis, she reached out to other women living with breast cancer. As she shared her fears with them, she found that their support and encouragement "opened a new way, a living way, through the curtain."

And she vowed, some day, to return the help she'd received: "I'm going to give in whatever way I can," she exclaimed. "I'll start Learn to Run clinics for breast cancer survivors!" Her body had shown her "a living way" to help others.

**Lord, when hurt and illness overwhelm me,
help me to find a living way through the darkness.**

Then Jesus' disciples said to him, "Now you are speaking plainly, without using figures of speech. We know now that you know everything; you do not need to have someone ask you questions. This makes us believe that you came from God."

Jesus answered them, "Do you believe now? The time is coming, and is already here, when all of you will be scattered, each of you to your own home, and I will be left all alone. But I am not really alone, because the Father is with me. I have told you this so that you will have peace by being united to me. The world will make you suffer. But be brave! I have defeated the world!"

John 16: 29-33

> "The time is coming…
> when all of you will be scattered..."

A strong foundation

There are times when I feel as though the last place of safety in the world is my own home. Outside, forces that seem as powerful and destructive as the forces of nature – consumerism, globalization, disposable relationships, our worship at the temple of the marketplace – join together and howl like a hurricane through the streets, scattering everything before them.

Some days, the foundations of my home creak and groan before their force. I feel as though it's only a matter of time before the strain will prove too great. How did this happen? What can I do?

And out of the whirlwind comes a voice that is both reassuring and more frightening than the blowing winds: "You will have peace by being united to me."

**Lord, give me the courage to trust in you,
as the foundation of my home.**

Jesus looked up to heaven and said, "Father, I have made you known to those you gave me out of the world. They belonged to you, and you gave them to me. They have obeyed your word, and now they know that everything you gave me comes from you....

"I pray for them. I do not pray for the world but for those you gave me, for they belong to you. All I have is yours, and all you have is mine; and my glory is shown through them. And now I am coming to you; I am no longer in the world, but they are in the world. Holy Father! Keep them safe by the power of your name, the name you gave me, so that they may be one just as you and I are one."

John 17: 1-11

> "Keep them safe..."

Out into the world

When I was a teenager, my mother waited up for me until I was home safely after a night out with my friends. When I was late, she met me at the door with the rosary in her hands, worried sick that I was lying in a ditch somewhere. At the time I would roll my eyes at her concern – after all, I knew that I was fine!

Now that I am a mother, I understand her fear. My son is not a teenager yet, but he will be in a few years. Then it will be my turn to send him out into the world, having taught him what I could about how to protect himself from harm. On my lips will be a silent prayer: "Keep him safe, God."

**Lord, sometimes the world can be a scary place.
Watch over the ones I love and keep them safe.**

"Holy Father! Keep them safe by the power of your name, the name you gave me, so that they may be one just as you and I are one. While I was with them, I kept them safe by the power of your name, the name you gave me…. And now I am coming to you, and I say these things in the world so that they might have my joy in their hearts in all its fullness…. Just as I do not belong to the world, they do not belong to the world. Dedicate them to yourself by means of the truth; your word is truth. I sent them into the world, just as you sent me into the world. And for their sake I dedicate myself to you, in order that they, too, may be truly dedicated to you."

John 17: 11-19

"Keep them safe by the power of your name…"

The power of a name

One of our wedding prayers asked that, in our marriage, we be kept safe in the meaning – 'the power' – of our names: that Margaret would always find herself to be a 'precious pearl,' and that I, David, would always know myself to be 'beloved.'

The power of God's name can be sensed in its meaning, "I will be who I will be." It is the name God revealed to Moses in the burning bush, and it carries the promise of both freedom and surprise: who can limit or even anticipate God?

When Jesus prays, "Keep them safe by the power of your name," he is asking that the disciples – including me – remain willing to be surprised by God's capacity to bring freedom where it is not yet.

God, keep me safe in your name. Let my words and actions show others your ability to surprise and to set free.

" I pray that they may all be one. Father! May they be in us, just as you are in me and I am in you. May they be one, so that the world will believe that you sent me. I gave them the same glory you gave me, so that they may be one, just as you and I are one: I in them and you in me, so that they may be completely one, in order that the world may know that you sent me and that you love them as you love me. Father... I made you known to them, and I will continue to do so, in order that the love you have for me may be in them."

John 17: 20-26

"I pray that they may all be one."

Gathered in love

Delicate, exquisitely beautiful, a gift from one of my dearest friends, the glass teacup lay shattered on my kitchen floor. The breakage was unmistakably final, and of my own doing. For twenty years I had treasured that cup. Now I longed to gather the tiny fragments and remould them into the vessel that had held the warm drinks over which friends had shared their stories. That simple cup represented so much to me!

But, in the end, it was just a cup. I try to imagine Jesus' sorrow and his love and longing as he contemplates our human brokenness! How his heart must ache: wanting to gather us to himself, to mould us into his one body, to fill us with the glorious warmth of God's love!

**Lord, forgive my thoughtless actions
that hurt those most precious to me.**

After they had eaten, Jesus said to Simon Peter, "Simon son of John, do you love me more than these others do?" "Yes, Lord," he answered, "you know that I love you."

Jesus said to him, "Take care of my lambs." A second time Jesus said to him, "Simon son of John, do you love me?" "Yes, Lord," he answered, "you know that I love you."

Jesus said to him, "Take care of my sheep." A third time Jesus said, "Simon son of John, do you love me?" Peter became sad because Jesus asked him the third time, "Do you love me?" and so he said to him, "Lord, you know everything; you know that I love you!"

Jesus said to him, "Take care of my sheep…." Then Jesus said to him, "Follow me!"

John 21: 15-19

> "Take care of my sheep."

The shepherd's helper

Our daughter saw sheep for the first time in Ireland. The rain drove horizontally across emerald green fields. "Dad," Sharon asked, as we drove along, "what are those fuzzy-looking grey rocks in those fields?"

Just then one of the 'rocks' shook itself. Sheep are not cute little balls of cotton wool. They smell. They feel like the inside of a vacuum cleaner bag. They can be stubborn and stupid. And they're what Jesus told Peter to take care of.

Not a particularly pleasant prospect for anyone. But Jesus told Peter – and through Peter, he told me – "I won't be around any more. You have to take my place. You have to be the Good Shepherd for them." What a job description!

Jesus, I can't be the Good Shepherd;
would you settle for a shepherd's helper?

Peter turned around and saw behind him that other disciple, whom Jesus loved…. When Peter saw him, he asked Jesus, "Lord, what about this man?" Jesus answered him, "If I want him to live until I come, what is that to you? Follow me…."

He is the disciple who spoke of these things, the one who also wrote them down; and we know that what he said is true.

Now, there are many other things that Jesus did. If they were all written down one by one, I suppose that the whole world could not hold the books that would be written.

John 21: 20-25

> "…the world could not hold the books that would be written."

A reader's quest

When I was a teenager, I determined to set aside what I'd been taught and find out for myself who this Jesus really was. So I read the gospels right through, one after another. This didn't help.

Then I found out about other gospels, like the gospel of Thomas, and read them, too. This didn't help, either. So I read other people's opinions, some sensible, some not – to see what they said about Jesus. This, too, didn't help.

But I didn't give up. I even took a whole university course on Mark's gospel. It was fascinating, but, of course, it didn't help.

Even if the world were filled with books about Jesus, it wouldn't help. The answer is not in what you read; the answer is in the reader.

Lord, help me read what you have written in my heart.

L ord, you have made so many things!
How wisely you made them all!
The earth is filled with your creatures....
When you turn away, they are afraid;
when you take away your breath, they die
and go back to the dust from which they came.
But when you give them breath, they are created;
you give new life to the earth.
May the glory of the Lord last forever!
May the Lord be happy with what he has made....
I will sing to the Lord all my life;
as long as I live I will sing praises to my God.
Psalm 104: 1, 24, 29-34

> "…as long as I live I will sing praises to my God."

Singing God's praise

I'm a biology teacher, so I spend my days reading and talking about life. How it works: dissolution and rebirth. Cycles: build it up, tear it down. Trees, insects and mammals – large and small – all wonders in their own way. All miracles.

Every day I learn something new, something amazing. Amazing enough that I should be in awe. And yet, and yet....

Papers and administrative duties. Go, go, go. So busy that, even surrounded by miracles, I forget to see them. The infinite variety of life: even that can become just so many words.

This is when I have to stop myself and say, "Look! Look at what has been given to you. It's spring. Go out and see your world. See the miracles that have been given to you. And sing praises to God."

**Lord, give me the wisdom to stop,
and to see the world you have given me.**

A man asked, "Good Teacher, what must I do to receive eternal life?" Jesus said, "You know the commandments: 'Do not commit murder; do not commit adultery; do not steal; do not accuse anyone falsely; do not cheat; respect your father and your mother.'"

"Teacher," the man said, "ever since I was young, I have obeyed all these commandments." Jesus looked straight at him with love and said, "You need only one thing. Go and sell all you have and give the money to the poor, and you will have riches in heaven; then come and follow me." When the man heard this, gloom spread over his face, and he went away sad, because he was very rich. Jesus said to his disciples, "How hard it will be for rich people to enter the kingdom of God!"

Mark 10: 17-27

> "You need only one thing."

A love that challenges

It seems contradictory that as soon as Jesus affirms this young man, he immediately demands of him the one thing that he is unable to do.

Many years ago I worked as a labourer on a construction site. Someone looked at me with the same penetrating gaze that Jesus turned on the young man, and challenged me – rather forcefully – to take my talents more seriously. I didn't forgive him for years.

Love is more comfortable when it's purely affirming; but love also challenges us to grow. Jesus shows me the barriers I've built against living fully in his love. Of course, they are the hardest things to take down; they feel like all the support I've got.

God, give me courage to see the barriers,
and the belief that you'll be there when I dismantle them.

P eter spoke up, "Look, we have left everything and followed you." "Yes," Jesus said to them, "and I tell you that those who leave home or brothers or sisters or mother or father or children or fields for me and for the gospel, will receive much more in this present age. They will receive a hundred times more houses, brothers, sisters, mothers, children, and fields – and persecutions as well; and in the age to come they will receive eternal life. But many who are now first will be last, and many who are now last will be first."

Mark 10: 28-31

"…and many who are now last will be first."

Reasonable, or not?

The reaction of those who heard Jesus speak must have been, "The last will be first? That just isn't logical."

A while ago, my daughter desperately needed new running shoes, so we went shopping. But when we got to the store, Katie suggested we wait until the next paycheque. Why? So that I could buy her younger brother a much needed and totally awesome new winter jacket that was on sale, half-price. Katie knew how thrilled Kevin would be.

I recounted this beautiful story to a relative who insisted on sending a cheque to Katie for shoes. Katie purchased shoes far superior to anything we could have afforded. Thinking of that experience, I was reminded of today's reading: it no longer seemed so illogical after all!

**Lord, grant that I may trust you enough
to put the needs of others before my own.**

J ames and John, the sons of Zebedee, came to Jesus. "Teacher," they said, "there is something we want you to do for us." "What is it?" Jesus asked them. They answered, "When you sit on your throne in your glorious Kingdom, we want you to let us sit with you, one at your right and one at your left." Jesus said to them, "You don't know what you are asking for. Can you drink the cup of suffering that I must drink…?"

"We can," they answered. Jesus said to them, "You will indeed drink the cup I must drink…. But I do not have the right to choose who will sit at my right and my left. It is God who will give these places to those for whom he has prepared them."

Mark 10: 32-45

> "You don't know what you are asking for."

In tough times

The disciples are, once again, acting like children! Two demanding, "Me first", and the others fighting about it. I can imagine Jesus sighing and explaining things – yet again.

When asked if they could suffer, James and John naively answer, "We can." They don't know what that suffering might entail, but with childlike bravado, they say, "Yes." For me, there are things I've done which, if I'd know then what I know now, I'd have never tried. But I'm glad I did.

Perhaps that's it. Not knowing what's in store for me, I say "Yes, Lord." Then, when things get difficult and I wonder what I've got myself into, I must strive to find the faith to keep saying "Yes, Lord. Yes."

Lord, help me to say "Yes" to difficult calls to love, and to not shy away out of fear.

"A blind beggar named Bartimaeus was sitting by the road. When he heard that it was Jesus of Nazareth, he began to shout, "Jesus! Son of David! Have mercy on me!"

Many of the people told him to be quiet. But he shouted even more loudly, "Son of David, have mercy on me!" Jesus stopped and said, "Call him." So they called the blind man. "Cheer up!" they said. "Get up, he is calling you." So he threw off his cloak, jumped up, and came to Jesus. "What do you want me to do for you?" Jesus asked him. "Teacher," the blind man answered, "I want to see again." "Go," Jesus told him, "your faith has made you well." At once he was able to see and followed Jesus.

Mark 10: 46-52

"Your faith has made you well."

Seeking wholeness

A friend of mine is celebrating his 37th birthday today. That is, he would be celebrating if he were feeling better. For over four years he has been struggling with chronic illness that leaves him exhausted and isolated. He finds it hard to trust doctors, he has lost touch with friends and his marriage has ended. Where can he turn? He feels so alone.

I imagine that this is how Bartimaeus felt – alone, helpless and desperate. Then Jesus walked by, and the blind man found hope. From that hope came the courage to call out to Jesus; from that courage came faith; from that faith came healing.

I hope that someday my friend can find this same hope, courage, faith and healing. I hope his faith can make him well.

**Jesus, help me find hope, courage,
faith and healing when I have lost my way.**

S ay to all the nations, "The Lord is king!
The earth is set firmly in place and cannot be moved;
he will judge the peoples with justice."
Be glad, earth and sky!
Roar, sea, and every creature in you;
be glad, fields, and everything in you!
The trees in the woods will shout for joy
when the Lord comes to rule the earth.
He will rule the peoples of the world
with justice and fairness.

Psalm 96: 10-13

"...with justice and fairness."

Are we all human?

Recently I attended a presentation by General Romeo Dallaire who was head of the United Nations Forces in Rwanda in the 1990s.

I was struck by his passion and compassion as he described his experiences, and how the world community failed to come to the aid of those being killed. He asked us repeatedly: "Are all humans human, or do some count more than others?" He challenged us, living in one of the wealthiest countries in the world, to consider our global perspective. Do we care enough to get involved?

Today's reading both reassures and challenges me. While God will rule with justice and fairness, what does God think of how we treat others now?

God of justice, forgive us our trespasses.
Let your kingdom come.

The chief priests, the teachers of the Law, and the elders came to [Jesus] and asked him, "What right do you have to do these things…?" Jesus answered them, "I will ask you just one question, and if you give me an answer, I will tell you…. Where did John's right to baptize come from: was it from God or from human beings?"

They started to argue among themselves: "What shall we say? If we answer 'From God,' he will say, 'Why, then, did you not believe John?' But if we say, 'From men….'" (They were afraid, because everyone was convinced that John had been a prophet.) So their answer to Jesus was, "We don't know." Jesus said to them, "Neither will I tell you, then, by what right I do these things."

Mark 11: 27-33

"If you give me an answer, I will tell you."

Let go, and trust

As a young child I loved to climb trees. Often going up was easier than coming down! On more than one occasion I remember my dad standing beneath me at the foot of the tree, while I clung somewhat fearfully to its branches. His arms were sure and strong, his hands were within inches of me, and he promised to catch me – if I only let go. But how I wanted to be caught first, before letting go.

Jesus' authority is not unlike my dad's; and there is no other way to discover it than an initial letting go, in trust. And yet, like the chief priests, the teachers and the elders of today's reading, how often I wish to be secure, before letting go!

**Jesus, help me trust
so that I might discover the truth of your good news.**

" I have much more to tell you, but now it would be too much for you to bear. When, however, the Spirit comes, who reveals the truth about God, he will lead you into all the truth. He will not speak on his own authority, but he will speak of what he hears and will tell you of things to come. He will give me glory, because he will take what I say and tell it to you. All that my Father has is mine; that is why I said that the Spirit will take what I give him and tell it to you."

John 16: 12-15

"The Spirit will lead you…"

Life: the process

A few years ago, when a friend was diagnosed with cancer, she wrote: "It's so dark. I don't know where this tunnel is going." Her comments were so vivid. How I longed for the Spirit to guide us in understanding.

I wrote to my friend: "We, the blind, are not alone. Without sight, we claim touch. We, the lonely, are not lost. Without guarantees, we claim trust. The tunnel of our life is a birth canal…. In darkness and solitude, we claim the process."

My friend and I stayed in touch throughout her time with cancer. The dark tunnel ended with healing. My friend continues to live, trusting the process of life. We continue to correspond, sharing our longings for the Spirit of Truth to guide us.

**Spirit of Truth, be with me
and lead me with your understanding.**

Mary hurried off to a town in the hill country of Judea. She went into Zechariah's house and greeted Elizabeth. When Elizabeth heard Mary's greeting, the baby moved within her. Elizabeth was filled with the Holy Spirit and said in a loud voice, "You are the most blessed of all women, and blessed is the child you will bear! Why should this great thing happen to me, that my Lord's mother comes to visit me? For as soon as I heard your greeting, the baby within me jumped with gladness. How happy you are to believe that the Lord's message to you will come true!" Mary said, "My heart praises the Lord; my soul is glad because of God my Saviour, for he has remembered me, his lowly servant."

Luke 1: 39-56

> "...the baby moved within her."

Time to prepare

Last fall Anne and Jane, both co-workers of mine, were pregnant at the same time. They each beamed with joy and wonder as their bellies swelled over the months.

Today's reading appears at the end of May on our calendar, but right before the Christmas story in Luke's gospel. Who thinks about Christmas in May? Mary and Elizabeth call us to, because their pregnancies begin well before our first thoughts about decorating for Christmas.

Watching the slow unfolding of new life in Jane and Anne, I remembered again how every birth – whether of a child or a nation, of friendship or freedom – is preceded by months (or more) of preparation. And it is as important to honour and celebrate the preparation as to rejoice at the birth itself.

Dear God, help me today to be quietly celebrating the birth of good things into this world.

S ome Pharisees and some members of Herod's party, sent to Jesus to trap him with questions, said, "Teacher, we know that you tell the truth. You pay no attention to anyone's status, but teach the truth about God's will for people. Tell us, is it against our Law to pay taxes to the Roman Emperor? Should we pay them or not?" But Jesus saw through their trick and answered, "Why are you trying to trap me? Bring a silver coin, and let me see it." They brought him one, and he asked, "Whose face and name are these?"

"The Emperor's," they answered. Jesus said, "Well, then, pay to the Emperor what belongs to the Emperor, and pay to God what belongs to God." *Mark 12: 13-17*

"...pay to God what belongs to God."

True generosity

I usually set aside a tenth of my income to give away. But little voices in my head, my own inner Pharisees and Herodians, are always trying to trick me into giving less. Where do Girl Guide cookies fit in? And is that honorarium really income, strictly speaking?

A friend, an African refugee, works in a factory earning $8 an hour. He regularly sends money to family members back in Africa. Recently, when he got a raise, the first thing he did was write 12 post-dated monthly cheques to his church for $100 each, outdoing even the wealthiest members of the congregation.

When I expressed astonishment, he said, "Money isn't for keeping; it's for sharing." That silenced my inner voices, for now.

**Lord, attune my ear to the voices of truth
instead of the voices of greed.**

S ome Sadducees said, "Teacher, Moses wrote this law for us: 'If a man dies and leaves a wife but no children, that man's brother must marry the widow'…. Then the second one married the woman, and he also died without having children. The same thing happened to the third brother, and then to the rest: all seven brothers married the woman and died without having children…. Now, when all the dead rise to life on the day of resurrection, whose wife will she be…?"

Jesus answered them, "How wrong you are! And do you know why? It is because you don't know the Scriptures or God's power. For when the dead rise to life, they will be like the angels in heaven and will not marry…. [God] is the God of the living, not of the dead."

Mark 12: 18-27

> "…the God of the living, not of the dead…"

Lost in the details

Have you ever found yourself in an argument where, having lost sight of the central issue, you become embroiled in debating details? At times, I've suddenly stopped and realized that the original, most important concern has been all but forgotten, and that neither side is really hearing the truth – hidden in the details.

Jesus was fielding questions about how we are to live, when he was suddenly sidetracked. I sense his anger, his impatience. How many of the Sadducees turned away to leave – smugly congratulating themselves on their clever question – while missing Jesus' answer to the next question, "What is the greatest commandment of all?"

How often have I turned away from wisdom while trying to show off my cleverness?

Lord, let me not be sidetracked by details.
Help me be silent long enough to hear your question.

A teacher of the Law asked Jesus: "Which commandment is the most important of all?" Jesus replied, "The most important one is this: 'Listen, Israel! The Lord our God is the only Lord. Love the Lord your God with all your heart, with all your soul, with all your mind, and with all your strength.' The second most important commandment is this: 'Love your neighbour as you love yourself.' There is no other commandment more important than these two."

The teacher of the Law said, "Well done, Teacher! It is true, as you say…. It is more important to obey these two commandments than to offer on the altar animals and other sacrifices to God."

Jesus noticed how wise his answer was, and so he told him, "You are not far from the kingdom of God."

Mark 12: 28-34

"Love your neighbour as you love yourself."

Hearing the cry

It's early in the morning, the sun just over the horizon. I awoke dreaming. A horrible dream of someone screaming, crying out for help. And I couldn't move. I couldn't speak. I was paralyzed with fear. Last night's news on my mind, I think.

As I consider the words of today's reading, the images of war keep coming back to me. The valour, the horror. Sons killing the sons of other mothers. Dying. How many cried out? How many stood like me in my dream? Hearing a cry, paralyzed by fear. How do I love my neighbour as myself'?

My life is so easy, so safe. Yet, how often I stand paralyzed by fear, hearing the cry. Or stand deafly, not hearing at all.

How hard it is to love.

Lord, help me overcome my fear. Help me to love.

But you have followed my teaching, my conduct, and my purpose in life; you have observed my faith, my patience, my love, my endurance, my persecutions and my sufferings.... But the Lord rescued me from them all. Everyone who wants to live a godly life in union with Christ Jesus will be persecuted; and evil persons and impostors will keep on going from bad to worse, deceiving others and being deceived themselves. But as for you, continue in the truths that you were taught and firmly believe.... All Scripture is inspired by God and is useful for teaching the truth, rebuking error, correcting faults, and giving instruction for right living, so that the person who serves God may be fully qualified and equipped to do every kind of good deed.

2 Timothy 3: 10-17

"...continue in the truths that you were taught..."

Tough advice

Paul's advice to a young man, Timothy, is penned at a dark time. Timothy is being persecuted, but he is also deflated by what he sees around him, especially in his own church. He has few friends, and some of the people he once trusted have not only deserted him, they have turned on him.

So Paul writes to his young apprentice, urging him to hang on. He then shares some advice, the fruit of his own experience. You will, he says, be persecuted for the faith. But don't lose sight of 'the truth.' There is no kind of good deed that you can say no to. And don't worry, he continues, whether the time is right or not. Just say it. Just do it.

**Lord, give me the strength to remain loyal,
not to my own biased assumptions, but to you alone.**

All day long I praise you
and proclaim your glory.
Do not reject me now that I am old;
do not abandon me now that I am feeble....
I will always put my hope in you;
I will praise you more and more.
I will tell of your goodness;
all day long I will speak of your salvation,
though it is more than I can understand.
I will go in the strength of the Lord God;
I will proclaim your goodness, yours alone.
You have taught me ever since I was young,
and I still tell of your wonderful acts.

Psalm 71: 8-9, 14-17, 22

"Do not reject me now that I am old..."

Honouring the elderly

"Do you have any thyme?" my daughter asked. She was helping me to make dinner. I enjoy my own puns, so I answered, "Yes, about thirty years," to which she responded, "I'll take them if they're good."

In seconds I went from joking to being hurt. I immediately jumped to the conclusion that she would like me to live thirty more years, *only* if I were healthy and no trouble to her. This was, of course, a ridiculous misinterpretation, but it made me think about my growing dread of being old and not being able to take care of myself as I'd like.

My mother-in-law is in her nineties, and my father, his eighties. How sensitive am I to the fears they must experience daily?

Lord, help me recognize the dignity and beauty of old age.

Whu hen the sun was beginning to set, the twelve disciples came to him and said, "Send the people away so that they can go to the villages and farms around here and find food and lodging, because this is a lonely place." But Jesus said to them, "You yourselves give them something to eat."

They answered, "All we have are five loaves and two fish. Do you want us to go and buy food for this whole crowd?"

Jesus said to his disciples, "Make the people sit down...." Then Jesus took the five loaves and two fish, looked up to heaven, thanked God for them, broke them, and gave them to the disciples to distribute to the people. They all ate and had enough, and the disciples took up twelve baskets of what was left over.

Luke 9: 11-17

"Send the people away..."

Give of yourself

He was a difficult child, a very difficult child. And his behaviour was becoming more and more destructive. It was tearing the family apart. The doctors' recommendation: "Send him away: for six months, for behaviour modification."

Several of her friends urged her to follow the doctors' advice: "Send him away. Think of your other children who need your attention. Think of your own health."

But somehow she stood firm, refusing to send him away. Perhaps she heard Jesus saying, "You yourself give him something to eat." With a determination she didn't know she possessed, she sought out and drew on resources in the community. And she provided the loving support her son needed – to heal the hurt he carried in his heart.

**Lord, when someone asks for help,
give me the strength to help in whatever way I can.**

"Happy are those who know they are spiritually poor; the kingdom of heaven belongs to them! Happy are those who mourn; God will comfort them! Happy are those who are humble; they will receive what God has promised! Happy are those whose greatest desire is to do what God requires; God will satisfy them fully! Happy are those who are merciful to others; God will be merciful to them! Happy are the pure in heart; they will see God! Happy are those who work for peace; God will call them his children! … Happy are you when people insult you and persecute you and tell all kinds of evil lies against you because you are my followers. Be happy and glad, for a great reward is kept for you in heaven."

Matthew 5: 1-12

> "Be happy and glad, for a great reward is kept for you in heaven."

Words that challenge

The Beatitudes – so familiar yet so startling – are some of the most quoted words in Scripture. While I've always respected them, I've tended to view them as classical literature, something to revere from a distance, like famous paintings in a gallery.

How wrong I've been! Jesus is not just crafting beautiful poetry. He's laying it on the line for the crowd – and for me. These powerful words make terrifying demands: live humbly, with a pure heart, showing mercy. They tell me I can expect to mourn, to have people insult me and persecute me for Jesus' sake. But they also make enticing promises.

I need to get beyond my passive respect for these words. Only then can they transform my life and, as Jesus promises, bring me real joy.

God, I need your help to translate these beautiful words into meaningful action.

" **Y**ou are like salt for the whole human race. But if salt loses its saltiness, there is no way to make it salty again. It has become worthless, so it is thrown out and people trample on it. You are like light for the whole world. A city built on a hill cannot be hid. No one lights a lamp and puts it under a bowl; instead it is put on the lamp stand, where it gives light for everyone in the house. In the same way your light must shine before people, so that they will see the good things you do and praise your Father in heaven."

Matthew 5: 13-16

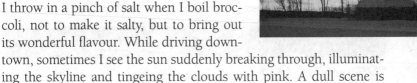

"You are like light for the whole world."

Salt and light

I throw in a pinch of salt when I boil broccoli, not to make it salty, but to bring out its wonderful flavour. While driving downtown, sometimes I see the sun suddenly breaking through, illuminating the skyline and tingeing the clouds with pink. A dull scene is transformed into breathtaking beauty.

Love can act like salt and like light. I have seen people, believing themselves unlovable, come into a community of love and be transformed: gradually beginning to smile, they stand erect and feel at home. When loved, my true self unfolds: I feel comfortable, free and beautiful.

Like salt and like light, I am called to be a presence of love in my home and at work, revealing to others their value and beauty.

Lord, give me eyes to see and love to affirm the truth and beauty of each person I meet.

How excellent are the Lord's faithful people!
My greatest pleasure is to be with them.
Those who rush to other gods
bring many troubles on themselves.
I will not take part in their sacrifices;
I will not worship their gods.
You, Lord, are all I have,
and you give me all I need;
my future is in your hands....
I am always aware of the Lord's presence;
he is near, and nothing can shake me....
You will show me the path that leads to life;
your presence fills me with joy
and brings me pleasure forever.

Psalm 16: 1-5, 8, 11

> "I am always aware of the Lord's presence…"

Where's Waldo?

At the end of the day, my daughter coaxes me into a game of *Where's Waldo*. She loves to sit with the big book on her lap, its pages open to the chaos of characters hiding the ever-smiling Waldo.

I get impatient: there are dishes to put away, lunches to be made and garbage to go out. I half-heartedly skim over the pages. She always finds Waldo before I do. I wonder if it is because she *believes*. She never tires of searching for him.

It dawns on me that God is like Waldo in my life: ever-present, hiding among the chaos. Perhaps the secret is to delight in the searching. God's presence will be revealed when I take the time to look.

God, I know you are with me.
Help me feel your presence today.

"You have heard that people were told in the past, 'Do not commit murder; anyone who does will be brought to trial.' But now I tell you: if you are angry with your brother you will be brought to trial, if you call your brother 'You good-for-nothing!' you will be brought before the Council, and if you call your brother a worthless fool you will be in danger of going to the fire of hell. So if you are about to offer your gift to God at the altar and there you remember that your brother has something against you, leave your gift there in front of the altar, go at once and make peace with your brother, and then come back and offer your gift to God."

Matthew 5: 20-26

"…go at once and make peace…"

Dealing with anger

I remember being in elementary school and preparing for first confession. The teacher put a list of sins on the board for us to choose from; one of the sins was 'anger.'

As a child, I was prone to temper tantrums – a euphemism for fits of blind rage. I probably listed 'anger' in every confession I ever made.

Later, when studying psychology, I discovered that anger is an emotion – one that can cloud your vision and cause a lot of pain. Anger in itself is not a sin. It is an emotion, a sign of deep frustration. Jesus must have known this for he teaches us to deal with our anger before doing anything else. He knew, as a person who got angry himself, how powerful an emotion it can be.

Lord, help me to recognize and deal with my anger before it causes me to hurt others.

The Lord is my shepherd;
I have everything I need.
He lets me rest in fields of green grass
and leads me to quiet pools of fresh water.
He gives me new strength.
He guides me in the right paths,
as he has promised.
Even if I go through the deepest darkness,
I will not be afraid, Lord,
for you are with me....
I know that your goodness and love
will be with me all my life;
and your house will be my home
as long as I live.

Psalm 23: 1-6

"I have everything I need."

All that I need

It's easy to nod in agreement with today's psalm when life is humming along smoothly. But when life gets a little rocky, it's much harder. Wouldn't it be wonderful to wake up each day and say, "I have everything I need!" But then, come to think of it, don't I?

I recall those dark times following my husband's death when friends supported me in my grieving. Or when faced with a difficult choice about my child's health, friends listened to my concerns. Or when I was sick and needed rest, a neighbour offered to drive my children to their music lessons and even pick up some groceries!

Indeed, I have everything I need. It's just that, at times, I need to look a little harder to recognize God at work in my life.

Lord, so often I focus on what I don't have.
Help me recognize all that I have, and give thanks.

W hen the festival was over, [Mary and Joseph] started back home, but the boy Jesus stayed in Jerusalem. His parents thought that he was with the group, so they travelled a whole day and then started looking for him among their relatives and friends. They did not find him, so they went back to Jerusalem looking for him. On the third day they found him in the Temple, sitting with the Jewish teachers, listening to them and asking questions. All who heard him were amazed at his intelligent answers. His parents were astonished when they saw him, and his mother said, "Son, your father and I have been terribly worried trying to find you." He answered them, "Why did you have to look for me? Didn't you know that I had to be in my Father's house?"

Luke 2: 41-51

"His parents were astonished when they saw him…"

Treasuring the mystery

The story about Mary and Joseph searching for Jesus, and then finding him in the Temple, is somewhat mystifying to me. But I find some keys to that mystery in the details of how the story is told.

Everyone who hears Jesus talk with the Temple teachers is 'amazed' at his answers. When his mother and father arrive, we hear that they are 'astonished' to find him there. But they were not, I think, astonished at his answers. They are astonished that he didn't tell them he was staying behind.

The relationship between Jesus, Mary and Joseph is, at times, very ordinary in spite of its cosmic significance. To me, that seems to be the real mystery.

**Lord, help me cherish the mystery of my children,
and all children.**

I n that town was a woman who lived a sinful life. She heard that Jesus was eating in the Pharisee's house, so she brought an alabaster jar full of perfume and stood behind Jesus, by his feet, crying and wetting his feet with her tears. Then she dried his feet with her hair, kissed them, and poured the perfume on them. When the Pharisee saw this, he said, "If this man really were a prophet, he would know what kind of sinful life this woman lives!"

Jesus said, "I came into your home, and you gave me no water for my feet, but she has washed my feet with her tears and dried them with her hair…. I tell you, then, the great love she has shown proves that her many sins have been forgiven."

Luke 7: 36 – 8: 3

"…the great love she has shown…"

True humility

She never said a word, yet she cried tears that wet his feet. I imagine they were silent tears. She never spoke in her defence; never tried to tell her side of the story. She, the nameless, speechless woman, came only to act, and her action spoke volumes.

I, on the other hand, am so preoccupied with telling my story – wrapped up in words and deep, meaningful discussions – that actions are often neglected. Or I get distracted by the presence and opinions of those who should not matter.

I'm sure I'd have cared too much about the other guests' opinions, and would not have focused on Jesus' presence and his offer of forgiveness. At the end of the day, it is all about faith and forgiveness.

**Forgiving God, help me to look directly at you,
and know your love.**

"You have heard that it was said, 'An eye for an eye, and a tooth for a tooth.' But now I tell you: do not take revenge on someone who wrongs you. If anyone slaps you on the right cheek, let him slap your left cheek too. And if someone takes you to court to sue you for your shirt, let him have your coat as well. And if one of the occupation troops forces you to carry his pack one mile, carry it two miles. When someone asks you for something, give it to him; when someone wants to borrow something, lend it to him."

Matthew 5: 38-42

> "...do not take revenge
> on someone who wrongs you."

Fully alive

I had worked on yearly contracts for a decade, when someone else was hired to do my job on a permanent basis. I was a little upset. No, I was incredibly angry! I couldn't believe colleagues could do such a thing. I lodged complaints, met with a lawyer – all to no avail. The embers of my anger flickered for a long time.

My instinct was to strike back immediately. But here Jesus insists that my response to unfairness must not create additional injustice. He challenges me not to live my life merely reacting to others, but to live it fully, actively and generously – in the real world of challenges and disappointments.

He's not telling me to stop feeling, but rather to find, with time, genuine forgiveness.

Dear God, when I'm caught between reacting badly and knowing what I should do, help me choose what is right and just.

" **Y**ou have heard that it was said, 'Love your friends, hate your enemies.' But now I tell you: love your enemies and pray for those who persecute you, so that you may become the children of your Father in heaven. For he makes his sun to shine on bad and good people alike, and gives rain to those who do good and to those who do evil. Why should God reward you if you love only the people who love you? Even the tax collectors do that! And if you speak only to your friends, have you done anything out of the ordinary? Even the pagans do that! You must be perfect – just as your Father in heaven is perfect."

Matthew 5: 43-48

"...pray for those who persecute you..."

Yes, but...

Today's reading calls me to task. As I consider my relationships, especially the 'difficult' ones in my life, I begin to squirm. "I agree with you, Jesus, but...."

How can I let him go on saying those things about me? They aren't true. I just want to correct him, tell him he's wrong....

She was so mean to me. I'll simply avoid seeing her in the future....

I have to set the record straight. I'm not to blame for the misunderstanding....

I am ashamed to admit that there are some people in my life for whom I can't pray. Can't even come close to it. Whenever I try, my righteous indignation rises to the surface.

Then I hear Jesus saying, "Yes, but...."

Dear God, I find it hard to love some people.
Grant me the courage to go beyond my hurt.

"Make certain you do not perform your religious duties in public so that people will see what you do…. When you give something to a needy person, do not make a big show of it, as the hypocrites do in the houses of worship…. But when you help a needy person, do it in such a way that even your closest friend will not know about it….

"And when you fast, do not put on a sad face as the hypocrites do. They neglect their appearance so that everyone will see that they are fasting…. When you go without food, wash your face and comb your hair, so that others cannot know that you are fasting – only your Father, who is unseen, will know. And your Father, who sees what you do in private, will reward you."

Matthew 6: 1-6, 16-18

> "…as the hypocrites do."

Today's hypocrites

"They back-talk you, Dad." This year my 13-year-old daughter has had to deal with 'back-talk' – false friends, hurtful comments, deceit and dishonesty. Someone who is a friend to your face, but will betray you behind your back.

I sympathize as best I can. I tell her the 'back-talkers' hurt them-selves more than they hurt her, but I also caution her not to get back at them with similar behaviour. It's part of becoming an adult, I suppose, but not a very welcome part.

The hypocrites Jesus speaks of are still common today, even if we have little interest in prayer, charity or fasting. Hypocrisy is as alive and well as ever, as my daughter is finding out to her sorrow – and mine.

Lord, give me the strength to overcome the hurt caused by hypocrites, and the courage to not hurt others in turn.

"When you pray, do not use a lot of meaningless words.... Your Father already knows what you need before you ask him. This, then, is how you should pray: 'Our Father in heaven: May your holy name be honoured; may your kingdom come; may your will be done on earth as it is in heaven. Give us today the food we need. Forgive us the wrongs we have done, as we forgive the wrongs that others have done to us. Do not bring us to hard testing, but keep us safe from the Evil One.' If you forgive others the wrongs they have done to you, your Father in heaven will also forgive you. But if you do not forgive others, then your Father will not forgive the wrongs you have done."

Matthew 6: 7-15

> "May your will be done on earth as it is in heaven."

Here on earth

A few months ago I was teaching my three-year-old daughter this prayer. The beginning of her version ran something like this: "Our Father, who aren't in heaven, hallowed be thy name." I tried to explain that the word was 'art' not 'aren't,' but her version prevailed. And perhaps she has a point.

Jesus knew God as his father so intimately that he called God 'abba' – which can be translated as 'daddy.' Like any dad (or mum), Jesus' Father worries about our daily bread, our broken relationships and our behaviour.

God's kingdom is not just about a later time; it is about this moment. Jesus invites us to be a part of that kingdom that 'aren't' just in heaven.

God, help me be aware of your nearness in all that I do today.

"Do not store up riches for yourselves here on earth, where moths and rust destroy, and robbers break in and steal. Instead, store up riches for yourselves in heaven, where moths and rust cannot destroy, and robbers cannot break in and steal. For your heart will always be where your riches are.

"The eyes are like a lamp for the body. If your eyes are sound, your whole body will be full of light; but if your eyes are no good, your body will be in darkness. So if the light in you is darkness, how terribly dark it will be!"

Matthew 6: 19-23

"Do not store up riches…"

Special moments

My mother died when I was young, and I was given her china, silver and linen. Because they were valuable, I kept them locked away in the basement, only to be used on special occasions.

After not using them for years, we hauled them up, enjoyed them, and then started wrapping each cup again.

In a moment of grace I realized that I had outlived my mother; that I was now a month older than the age at which she had died. I sat and wept. Then, I went out and bought a china cabinet.

Now we use the china, silver and linen often. Everyday moments are just as 'special,' and create precious memories that will light up our hearts in the future.

**God of all beauty,
help me to treasure the present moment, now.**

"You cannot be a slave of two masters; you will hate one and love the other; you will be loyal to one and despise the other. You cannot serve both God and money....

"Look how the wild flowers grow: they do not work or make clothes for themselves. But I tell you that not even King Solomon with all his wealth had clothes as beautiful as one of these flowers.... Won't [God] be all the more sure to clothe you?

"So do not start worrying: 'Where will my food come from? or my drink? or my clothes?' Your Father in heaven knows that you need all these things. Instead, be concerned above everything else with the kingdom of God and with what he requires of you, and he will provide you with all these other things. So do not worry about tomorrow."

Matthew 6: 24-34

> "So do not worry about tomorrow."

Trust in God

I have spent too much of my life worrying about money. I have been broke and in debt several times – a fact I'm not proud of. I have lain awake many nights worrying about how I was going to make ends meet, how I was going to get out of the current crisis.

After all these years of struggling financially, I've begun to realize one thing – I'm still here! These financial crises did not destroy me. My family has had food, clothing and shelter – however humble or simple.

I think that today's reading is true. God takes care of us– in so many ways. There's a twelve-step-program saying that goes: "If you worry, you do not trust. If you trust, you do not worry."

I trust in you, my God.
Let my worry be replaced with even greater trust.

J esus asked the disciples, "Who do the crowds say I am?" "Some say that you are John the Baptist. Others say that you are Elijah, while others say that one of the prophets of long ago has come back to life." "Who do you say I am?" Peter answered, "You are God's Messiah."

Jesus gave them strict orders not to tell this to anyone. He also told them, "The Son of Man must suffer.... He will be put to death, but three days later he will be raised to life. If you want to come with me, you must forget yourself, take up your cross every day, and follow me. For if you want to save your own life, you will lose it, but if you lose your life for my sake, you will save it."

Luke 9: 18-24

> "Take up your cross every day, and follow me."

Each day's cross

Each day provides its cross: a whining child, a hard day's work, an unexpected bill. Other days, rejection or loss enters my life. Still, the gospel invites me to follow Jesus and behave as Jesus did.

When the soldiers actually nailed him to his cross, Jesus forgave them. Then he made sure that someone would take care of his mother. And finally he reassured the thief who was dying beside him.

Even when the cross weighs heavily on me, God calls on me to forgive, to act responsibly, and to give generously, as Jesus did. The cross won't go away, but I'll find that I'm able to leave some of my resentment and self-pity behind when I focus on doing what Jesus would do.

**Dear God, teach me to focus on you
and on your loving plan for my life.**

"Do not judge others, so that God will not judge you, for God will judge you in the same way you judge others, and he will apply to you the same rules you apply to others. Why, then, do you look at the speck in your brother's eye and pay no attention to the log in your own eye? How dare you say to your brother, 'Please, let me take that speck out of your eye,' when you have a log in your own eye? You hypocrite! First take the log out of your own eye, and then you will be able to see clearly to take the speck out of your brother's eye."

Matthew 7: 1-5

"Do not judge others…"

Judge with care

I came across the opening lines of today's reading just as I was about to hand my students their year-end report cards. The words made me squirm.

I had neatly labelled and boxed each child into letter grades with appropriate comments. Yet I *know* they are more than what is reflected on their report cards.

I think of how I evaluate others – family and friends – placing them in neat categories. Judging them. But isn't making judgments part of being human?

Reading on, I find some comfort: "God will judge you in the same way as you judge others." This is the challenge. How might I look at others with eyes as compassionate as God's? How might I look at myself in the same way?

**Loving God, grant me wisdom and compassion
in my judgment of others, and of myself.**

"**D**o not give what is holy to dogs – they will only turn and attack you. Do not throw your pearls in front of pigs – they will only trample them underfoot….

"Do for others what you want them to do for you: this is the meaning of the Law of Moses and of the teachings of the prophets.

"Go in through the narrow gate, because the gate to hell is wide and the road that leads to it is easy, and there are many who travel it. But the gate to life is narrow and the way that leads to it is hard, and there are few people who find it."

Matthew 7: 6, 12-14

> "But the gate to life is narrow…"

The narrow gate

Sports can be a metaphor for life. The stories are all the same. Gordie Howe stays on the ice long after everyone else. Lance Armstrong trains to exhaustion on every climb for the next Tour de France. And a more obscure example: George 'Shotgun' Shuba, of the old Brooklyn Dodgers, swings at a hanging knot of string 600 times a night in the off-season, to get his 'natural' swing.

It seems it's the same with virtue. It's not easy. It requires taking the hard path.

Every time I join in gossip, I take the easy path.

Every time I'm jealous of another's good fortune, I take the easy path.

Every time I refuse to see that my wealth is based on another's poverty, I take the easy path.

Lord, give me the strength for the hard road of virtue.

"Be on your guard against false prophets; they come to you looking like sheep on the outside, but on the inside they are really like wild wolves. You will know them by what they do. Thorn bushes do not bear grapes, and briers do not bear figs. A healthy tree bears good fruit, but a poor tree bears bad fruit. A healthy tree cannot bear bad fruit, and a poor tree cannot bear good fruit. And any tree that does not bear good fruit is cut down and thrown in the fire. So then, you will know the false prophets by what they do."

Matthew 7: 15-20

"You will know them by what they do."

Know by what I do

I talked to a teen the other day. He'd had a lot of troubles for a person his age. I could see it in his face, and in the way he looked at me when I started talking to him. Waiting. Waiting for the con.

When I asked him what was up, he said, "Well, people either say they like you and never prove it, or tell you they don't and always prove it. You just have to watch long enough."

Well, I hope the longer he watches, the better I look. I hope I'm not just another false prophet, another person who proves to him that nobody's there for the long haul. It's not by what I say that I'll prove myself. It's by what I do.

**Lord, if I'm to be known for what I do,
help me do what's right and good.**

The time came for Elizabeth to have her baby, and she gave birth to a son. Her neighbours and relatives heard how wonderfully good the Lord had been to her, and they all rejoiced with her. When the baby was a week old, they came to circumcise him, and they were going to name him Zechariah, after his Father. But his mother said, "No! His name is to be John." They said to her, "But you don't have any relatives with that name!" Then they made signs to his father, asking him what name he would like the boy to have.

Zechariah asked for a writing pad and wrote, "His name is John." How surprised they all were! At that moment Zechariah was able to speak again, and he started praising God.

Luke 1: 57-66, 80

> "No! His name is to be John."

Faced with a choice

A baby is born! With care, parents consider possible names – of their parents, grandparents, uncles or aunts, and of people who have touched their lives in a special way. They can be pulled in so many directions! And what a difficult decision this can be if others feel slighted or hurt by their final choice.

Elizabeth and Zechariah had been told by an angel to name their baby John. Faced with the disapproval of neighbours and relatives, they remain true – to that quiet voice speaking in their hearts.

In parenting, as in any relationship, there are many demands placed on us. I struggle to live what is in my heart, to be true to God's Spirit dwelling within. To listen to God's voice guiding me, giving me direction.

**God, help me recognize you in the unexpected
and to follow your lead today.**

By the rivers of Babylon we sat down;
there we wept when we remembered Zion.
On the willows near by
we hung up our harps.
Those who captured us told us to sing;
they told us to entertain them:
"Sing us a song about Zion."
How can we sing a song to the Lord
in a foreign land?
May I never be able to play the harp again
if I forget you, Jerusalem!
May I never be able to sing again
if I do not remember you,
if I do not think of you as my greatest joy!   *Psalm 137: 1-6*

"…we hung up our harps."

Entertainment, or not?

Today's reading is so evocative. I picture the Israelites in captivity: hanging their harps in the willow trees because they've lost the heart to sing. Yet their captors demand that their prisoners entertain them with song.

Recently I attended a pow-wow at the Rogers Centre in Toronto. It made me remember my time in aboriginal communities – of a sick woman who had to carry water from a well; a young man who drank to forget his childhood; an old man who lived in a cold, falling-down shack.

Although the colourful dances at the pow-wow were beautiful, I thought of the faces I'd seen and how we still expect aboriginal peoples to entertain us with their songs.

God, grant me the ability to walk in another person's moccasins.

A Roman officer met Jesus and begged: "Sir, my servant is sick in bed at home, unable to move and suffering terribly." "I will go and make him well," Jesus said. "Oh no, sir," answered the officer. "I do not deserve to have you come into my house. Just give the order, and my servant will get well."

When Jesus heard this, he was surprised and said to the people, "I tell you, I have never found anyone in Israel with faith like this…." Then Jesus said to the officer, "Go home, and what you believe will be done for you." And the officer's servant was healed that very moment.

People brought to Jesus many who had demons in them. Jesus drove out the evil spirits with a word and healed all who were sick.

Matthew 8: 5-17

> "What you believe will be done for you."

Surprised by faith

Having a handicapped child in our society is not easy. It's a struggle to have the child accepted in schools, churches and workplaces. I see parents who have given their lives to that struggle, believing deeply that something could happen for their child. They have deep faith.

The Roman officer came to Jesus, convinced that something could happen for his servant. Jesus was not only moved by the man's faith: he was *surprised* to find such faith in a Roman soldier!

Where are the unexpected places faith is found today – in those who believe refugees deserve dignity; that the sick and the elderly are entitled to care; that the dying must be honoured?

Jesus is moved by our faith. Miracles can happen.

**Lord, may my deepest aspirations give me the courage
to believe that things can be better.**

Jesus set out to Jerusalem. He sent messengers ahead of him, who went into a village to get everything ready for him. But the people there would not receive him. When the disciples James and John saw this, they said, "Lord, do you want us to call fire down from heaven to destroy them?"

Jesus rebuked them. Then Jesus and his disciples went on to another village. A man said to Jesus, "I will follow you wherever you go." Jesus said, "Foxes have holes, and birds have nests, but the Son of Man has no place to lie down and rest." He said to another, "Follow me." But that man said, "Sir, first let me go back and bury my father." Jesus answered, "Let the dead bury their own dead. Go and proclaim the kingdom of God."

Luke 9: 51-62

"I will follow you wherever you go."

Faith and understanding

My youngest son is a 'spirited' child. He lives at the extremes of his emotions, and his actions usually follow suit! While I delight in channelling the marvellous creativity of his passions to goodness, I fear the potential of his misdirected energies.

My son is a lot like the disciples in today's reading. James and John have an endearing zeal, with energy and faith in what they can accomplish in Jesus' name. But they don't yet understand exactly what he is asking of them.

Jesus tells his would-be followers what it takes to 'get with the program' of his kingdom: immediate, wholehearted, unconditional commitment. Can we place whatever we have – passions, talents and family – at the service of whatever he asks?

Lord, all that I am and have is yours today.
Help me to listen for what you want of me!

When Jesus noticed the crowd around him, he ordered his disciples to go to the other side of the lake. A teacher of the Law came to him. "Teacher," he said, "I am ready to go with you wherever you go."

Jesus answered him, "Foxes have holes, and birds have nests, but the Son of Man has no place to lie down and rest."

Another man, who was a disciple, said, "Sir, first let me go back and bury my father."

"Follow me," Jesus answered, "and let the dead bury their own dead."

Matthew 8: 18-22

"Let the dead bury their own dead."

The living dead

Pretty sharp remarks… and from Jesus, a man of such empathy. Think of someone whose father has just died, and consider his answer.

Maybe Jesus was tired: tired of people not understanding. But he sure made it clear – what a big step it was to follow him.

I'm not a scholar, but I think 'the dead' are the people Jesus saw mired in a dead-end way of thinking about spiritual life. I wonder how he'd respond today were he to see what has become of his message.

Are we 'the dead' Jesus spoke of? We claim to be virtuous because we follow all the rules – but often die to his great commandment of love. Are we 'the dead'?

Dear God, keep me alive, and help me to keep growing.

A s for me, the hour has come for me to be sacrificed; the time is here for me to leave this life. I have done my best in the race, I have run the full distance, and I have kept the faith. And now there is waiting for me the victory prize of being put right with God, which the Lord, the righteous Judge, will give me on that Day....

But the Lord stayed with me and gave me strength, so that I was able to proclaim the full message for all the Gentiles to hear; and I was rescued from being sentenced to death. And the Lord will rescue me from all evil and take me safely into his heavenly kingdom. To him be the glory forever and ever! Amen.

2 Timothy 4: 6-8, 17-18

> "I have done my best..."

Keeping the faith

My friend Tom is dying of prostate cancer. He knows his time is limited. He's not famous, but he *has* done a great deal in his 80 years: a missionary in Angola, a teacher in adult education programs, administrator for a group of Native churches, director of a publishing house. He has lived through his wife's death from cancer. Now he faces his own death with courage.

I find Tom deeply moving. Just as, for the same reasons, I find Paul's letter to Timothy moving. In many ways, this is Paul's Last Will and Testament. Soon, he will go out from his prison cell, to his death. And he looks back, and is grateful. He has done his best; he has kept the faith.

When my time comes, God, may I look back without regrets, and look forward with confidence.

J esus was met by two men who came out of the burial caves.... These men had demons in them and were so fierce that no one dared travel on that road. At once they screamed, "What do you want with us, you Son of God? Have you come to punish us before the right time?"

Not far away there was a large herd of pigs feeding. So the demons begged Jesus, "If you are going to drive us out, send us into that herd of pigs."

"Go," Jesus told them; so they left and went off into the pigs. The whole herd rushed down the side of the cliff into the lake and was drowned.

The men who had been taking care of the pigs ran away and went into the town, where they told the whole story.

Matthew 8: 28-34

"The men who had been taking care of the pigs…"

What is fair?

I've always felt sorry for the guy with the pigs. In the past, when I heard this story, I'd nod in agreement. But I never really could understand why the pigs had to go. I can imagine myself as the owner of those pigs: "That guy gets possessed and my pigs get drowned?" To be honest, I don't get it, but....

When I was growing up, there was a girl who was having serious problems at home – a complicated situation. My parents took her in, and then *they* had the major problems.

Today, as I'm raising my own children, I think of my parents: sweating it out with problems they didn't cause. Like the owner of those pigs. Fair? Is life fair? But they did help turn her life around.

**Lord, help me put my notions of 'fairness' aside,
so I can give more freely.**

Some people brought Jesus a paralyzed man, lying on a bed. When Jesus saw how much faith they had, he said to the paralyzed man, "Courage, my son! Your sins are forgiven."

Then some teachers of the Law said to themselves, "This man is speaking blasphemy!" Jesus perceived what they were thinking, and so he said, "Why are you thinking such evil things? Is it easier to say, 'Your sins are forgiven,' or to say, 'Get up and walk'? I will prove to you, then, that the Son of Man has authority on earth to forgive sins." So he said to the paralyzed man, "Get up, pick up your bed, and go home!"

The man got up and went home. When the people saw it, they were afraid, and praised God for giving such authority to people.

Matthew 9: 1-8

> "Courage… your sins are forgiven."

Healing life's hurts

Usually I'm a very healthy, energetic person. But for the past few weeks, I've been sick: unable to work, to care for my family, to go for a walk even. At the risk of sounding ungrateful, if Jesus were to stand before me and say, "Your sins are forgiven," I think I'd ask him to reconsider. Couldn't he restore my physical health instead?

My body has forced me to take notice of what's happening at other levels – within my heart and my soul. Physical limitations have given me the opportunity to look at my life: at truths that I've not wanted, or taken the time, to consider.

Indeed, Jesus offers to heal me where I most need healing. It's just that, in my busyness, I don't always recognize it.

**Lord, help me to seek healing at all levels of my being:
body, mind, heart and soul.**

A s he walked along, Jesus saw a tax collector, named Matthew, sitting in his office. He said to him, "Follow me." Matthew got up and followed him.

While Jesus was having a meal in Matthew's house, many tax collectors and other outcasts came and joined Jesus and his disciples at the table. Some Pharisees saw this and asked his disciples, "Why does your teacher eat with such people?"

Jesus heard them and answered, "People who are well do not need a doctor, but only those who are sick. Go and find out what is meant by the scripture that says: 'It is kindness that I want, not animal sacrifices.' I have not come to call respectable people, but outcasts."　　*Matthew 9: 9-13*

"Why does your teacher eat with such people?"

Worthy of love

I think the tax collectors of Jesus' day must have been like today's middle managers: the 'in-between' people. They are the supervisors who are not completely 'workers,' nor are they completely 'management.'

I know what a hard role that is to play. I make decisions that affect people's daily lives: scheduling work hours, deciding who does what job, deciding whose opinions will get priority. I also end up being the messenger for a lot of unwelcome news from 'up above' – whether or not I agree with the decisions.

I am heartened by the fact that Jesus was so kind to the 'in-between' people. They may have been seen as 'sell outs' by their peers, but Jesus saw them as worthy of love.

Lord, help me to be compassionate to everyone I meet today, regardless of their status.

So then, you Gentiles are not foreigners or strangers any longer; you are now citizens together with God's people and members of the family of God. You, too, are built upon the foundation laid by the apostles and prophets, the cornerstone being Christ Jesus himself. He is the one who holds the whole building together and makes it grow into a sacred temple dedicated to the Lord. In union with him you too are being built together with all the others into a place where God lives through his Spirit.

Ephesians 2: 19-22

"You Gentiles are not foreigners or strangers any longer…"

Welcoming the outsider

Last year my son started Grade 7 at a new school. It was a terrible experience. From the very beginning, he was labelled as the 'outsider,' and was never welcomed into any group. Even the kids who had been on the fringes the previous year gained status by banding together against 'the new kid.'

Of course, most were friendly one-on-one. And they didn't hesitate to call and ask for help with homework. But, in public, when two or more were together in the schoolyard, he became their target.

Whom do I consider to be the 'outsider'? When I've tried to fit in, have I done it at another's expense? Believing that we are all one family, how can I welcome the 'outsider' today?

**Dear God, I believe that we are all members of your family.
Show me ways to welcome the 'outsider.'**

"The Lord chose another seventy-two and sent them out two by two, to go ahead of him to every town where he himself was about to go. He said, "Go! I am sending you like lambs among wolves. Don't take a purse or a beggar's bag or shoes; don't stop to greet anyone on the road. Whenever you go into a house, first say, 'Peace be with this house.' If someone who is peace-loving lives there, let your greeting of peace remain on that person; if not, take back your greeting of peace. Stay in that same house, eating and drinking whatever they offer you, for workers should be given their pay…. Whenever you go into a town and are made welcome, eat what is set before you, heal the sick in that town."

Luke 10: 1-12, 17-20

> "I am sending you like lambs among wolves."

Too much baggage

Whenever we take a trip, I over-pack. There are just so many contingencies to consider! Multiply that by each family member, and you've got enough baggage for a world cruise!

I carry extra baggage with me every day, too. It's impossible not to. Everyone I've known has shaped the person I am today. Sadly, not all of this has been for the good. Past troubles can stand in the way of present relationships.

Jesus told the disciples to travel light. No luggage! No preconceptions! Take people as they are, and accept that some people won't want to listen. My life would be simpler if I followed these instructions. I could focus on listening and healing, and the journey would take care of itself.

Lord, help me to let go of my extra 'baggage'
so I might recognize you more clearly in the people I meet.

A Jewish official came to Jesus, knelt before him, and said, "My daughter has just died; but come and place your hands on her, and she will live…."

A woman who had suffered from severe bleeding for twelve years came up behind Jesus and touched the edge of his cloak. She said to herself, "If only I touch his cloak, I will get well." Jesus turned around and saw her, and said, "Courage, my daughter! Your faith has made you well." At that very moment the woman became well.

Then Jesus went into the official's house…. He said, "Get out, everybody! The little girl is not dead – she is only sleeping!" As soon as the people had left, Jesus went into the girl's room and took hold of her hand, and she got up.

Matthew 9: 18-26

> "Jesus turned around and saw her…"

In the moment

At times I find it hard to stay focused on the present moment. I am easily distracted by where I have to be, by what I am going to do – all the important tasks that lie ahead of me.

Surrounded by crowds – all expecting to see if he was going to perform a miracle – Jesus was very aware of the people pressing close to him. When the woman touched his cloak, he knew it. He stopped and looked at her. Only *after* he had spoken to her tenderly, encouraged her and complimented her on her faith, did he go on his way and raise the little girl.

Today's reading is a fine example of being open to doing good – on the way to doing good.

**God, help me not to get too wrapped up in my plans
so that I have no time for yours.**

S ome people brought to Jesus a man who could not talk because he had a demon. As soon as the demon was driven out, the man started talking, and everyone was amazed. But the Pharisees said, "It is the chief of the demons who gives Jesus the power to drive out demons."

Jesus taught in the synagogues, preached the Good News about the kingdom, and healed people with every kind of disease and sickness. As he saw the crowds, his heart was filled with pity for them, because they were worried and helpless, like sheep without a shepherd. He said to his disciples, "The harvest is large, but there are few workers to gather it in. Pray to the owner of the harvest that he will send out workers to gather in his harvest."

Matthew 9: 32-38

> "His heart was filled with pity for them."

To suffer with

At the heart of Jesus' teaching is his commitment to a life of compassion. The word 'compassion' is formed from the Latin words *cum* and *pasti*, literally meaning 'to suffer with.' Jesus challenges us 'to suffer with' one another by sharing our common vulnerability, pain and brokenness.

In today's passage, we read that Jesus heals a man possessed by a demon. The Pharisees accuse Jesus of being an agent of evil. Jesus does not take the time to challenge his accusers, nor to repudiate the charges. His commitment to compassion is not about himself but about others.

As disciples, we, too, are called to be with people who are hurting – recognizing and sharing our common brokenness along the way.

Lord, give me the courage to share my vulnerability with another person today. Help me listen to their pain, also.

T he people of Israel were like a grapevine that was full of grapes. The more prosperous they were, the more altars they built. The more productive their land was, the more beautiful they made the sacred stone pillars they worship. The people whose hearts are deceitful must now suffer for their sins. God will break down their altars and destroy their sacred pillars.

These people will soon be saying, "We have no king because we did not fear the Lord…." I said, "Plow new ground for yourselves; plant righteousness, and reap the blessings that your devotion to me will produce. It is time for you to turn to me, your Lord, and I will come and pour out blessings upon you."

Hosea 10: 1-3, 7-8, 12

"The more prosperous they were…"

True security

I am a member of the richest society in the entire history of humanity. For me, prosperity is a given. Most of the time I don't even think about it.

Yet, in my quiet moments, I understand the failing of the people of Israel only too well. Like them, I forget that this prosperity is not of my doing. The altars before which I bow down – an ever-rising standard of living, secure pensions, more and more entertainment – are as fragile as the sacred stone pillars the Israelites foolishly worshipped.

When the wealth ends – as it does for each of us, if only at death – where will I find my security? What will my foundation be then?

**Lord, help me remember
that you are my only sure foundation.**

The Lord says, "When Israel was a child, I loved him and called him out of Egypt as my son.... Yet I was the one who taught Israel to walk.... I drew them to me with affection and love. I picked them up and held them to my cheek; I bent down to them and fed them....

"How can I give you up, Israel? How can I abandon you? Could I ever destroy you as I did Admah, or treat you as I did Zeboiim? My heart will not let me do it! My love for you is too strong. I will not punish you in my anger; I will not destroy Israel again. For I am God and not a mere human being. I, the Holy One, am with you. I will not come to you in anger."

Hosea 11: 1, 3-5, 8-9

> "I was the one who taught Israel to walk."

A tender and caring love

I love this passage. Most of the Bible portrays fathers as distant autocrats and rulers of the household. Hosea reveals a father's tender and loving side.

Helping a child learn to walk is such a satisfying accomplishment! Recently, our granddaughter took her first steps. At first, we had to hold her hand. Then she launched out on her own. Her face showed a wild joy, an ecstacy. As her confidence grew, she went from tentative steps to a trot to a gallop. In a single weekend, she taught herself three different ways of going down stairs: backwards, facing frontwards on her rear, and standing up holding the handrail.

As I read Hosea's words, I can identify with him, and with his love.

**Tenderly and gently, you taught me
to take my first tentative steps in faith. Thank you!**

" isten! I am sending you out just like sheep to a pack of wolves. You must be as cautious as snakes and as gentle as doves. Watch out, for there will be those who will arrest you and take you to court…. For my sake you will be brought to trial before rulers and kings, to tell the Good News to them and to the Gentiles. When they bring you to trial, do not worry about what you are going to say or how you will say it; when the time comes, you will be given what you will say. For the words you will speak will not be yours; they will come from the Spirit of your Father speaking through you."

Matthew 10: 16-23

"…do not worry about what you are going to say…"

Spirit words

When I was younger, speaking in public was one of my biggest nightmares. Fortunately, mid-life has allowed me to become considerably less inhibited in that regard.

But often, in more personal situations, I still find it hard to know what to say. What words of comfort can I offer to the friend whose child has just died? Do I have the courage to speak words of protest when I recognize an injustice in my workplace or my community? Am I able to extend a much-needed word of reconciliation in the face of misunderstanding or a strained relationship?

I need to recognize those circumstances where silence is not an option, and to trust that God will help me find the necessary words.

O Lord, be in my heart and on my lips,
so that I may speak words of healing where they are needed.

"No pupil is greater than his teacher; no slave is greater than his master. So a pupil should be satisfied to become like his teacher, and a slave like his master....

"Whatever is now covered up will be uncovered, and every secret will be made known. What I am telling you in the dark you must repeat in broad daylight, and what you have heard in private you must announce from the housetops. Do not be afraid of those who kill the body but cannot kill the soul.... For only a penny you can buy two sparrows, yet not one sparrow falls to the ground without your Father's consent. As for you, even the hairs of your head have all been counted. So do not be afraid; you are worth much more than many sparrows!"

Matthew 10: 24-33

> "...even the hairs of your head have all been counted."

Truth and justice

Bill had a profound influence on the students at the school where he taught. They admired him for always speaking the truth and insisting on fairness and justice.

Bill sometimes annoyed school administrators, however, because he refused to compromise the values that he had learned from his own teachers. And through his career as a teacher, Bill learned some new lessons: fulfillment in life does not depend on being popular, or on getting ahead with promotions. What matters is how well he serves his students and cares for them.

What also matters for Bill is the knowledge that he is loved by family, former students and by God – who assures him that even the hairs on his head have been counted.

Lord, open my heart and mind,
and teach me how to care for those entrusted to my care.

The teacher of the Law asked Jesus, "Who is my neighbour?" Jesus answered, "There was once a man who was going down from Jerusalem to Jericho when robbers attacked him, stripped him, and beat him up, leaving him half dead…. A priest was going down that road; but when he saw the man, he walked on by on the other side. A Levite also came there, went over and looked at the man, and then walked on by on the other side. But a Samaritan who was travelling that way came upon the man, and when he saw him, his heart was filled with pity. He went over to him, poured oil and wine on his wounds and bandaged them."

Luke 10: 25-37

"…his heart was filled with pity."

Not just a nice story

My high-school English class got into a discussion about bullying. One of the school's leading athletes told about seeing others publicly humiliated in the locker room. The most vocal social justice advocate told about racial slurs on the bus. When I asked them what they did, they were silent. They squirmed. "It's part of life." "What can we do?" "They won't listen."

I kept those kids after class, got the names of the bullies and spoke to them. I did it for the bullied kids, but more so to challenge those 'star' students. In our look-out-for-number-one world, they need to see adults living their faith. They need to see that the Good Samaritan isn't just a nice story!

**Lord, let me model your love for others
– in my actions as well as in my words.**

"Do not think that I have come to bring peace to the world. No, I did not come to bring peace, but a sword. I came to set sons against their fathers, daughters against their mothers, daughters-in-law against their mothers-in-law; your worst enemies will be the members of your own family.

"Those who love their father or mother more than me are not fit to be my disciples; those who love their son or daughter more than me are not fit to be my disciples. Those who do not take up their cross and follow in my steps are not fit to be my disciples. Those who try to gain their own life will lose it; but those who lose their life for my sake will gain it."

Matthew 10: 34 – 11: 1

> "I did not come to bring peace, but a sword."

Honesty and peace

Here Jesus says, "I did not come to bring peace…." But didn't he also say, "I leave you peace. My peace I leave you"? I want peace in my life, but perhaps the peace I seek is not what Jesus means by "peace."

I remember an argument I had with my mother. Up to that moment I had always avoided conflict with her. But this time there was no avoiding it. It wasn't easy: I didn't know how to tell her what I felt or all that I held deep in my heart.

However, with time, my mother and I have come to know a deep peace, deeper than I ever imagined possible. Jesus' kind of peace challenges me to speak with honesty – especially when it seems too hard.

**God, give me the courage to speak with honesty.
Help me trust that honesty is the only pathway to peace.**

The people in the towns where Jesus had performed most of his miracles did not turn from their sins, so he reproached those towns. "How terrible it will be for you…! If the miracles which were performed in you had been performed in Tyre and Sidon, the people there would have long ago put on sackcloth and sprinkled ashes on themselves, to show that they had turned from their sins! I assure you that on the Judgment Day God will show more mercy to the people of Tyre and Sidon than to you…! If the miracles which were performed in you had been performed in Sodom, it would still be in existence today! You can be sure that on the Judgment Day God will show more mercy to Sodom than to you!"

Matthew 11: 20-24

> "God will show mercy to the people…"

A merciful God

This morning I awoke to a little miracle. Impinging upon my senses was a chorus of eager birds greeting the morning with unbridled passion. Startling enthusiasm! Contagious joy! God's gift of morning love surrounded me while I was still within the warmth and comfort of my bed.

How could I share the wonder of my first waking moment? How could I concretely pass along the love that greeted me?

Others nearby awakened to the stench of a back alley and the chill of the morning breeze. I know God's gentle judgment and mercy are rightly assured for them. But what about people like me, privileged to waken to the daily miracle of comfort? Will God's judgment of me be as merciful?

**God, grant me an appreciation of the comforts I have received.
Let this lead me to acts of mercy.**

A t that time Jesus said, "Father, Lord of heaven and earth! I thank you because you have shown to the unlearned what you have hidden from the wise and learned. Yes, Father, this was how you were pleased to have it happen. My Father has given me all things. No one knows the Son except the Father, and no one knows the Father except the Son and those to whom the Son chooses to reveal him."

Matthew 11: 25-27

"...you have shown to the unlearned..."

A loving parent

The little boy had probably become too rowdy for the folks inside the church. His dad had him on his knee on a bench outside the church and was showing him one of the most ancient of rituals: "This is the church and this is the steeple. Open the doors and see all the people!" The boy's stubby little fingers had some difficulty in opening up to "show all the people." He whooped with joy when he was able to do it for the first time.

As I watched, I recalled similar times spent with my father, and I was reminded of how aware Christ was of that kind of tender care. And I said a quiet prayer for the little boys and girls who do not have a kind and loving parent.

Lord, help all parents and children as they negotiate the difficult passages involved in their relationships.

"Come to me, all of you who are tired from carrying heavy loads, and I will give you rest. Take my yoke and put it on you, and learn from me, because I am gentle and humble in spirit; and you will find rest. For the yoke I will give you is easy, and the load I will put on you is light."

Matthew 11: 2-30

"Come to me, all of you who are tired…"

A heavy load

I remember when the biggest load I carried was a bag labelled 'father.' Making sure there was food, clothing and a home for my children took up a lot of space. It held a huge supply of patience, which I dipped into regularly. Fatigue took up a lot of room, too, crushing many things under its weight. This bag was large and full, but I didn't mind. It had been my choice to pick it up, and love gave me strength.

I carry another burden, too, heavy even though it contains… nothing. In it are words I didn't say, but should have; and things I didn't do, but wish I had. This load I also chose, but oh, I would put it down if I could.

Lord, this heavy load wears me out. Give me rest.

Jesus was walking through some wheat fields on a Sabbath. His disciples were hungry, so they began to pick heads of wheat and eat the grain. When the Pharisees saw this, they said, "Look, it is against our Law for your disciples to do this on the Sabbath!"

Jesus answered, "Have you never read what David did that time when he and his men were hungry? He went into the house of God, and he and his men ate the bread offered to God.... I tell you that there is something here greater than the Temple. The scripture says, 'It is kindness that I want, not animal sacrifices.' If you really knew what this means, you would not condemn people who are not guilty; for the Son of Man is Lord of the Sabbath."

Matthew 12: 1-8

> "It is kindness that I want..."

A kind heart

Kindness. It's that lovely and simple! I go through elaborate lists of rules for my classroom, and everyone gets caught up in the details regarding infractions. Family meetings result in contracts for particular behaviours resulting in specific rewards and consequences. But we always need to go back and refer to the words, lists and legalities. I never realized what a Pharisee I am!

How can I live at the heart of my relationships – at home and at work – and live this principle of kindness? Respect, co-operation, inclusiveness and responsibility would all flow from kindness.

The Dalai Lama has said, "My religion is kindness." And here is Jesus, drawing on the Hebrew scripture, saying the same thing. I must take this to heart.

Lord of all kindness, help me to be kind.

T he Pharisees made plans to kill Jesus. When Jesus heard about the plot against him, he went away from that place; and large crowds followed him. He healed all the sick and gave them orders not to tell others about him. He did this so as to make come true what God had said through the prophet Isaiah: "Here is my servant, whom I have chosen, the one I love, and with whom I am pleased. I will send my Spirit upon him, and he will announce my judgment to the nations. He will not argue or shout, or make loud speeches in the streets. He will not break off a bent reed, nor put out a flickering lamp. He will persist until he causes justice to triumph, and on him all peoples will put their hope."

Matthew 12: 14-21

> "He will persist until he causes justice to triumph."

Loving patience

The neighbourhood bully preys on the misfit. An aggressive, power-ful nation overtakes one that is defenceless. There is a vicious streak within us that finds expression whenever we trample on the vulner-able in an attempt to strengthen ourselves. We are all capable of it at some level – manipulating our family with angry moods, gossiping to defame our neighbour, buying 'cheap' and perpetuating economic exploitation of others.

Jesus is clear that this is not his way. He does not despise or reject us for our weakness; neither does he take advantage of us, forcing us to follow him. Patiently, persistently, he confronts us with his truth until our love ignites, and we freely place our hope in him.

Do we do the same for one another?

**Lord, fill me with your strength when I am weak.
Help me be patient and loving with others when they are weak.**

As Jesus and his disciples went on their way, he came to a village where a woman named Martha welcomed him in her home. She had a sister named Mary, who sat down at the feet of the Lord and listened to his teaching. Martha was upset over all the work she had to do, so she came and said, "Lord, don't you care that my sister has left me to do all the work by myself? Tell her to come and help me!"

The Lord answered her, "Martha, Martha! You are worried and troubled over so many things, but just one is needed. Mary has chosen the right thing, and it will not be taken away from her."

Luke 10: 38-42

"You are worried and troubled..."

Listen, and be still

Often this story is seen to portray the tension that exists between two aspects of Christian life: the active and the contemplative. But notice that Jesus does not criticize Martha for her activity; rather he gently reminds her that she has lost her focus, the reason for all her labours. She has become consumed by the minutiae of the household.

How easy it is for us, as well, to be so preoccupied by the many obligations and concerns of the day that we lose our grounding, our sense of the sacred in the ordinary.

Jesus invites us to sit at his feet, even if it is for a few minutes in a hectic day, to listen to him and to be still.

**Lord, help me take a few moments to be quiet
and to listen for your voice amidst the busyness of my day.**

"How evil and godless are the people of this day!" Jesus exclaimed. "You ask me for a miracle? The only miracle you will be given is the miracle of the prophet Jonah. In the same way that Jonah spent three days and nights in the big fish, so will the Son of Man spend three days and nights in the depths of the earth. On Judgment Day the people of Nineveh will accuse you, because they turned from their sins when they heard Jonah preach; I tell you that there is something here greater than Jonah! On Judgment Day the Queen of Sheba will accuse you, because she travelled all the way from her country to listen to King Solomon's wise teaching; I assure you that there is something here greater than Solomon!"

Matthew 12: 38-42

> "You ask me for a miracle?"

The miracle of life

It's so easy to lose sight of God's gifts to me. Duty and obligation can blind me: the jobs I have to finish; the bills I need to pay; the time I have to spend with people I don't like. Ambition, envy, anger and discouragement are just a few of the failings that can distract me. I forget there is 'something greater' here.

It is God who created the beauty of this world in which I live: each dawn is a miracle. It is God who gives me life and breath and a beating heart. It is God who brings courageous and generous people into my life.

Today I will find time to appreciate God's gracious gifts – and to react fittingly: with awe and wonder.

Make me constantly aware of your gifts.
Help me be grateful for the life and the love that you give me.

J esus was still talking to the people when his mother and brothers arrived. They stood outside, asking to speak with him. So one of the people there said to him, "Look, your mother and brothers are standing outside, and they want to speak with you."

Jesus answered, "Who is my mother? Who are my brothers?" Then he pointed to his disciples and said, "Look! Here are my mother and my brothers! Whoever does what my Father in heaven wants is my brother, my sister, and my mother."

Matthew 12: 46-50

"Who is my mother?"

Family ties

What shocking words – so naked and so harsh! I know Jesus is making a point about the urgency of his mission, and the importance of our response. But such roughness is hard to understand.

I'm a father, and this story makes me feel for Jesus' mother. Why had she come? What did she want to say to him?

Maybe she hadn't seen her son for a long time and wanted to give him a greeting. Perhaps she was worried and wanted to reassure herself that he was all right. Maybe there was important family news to share. We're not told. And we're not told what happened when she heard his response. But I can guess.

**We mothers and fathers need special strength sometimes.
Lord, give us that strength.**

J esus sat down to teach…. He used parables to tell them many things.

"Once there was a man who went out to sow grain. As he scattered the seed in the field, some of it fell along the path, and the birds came and ate it up. Some of it fell on rocky ground, where there was little soil. The seeds soon sprouted, because the soil wasn't deep. But when the sun came up, it burned the young plants; and because the roots had not grown deep enough, the plants soon dried up. Some of the seed fell among thorn bushes, which grew up and choked the plants. But some seeds fell in good soil, and the plants bore grain: some had one hundred grains, others sixty, and others thirty." Jesus concluded, "Listen, then, if you have ears!"

Matthew 13: 1-9

> "…some seeds fell in good soil, and the plants bore grain…"

Matching seed with soil

Like the man in Jesus' parable, I too go out to sow. My words and actions are my seeds, and my children's souls are my soil.

I try to make sure that what I'm sowing is suited to the soil, but it's hard to tell which seeds will take root or whether the harvest of their lives will be a bountiful one. Sometimes I know the soil needs lots of seeds – and water too! And fertile soil may need only one seed and no tending at all for a rich crop to flourish.

Like a good farmer, my job is to match the seed with the soil, tend it carefully, and then wait patiently and in hope for the harvest to come.

**Lord, please help me plant wisely –
and give me the patience to wait for the harvest to grow.**

E arly on Sunday morning, Mary Magdalene went to the tomb and saw that the stone had been taken away from the entrance.

Mary stood crying outside the tomb. While she was still crying, she bent over and looked in the tomb and saw two angels there dressed in white, sitting where the body of Jesus had been. "Woman, why are you crying?" they asked. She answered, "They have taken my Lord away, and I do not know where they have put him!" Then she turned around and saw Jesus standing there; but she did not know that it was Jesus. "Woman, why are you crying?" Jesus asked her. "Who is it that you are looking for...?"

Jesus said to her, "Mary!" She turned toward him and said in Hebrew, "Rabboni!" (This means "Teacher.")

John 20: 1, 11-18

> "Who is it that you are looking for?"

Present to others

My life is so cluttered – with things to do or to buy, with news to catch up on – that it is hard to stay focused like Mary Magdalene in her grief over Jesus' death, and in her joy when she recognized him after his resurrection. She had stood by the cross and watched Jesus' agonizing death. She was the first to proclaim that he had risen: he is alive!

How can I recognize Jesus in the pain and sorrow of others? Maybe I won't see it at first – after all, Mary Magdalene thought Jesus was the gardener! But if I try to simplify my life, so that people always come first, then perhaps I will be able to see Jesus in everyone I meet.

Lord, may I learn to be present – in small ways – to those who suffer within my community.

L isten, then, and learn what the parable of the sower means. Those who hear the message about the kingdom but do not understand it are like the seeds that fell along the path. The Evil One comes and snatches away what was sown in them. The seeds that fell on rocky ground stand for those who receive the message gladly as soon as they hear it. But it does not sink deep into them.... So when trouble or persecution comes because of the message, they give up at once. The seeds that fell among thorn bushes stand for those who hear the message; but the worries about this life and the love for riches choke the message, and they don't bear fruit. And the seeds sown in the good soil stand for those who hear the message and understand it: they bear fruit."

Matthew 13: 18-23

> "...what the parable of the sower means."

Nurturing the seeds

Last year my children planted sunflower seeds. When the seedlings were about eight inches high, a slug chewed through the main stalk of one of them. The plant leaned over sadly. I was going to pull it out, but my kids fashioned a splint out of two popsicle sticks and some tape.

The sunflower survived! It only grew to about a third of the height of the others, and it bloomed later, but it was the most perfect bloom! I took such pleasure from looking at that 'saved' sunflower.

Today's reading talks about the seeds that don't 'take.' But there are also seeds that get off to a good start and then experience some kind of hurt. There is hope for them too – hope for the late bloomers.

**Dear Lord, help me to nurture
and feed whatever seeds you've planted in me.**

"The kingdom of heaven is like this. A man sowed good seed in his field. One night, when everyone was asleep, an enemy came and sowed weeds among the wheat and went away. When the plants grew and the heads of grain began to form, then the weeds showed up. The man's servants said, 'Sir, where did the weeds come from?' 'It was some enemy who did this,' he answered. 'Do you want us to go and pull up the weeds?' they asked him. 'No,' he answered, 'because as you gather the weeds you might pull up some of the wheat along with them. Let the wheat and the weeds both grow together until harvest. Then I will tell the harvest workers to pull up the weeds first, tie them in bundles and burn them, and then to gather in the wheat and put it in my barn.'"

Matthew 13: 24-30

> "...then the weeds showed up."

Identifying the weeds

Year one: in late spring, I weed my young garden. I am, at the time, a rank beginner. Hmm, this looks 'weedish' – out you come. As summer progresses, much of what I planted is gone.

Year two: I've learned. I wait a few days, until I'm sure they're weeds. Up they come… and with them, many plants I want! Their roots still tiny, they come together in clumps of sod. As summer progresses, most of what I planted is gone.

Life! What are weeds? What are plants? Even when you think you know, how do you untangle them? With plants you can wait until you're sure. In life? Not so clear; sometimes you have to choose. And if you're wrong, to have the faith that you can plant again.

God, give me eyes to see.
Help me untangle the weeds from the wheat.

One day Jesus was praying. When he had finished, one of his disciples said, "Lord, teach us to pray...."

Jesus said, "Ask, and you will receive; seek, and you will find; knock, and the door will be opened to you. For those who ask will receive, and those who seek will find, and the door will be opened to anyone who knocks. Would any of you who are fathers give your son a snake when he asks for fish? Or would you give him a scorpion when he asks for an egg? As bad as you are, you know how to give good things to your children. How much more, then, will the Father in heaven give the Holy Spirit to those who ask him!"

Luke 11: 1-13

"Ask, and you will receive..."

Abundant love

I can barely remember the details surrounding the days when my husband was diagnosed with terminal cancer. However, I do remember praying, "God, help us."

And God provided help in so many ways! We knew ourselves supported by the thoughts and prayers of others, both near and far. We knew ourselves loved in such tangible ways: food kept arriving at our door; friends and family took our children on outings; teachers and classmates wove a supportive net for them at school; co-workers even re-roofed our house! The list goes on....

I can say with deep conviction that, throughout my husband's illness and since his death, God did answer my prayer – through the love and caring of friends and family. For that I am truly thankful.

God, give me the courage to ask for what I need.
Help me recognize the different ways you respond.

"As for you, how fortunate you are! Your eyes see and your ears hear. I assure you that many prophets and many of God's people wanted very much to see what you see, but they could not, and to hear what you hear, but they did not."

Matthew 13:16-17

> "God's people wanted very much to see…"

Look again

A few years ago my husband gave me one of those optical illusion plaques. The image looks like scrambled lines but apparently if you stare at it long enough a three-dimensional figure will appear.

Many of our friends have stood before it oohing and ahhhing in amazement. I have never seen anything but squiggly lines. But something in me says: "Keep trying!"

It's that way with the parables for me. Some of them evade me; many frustrate me. But every once in awhile I will read or hear a commentary that sheds some light on the parable's message, and I am encouraged to look again.

God, open my eyes, ears and heart to your words.

" The man who sowed the good seed is the Son of Man; the field is the world; the good seed is the people who belong to the kingdom; the weeds are the people who belong to the Evil One; and the enemy who sowed the weeds is the Devil…. Just as the weeds are gathered up and burned in the fire, so the same thing will happen at the end of the age: the Son of Man will send out his angels to gather up out of his kingdom all those who cause people to sin and all others who do evil things, and they will throw them into the fiery furnace, where they will cry and gnash their teeth. Then God's people will shine like the sun in their Father's kingdom."

Matthew 13: 36-43

"Then God's people will shine like the sun…"

Right and wrong

Sometimes I find Jesus' words so confusing. One day I read how "my burden is light," and another how "they will cry and gnash their teeth." It sounds so foreign two thousand years later.

Yet it is consistent with how Jesus drew his lines around right and wrong. I think of his defence of the woman about to be stoned and how he challenged the crowd; the healing on the Sabbath and his response: "Is it right to save life or to kill?" His position is so clear.

I like to think of Jesus' unending forgiveness and his warmth. But I must be reminded of his piercing honesty and his challenge to do what I know to be right – no matter how hard.

**Lord, help me see things your way.
Help me to know what is right, and to do it.**

"The kingdom of heaven is like this. A man happens to find a treasure hidden in a field. He covers it up again, and is so happy that he goes and sells everything he has, and then goes back and buys that field.

"Also, the kingdom of heaven is like this. A man is looking for fine pearls, and when he finds one that is unusually fine, he goes and sells everything he has, and buys that pearl."

Matthew 13: 44-46

"...looking for fine pearls."

Fine pearls

My five-year-old daughter likes to play while she's getting dressed. She pulls her pyjama-top half off so it's stuck on her head, pretending to be Cleopatra. She puts both legs down one leg of her pants. She does a somersault, or runs off to catch the cat. I say continually, "Come on, hurry up, we're late," and we always are.

She follows a different rhythm than mine. It's infuriating, but sometimes I long to ditch my schedule and follow hers. Is mine really so important?

Giving up my agenda can seem like a sacrifice – when I'm living by this world's rules. But at those times when I recognize the glint of pearls, I'm eager to go with God's kingdom. So what if we miss the bus!

**Lord, give me the freedom to close my agenda book,
and to open my eyes to see your pearls.**

As Jesus and his disciples went on their way, he came to a village where a woman named Martha welcomed him in her home. She had a sister named Mary, who sat down at the feet of the Lord and listened to his teaching. Martha was upset over all the work she had to do, so she came and said, "Lord, don't you care that my sister has left me to do all the work by myself? Tell her to come and help me!"

The Lord answered her, "Martha, Martha! You are worried and troubled over so many things, but just one is needed. Mary has chosen the right thing, and it will not be taken away from her."   *Luke 10: 38-42*

> "You are worried and troubled over so many things..."

Faced with a choice

Last night I looked over the journals that I've kept about our children's lives. When our daughters were young, I diligently made time in the evenings to write. Skimming through their journals last night, I realized that I haven't written in over a year and a half! What has filled my evenings? Probably the kind of housework that Martha, God bless her, fretted over.

I wonder if Martha was angered by the words of Jesus. Was he dismissing her work? Or was he encouraging her to free herself from getting caught up with the housework?

Looking at those empty journal pages, I realize that I have missed an opportunity, not only to capture something precious, but to give myself the gift of quiet reflection.

Lord, today the housework can wait.
I will give myself the gift of quiet reflection.

When Jesus finished telling these parables, he left that place and went back to his hometown. He taught in the synagogue, and those who heard him were amazed. "Where did he get such wisdom?" they asked. "And what about his miracles? Isn't he the carpenter's son? Isn't Mary his mother, and aren't James, Joseph, Simon, and Judas his brothers? Aren't all his sisters living here? Where did he get all this?" And so they rejected him.

Jesus said to them, "A prophet is respected everywhere except in his hometown and by his own family." Because they did not have faith, he did not perform many miracles there.

Matthew 13: 54-58

> "Isn't he the carpenter's son?"

Look for the miracle

It's strange, perhaps, to think of the Olympics when you're reading the Bible. But today's reading made me think of past Winter Olympics. As I watched the athletes perform such amazing feats, I found it hard to think that they were once 'the kid next door.' Catriona LeMay Doan, with her power, poise and beauty, was once a little kid, growing up in Saskatchewan.

One of the valuable things I learn from Jesus, 'the carpenter's kid from next door,' is that within the most ordinary of us there is something miraculous – and that I need to look for it, to be aware of its presence in others.

There's a country song that goes, "Miracles occur in the strangest of places." I guess that's why I need to keep my eyes open.

**Lord, help me see the amazing potential
of the people around me.**

For some time John the Baptist had told Herod, "It isn't right for you to be married to Herodias!" Herod wanted to kill him....

On Herod's birthday the daughter of Herodias danced [and] Herod was so pleased that he promised her, "I swear that I will give you anything you ask for!" At her mother's suggestion she asked him, "Give me here and now the head of John the Baptist on a plate!"

The king was sad, but because of the promise he had made in front of all his guests he gave orders that her wish be granted. So he had John beheaded in prison. The head was brought in on a plate and given to the girl, who took it to her mother.

Matthew 14: 1-12

"So he had John beheaded…"

Speaking out

How strange life is – particularly for those who have no power. John the Baptist: incarcerated, rotting in a dungeon, because he spoke the truth as he saw it. And then, a girl dances, and on a whim he loses his head! It's a tough life being a prophet.

Years ago, I met a man who had spent four years in a Latin American prison – beaten, shocked with electric probes, fingers broken. His crime: speaking out and having no power. He said he knew it was a risk, but he knew what he believed, and he wanted a better world.

And me? When I see injustice, do I speak out, or do I look away?

Lord, help those who speak the truth.
Give them strength.

J esus said, "Watch out and guard yourselves from every kind of greed; because your true life is not made up of the things you own."

Jesus told this parable: "There was once a rich man who had land which bore good crops. He began to think to himself, 'I don't have a place to keep all my crops… so I will tear down my barns and build bigger ones. Then I will say to myself, Lucky man! You have all the good things you need for many years. Take life easy, eat, drink, and enjoy yourself !' But God said to him, 'You fool! This very night you will have to give up your life….'" And Jesus concluded, "This is how it is with those who pile up riches for themselves but are not rich in God's sight."

Luke 12: 13-21

> "…true life is not made up of the things you own."

Less rich and less foolish

These days I live close to the poverty line, and am struggling to make ends meet. Let me clarify that: I am *trying* to move down the economic ladder – closer to global justice.

The statistics haunt me: for everyone to live at the level enjoyed (and expected) by the average North American would require the resources of four planet Earths! To be 'average' here is to use four times our share of global resources. It is to be a 'rich fool' with bigger and bigger barns – garages, houses, closets – filled with possessions that cannot bring me closer to God, others or real happiness.

It's easy to see 'rich fools' among the wealthy. My task is to see a rich fool in the mirror – and to struggle daily to be less rich and less foolish.

**Dear God, help me to live more simply,
so that others may simply live.**

Wh“hen Jesus heard the news about John, he left in a boat and went to a lonely place by himself. The people heard about it, and so they followed him by land. Jesus got out of the boat, and when he saw the large crowd, his heart was filled with pity for them, and he healed their sick....

Jesus' disciples said, "Send the people away and let them go to the villages to buy food for themselves.... All we have here are five loaves and two fish."

"Then bring them here to me," Jesus said. He took the five loaves and the two fish, looked up to heaven, and gave thanks to God. He broke the loaves and gave them to the disciples, and the disciples gave them to the people. Everyone ate and had enough. *Matthew 14: 13-21*

"…his heart was filled with pity for them…"

Enough to share

I've come to accept that bad timing is part of life. After a slow period, four good contracts will appear, each with the same deadline. In the middle of a joyous dinner with friends, the phone rings. It's the hospital, and the news is bad.

Jesus wants to be alone to mourn John's death. He even takes a boat to get away, but he can't escape. When faced with the overwhelming needs of the people, he reaches down – into his inner resources – to give of himself. And because he gives freely, what little he has is more than enough.

I often feel the need to get away by myself, away from the demands of life. But, even when I have little to offer, I'm most fully alive when I give of myself.

Lord, you understand despair and emptiness.
When I feel completely drained,
may I remember to pray to you from that lonely place.

J esus made the disciples get into the boat and go on ahead to the other side of the lake…. Between three and six o'clock in the morning Jesus came to the disciples, walking on the water…. "It's a ghost!" they screamed with fear.

Jesus spoke. "Courage! It is I. Don't be afraid!" Then Peter spoke up. "Lord, if it is really you, order me to come out on the water to you." "Come!" answered Jesus. So Peter got out of the boat and started walking on the water to Jesus. But when he noticed the strong wind, he was afraid…. "Save me, Lord!" he cried. At once Jesus reached out and grabbed hold of him and said, "What little faith you have! Why did you doubt?"

They both got into the boat, and the wind died down.

Matthew 14: 22-36

> "What little faith you have!"

Infinite trust

As a writing exercise, I often pick a topic, put my pen on the paper, and write whatever comes. When I give myself over to this experience, I am often surprised by the results!

My writing unfolds as the Spirit moves me. I open up and let go, and beauty, passion, humour, pain – whatever – emerge. It is a place of infinite trust, requiring great courage. However, when I let myself get distracted by feelings of fear and inadequacy, then I sink like a rock.

As I practise being present to the moment – whether in writing or in life – I develop the trust needed to see the Spirit at work in the world around me, and the courage to respond to the challenges before me.

God, may I always be open to your Spirit at work in my life.

A Canaanite woman came to Jesus. "Son of David!" she cried out. "Have mercy on me, sir! My daughter has a demon and is in a terrible condition...." His disciples came to him and begged him, "Send her away! She is following us and making all this noise!" Then Jesus replied, "I have been sent only to the lost sheep of the people of Israel."

At this the woman came and fell at his feet. "Help me, sir!" she said. Jesus answered, "It isn't right to take the children's food and throw it to the dogs."

"That's true, sir," she answered, "but even the dogs eat the left-overs that fall from their masters' table." Jesus answered her, "You are a woman of great faith! What you want will be done for you." And at that very moment her daughter was healed.   *Matthew 15: 21-28*

> "...the woman came and fell at his feet."

Parental love

I know this Canaanite woman. She's one of the other parents I've met in hospital emergency rooms waiting anxiously with a sick child. She's one of the parents I've talked to whose heart has bled when their child was hurt or disappointed or who failed at something important. She's one of the parents I've been humbled to see live uncomplainingly and even joyfully with a child who has been given enormous challenges in life.

She is as ordinary and familiar as they are – and as heroic. Twelve angry men blocking her way? Not a problem. The Son of God brushing her off? A minor setback.

Is there anything as powerful as the love of parents for their children? Not that I've seen.

**Loving God, continue to support and inspire all parents
as they care for the needs of their children.**

J esus asked his disciples, "Who do people say the Son of Man is?"

"Some say John the Baptist," they answered. "Others say Elijah, while others say Jeremiah or some other prophet."

"What about you?" he asked them. "Who do you say I am?" Simon Peter answered, "You are the Messiah, the Son of the living God."

"Good for you, Simon son of John!" answered Jesus. "For this truth did not come to you from any human being, but it was given to you directly by my Father in heaven. And so I tell you, Peter: you are a rock, and on this rock foundation I will build my church, and not even death will ever be able to overcome it. I will give you the keys of the kingdom of heaven."

Matthew 16: 13-23

"...on this rock foundation..."

Doing God's work

When Peter gets it right, Jesus praises him and when he gets it wrong, Jesus reprimands him. Peter never stops trying: he doesn't rest on his laurels after success, and he doesn't fall apart after his failures.

Jesus doesn't call Peter 'a rock' because he's never wrong. Rather, Jesus recognizes in Peter his unfaltering love for God and his willingness to keep going.

Like Peter, I don't need to be perfect to do God's work. I admit it feels good to be praised and it feels lousy to fail. And both boasting and wallowing in self-pity are seductive in their own ways. It's only when I dig more deeply that I find the love and resilience I need to continue doing God's work.

God, give me strength to continue doing your work.

Jesus took Peter, John, and James with him and went up a hill to pray. While he was praying, his face changed its appearance, and his clothes became dazzling white. Suddenly two men were there talking with him. They were Moses and Elijah, who appeared in heavenly glory and talked with Jesus about the way in which he would soon fulfill God's purpose by dying in Jerusalem. Peter and his companions were sound asleep, but they woke up and saw Jesus' glory and the two men who were standing with him....

While he was still speaking, a cloud appeared and covered them with its shadow; and the disciples were afraid as the cloud came over them. A voice said from the cloud, "This is my Son, whom I have chosen – listen to him!"   *Luke 9: 28-36*

"...his clothes became dazzling white."

Dazzling light

Today is the anniversary of the bombing of Hiroshima. Last year I attended a prayer service commemorating this tragedy. A survivor spoke, describing the flash of light as the bomb exploded, and its unbelievable brightness. The next speaker reminded us that the bomb was dropped on the Feast of the Transfiguration – a moment of unbelievable light.

Hiroshima was the result of human beings seeking ultimate power through destruction. The Transfiguration was the reflection of God's presence, which does not diminish or destroy.

I am drawn to brilliant minds and bright ideas. I am easily dazzled by lights of this world: celebrity, power, wealth. But these usually come at the cost of people's suffering, somewhere in the world. Today's reading reminds me which light I must try to follow.

**God, guide my steps
so that I may walk with confidence in your light.**

A man came to Jesus and said, "Sir, have mercy on my son! He is an epileptic and has such terrible attacks…. I brought him to your disciples, but they could not heal him."

Jesus answered, "How unbelieving and wrong you people are! … How long do I have to put up with you? Bring the boy here to me!" Jesus gave a command to the demon, and it went out of the boy, and at that very moment he was healed.

Then the disciples asked Jesus, "Why couldn't we drive the demon out?" "It was because you do not have enough faith," answered Jesus. "I assure you that if you have faith as big as a mustard seed, you can say to this hill, 'Go from here to there!' and it will go. You could do anything!"

Matthew 17: 14-20

"You could do anything!"

Faith and hope

The computer breaks down, the babysitting arrangements fall through, the bills need paying, a deadline looms. And I miss my daughter growing up… as my face is anxiously glued to the computer screen.

In trying to balance loving my daughter and running my own business, I often get furiously impatient with myself, as Jesus does when his disciples fail to heal this sick man. But he's not asking them to be stronger, better qualified or more organized. He's simply asking them to have more faith.

When I remember to ask God for what I need, I see my own frustrations and failures in a different light. The possibilities of what I can do – with just a tiny seed of faith – fill me with hope instead of disappointment.

**Lord, teach me to exchange my impatience with myself
for a mustard seed of faith in you.**

"**B**e ready for whatever comes, dressed for action and with your lamps lit, like servants who are waiting for their master to come back from a wedding feast. When he comes and knocks, they will open the door for him at once. How happy are those servants whose master finds them awake and ready when he returns! I tell you, he will take off his coat, have them sit down, and will wait on them. How happy they are if he finds them ready, even if he should come at midnight or even later! … You, too, must be ready, because the Son of Man will come at an hour when you are not expecting him."

Luke 12: 32-48

"Be ready for whatever comes…"

Ready to listen

When my daughter practises the violin, she gets furious if I interrupt her before she's finished playing a piece. And I get furious that she insists on playing it to the end.

One day I asked her what we could both do to improve her practice time. She thought for awhile and then said, "You talk less, and I'll listen more."

I'm taking this as a fine lesson for life in general, especially prayer. I suspect I drown God out – with how my life is going and what I need to make it go better. I'm not used to being still, listening and keeping quiet. Will I even *hear* the master's knock, let alone be dressed and ready?

Lord, I want to hear your voice.
Teach me to be still and to listen.

J esus said, "The Son of Man is about to be handed over to those who will kill him; but three days later he will be raised to life…."

The collectors of the Temple tax came to Peter and asked, "Does your teacher pay the Temple tax?" "Of course," Peter answered…. Jesus spoke up, "Simon, who pays duties or taxes to the kings of this world? The citizens of the country or the foreigners?" "The foreigners," answered Peter. "Well, then," replied Jesus, "that means that the citizens don't have to pay. But we don't want to offend these people. So go to the lake and drop in a line. Pull up the first fish you hook, and in its mouth you will find a coin worth enough for my Temple tax and yours. Take it and pay them our taxes."

Matthew 17: 22-27

> "Who pays duties or taxes to the kings of this world?"

Lost in the details

When I started my own business I received a lot of advice about taxes. The language was very mundane and uninspiring: "This decision leads to that… but avoid that by doing this…." Launching a business calls for dreams and ambitions that can be eclipsed by dry tax manuals.

Today's reading captures a similar tension. Jesus predicts his death and resurrection, and a little later he and the disciples end up discussing who pays what tax. And there's the additional jolt about a mysterious coin to be found in the mouth of a fish. Everyday concerns and inexplicable mystery vie for the disciples' attention.

How like my life today, where the demands of my business and family jostle for attention, threatening to eclipse Jesus' presence in my life.

**God, never let me get so wrapped up in the details
of household chores that I leave no space for you in my life.**

" I am telling you the truth: a grain of wheat remains no more than a single grain unless it is dropped into the ground and dies. If it does die, then it produces many grains. Those who love their own life will lose it; those who hate their own life in this world will keep it for life eternal. Whoever wants to serve me must follow me, so that my servant will be with me where I am. And my Father will honour anyone who serves me."

John 12: 24-26

"If it does die, then it produces many grains."

Dying to self

Jesus challenges us to risk. To risk is to enter the realm of uncertainty, and that may mean the death of my long-held beliefs. I find myself caught up in the expected, comfortable patterns of behaviour. I do not like to disturb myself, or those around me, by choosing the unexpected, the uncomfortable.

However, just as the seed, in the dark of the soil, is broken open, so too must I enter the unknown areas of my life, in order to grow. It is precisely in breaking through the bonds that hold me captive that the seeds of God's kingdom can germinate.

Maryanne Williamson once wrote, "Our deepest fear is not that we are inadequate. Our deepest fear is that we are powerful beyond measure."

Lord, help me consider what makes me uncomfortable.
Give me the courage to look for your presence in those situations.

" If your brother sins against you, go to him and show him his fault. But do it privately, just between yourselves. If he listens to you, you have won your brother back. But if he will not listen to you, take one or two other persons with you, so that 'every accusation may be upheld by the testimony of two or more witnesses,' as the scripture says. And if he will not listen to them, then tell the whole thing to the church. Finally, if he will not listen to the church, treat him as though he were a pagan or a tax collector. And so I tell all of you: what you prohibit on earth will be prohibited in heaven, and what you permit on earth will be permitted in heaven."

Matthew 18: 15-20

> "…take one or two other persons with you…"

True reconciliation

I would have a terrible time maintaining my list of enemies and my resentments if I were to follow the 'Four-Step Plan' that Jesus describes in today's reading!

Just taking that first step – discussing the matter with a brother or sister – would leave me open to the possibility of being wrong, or that there may be two sides to the issue. The second step of bringing in a couple of witnesses would be even more dangerous. What if they did not side with me? And that third step of telling the whole thing to the church – well! We've all experienced what happens when any kind of committee gets together to discuss an issue!

True reconciliation is a dangerous, but necessary, process.

**God, it is much easier to hold on to resentment
than to risk letting it go. Help me to let go.**

P eter asked Jesus, "Lord, if my brother keeps on sinning against me, how many times do I have to forgive him? Seven times?"

"No, not seven times," answered Jesus, "but seventy times seven, because the kingdom of heaven is like this. Once there was a king who decided to check on his servants' accounts…. One of them was brought in who owed him millions of dollars. The servant did not have enough to pay his debt, so the king ordered him to be sold as a slave, with his wife and his children and all that he had, in order to pay the debt. The servant fell on his knees before the king. 'Be patient with me,' he begged, 'and I will pay you everything!' The king felt sorry for him, so he forgave him the debt and let him go."

Matthew 18: 21 – 19: 1

"…so he forgave him…"

Asking for forgiveness

Phil was very angry about a decision that John, his boss, had made without consulting him. For days, Phil steamed about it and complained at length to others.

The following week, at a meeting with John and others, Phil was silent, not participating as he usually did. John noticed this and asked, "Is something wrong?" Phil blurted out angrily, "I've never been so angry! You didn't consult us. Aren't we important?"

John listened. Then, after a few minutes of silence, he said, "You're right. I messed up. Can you forgive me?" Phil was stunned to hear those words. Right away his anger melted and he said, "Yes, I forgive you."

Phil came away with a new respect for his boss and a greater gentleness towards others.

**O God, give me the humility to recognize
when I've hurt someone and to ask for forgiveness.**

T he Sovereign Lord says, "I will treat you the way you deserve, because you ignored your promises and broke the covenant. But I will honour the covenant I made with you when you were young, and I will make a covenant with you that will last forever. You will remember how you have acted, and be ashamed of it when you get your older sister and your younger sister back. I will let them be like daughters to you, even though this was not part of my covenant with you. I will renew my covenant with you, and you will know that I am the Lord…." The Sovereign Lord has spoken.

Ezekiel 16: 59-63

> "I will honour the covenant
> I made with you…"

Faithful love

I like this: the Sovereign Lord assesses the situation, applies consequences, but continues to forgive and remain committed to his covenant.

I'm a teacher. In my business, we have to deliver the message: "I'll treat you the way you deserve." Sometimes it's hard to remember the second part: "I will honour the covenant I made with you."

A covenant is not a contract – it's not *quid pro quo*. It doesn't give up. It doesn't say, "You've had your chance." Instead, it says, "I am committed to you. Even when you've given up on yourself."

What a wonderful model for relationships: I will be truthful, but I will forgive. And I will be there. Committed.

Lord, make me mindful of my covenants.
Keep me faithful to them.

S ome people brought children to Jesus for him to place his hands on them and to pray for them, but the disciples scolded the people. Jesus said, "Let the children come to me and do not stop them, because the kingdom of heaven belongs to such as these."

He placed his hands on them, and then went away.

Matthew 19: 13-15

"…the kingdom of heaven belongs to such as these."

Children

A line from a country song: "My old man is just another child that's grown old." As we all are – children growing old.

It's hard to remain a child. And glib to pretend that's what we are, for the child in us goes. Those mornings: rushing off to work after too little sleep. Those bills to pay. Those compromises made – right and wrong not as clear as they once were. All the pain of lost love, sick children, loved ones gone. As time, that thief, steals our childhood from us.

But, perhaps… if I stop and listen to the wind. Give spontaneously. Say Yes to an invitation without stopping to think it over. Live only today. Only right now. Laugh. Perhaps… just for a moment, the kingdom can begin, right now.

Dear God, let me see your creation with a child's eyes.

Soon afterward Mary got ready and hurried off to a town in the hill country of Judea. She went into Zechariah's house and greeted Elizabeth. When Elizabeth heard Mary's greeting, the baby moved within her. Elizabeth was filled with the Holy Spirit and said in a loud voice, "You are the most blessed of all women, and blessed is the child you will bear! Why should this great thing happen to me, that my Lord's mother comes to visit me? For as soon as I heard your greeting, the baby within me jumped with gladness. How happy you are to believe that the Lord's message to you will come true...."

Mary stayed about three months with Elizabeth and then went back home.

Luke 1: 39-56

"...the baby moved within her."

Within the womb

As an unexpected Christmas present, my wife Joan became pregnant. While she knew the baby was there, it took time for his presence to become real to me. Joan could recognize the changes in her body – including a sudden aversion to her usual morning coffee – long before I could detect anything different.

Then her belly began to swell. And then, one day, I saw movement. A tiny foot, or hand, or something, pressed outward from within her womb. I saw her skin bulge. I felt the new life push against my hand. I was awestruck.

Our son lived twenty-one years. The day we committed his ashes to the sea, Joan said a few broken sentences. They began, "When I first felt you move in my womb...."

Holy One, may I always be open to the signs of new life leaping into being – in me and in others.

Once a man asked Jesus. "Teacher, what good thing must I do to receive eternal life?"

"Why do you ask me concerning what is good?" answered Jesus. "There is only One who is good. Keep the commandments if you want to enter life…." "I have obeyed all the commandments," the young man replied. "What else do I need to do?"

Jesus said to him, "If you want to be perfect, go and sell all you have and give the money to the poor, and you will have riches in heaven; then come and follow me."

When the young man heard this, he went away sad, because he was very rich.

Matthew 19: 16-22

"…because he was very rich."

Follow me

I like to think that today's passage has nothing to do with me. In fact, I can be quite smug about it. Why? Because I'm not rich like the young man. And I'm definitely not *very* rich.

Then I ask myself what, if not money, keeps me from following Jesus? Immediately I think of my home: could I leave the comfort, the beauty, the sense of rootedness that my home gives me? And I think of my physical health: could I accept a loss of independence, of physical activity, of sensual pleasure?

Jesus asks me, every day, to let go of anything that keeps me from truly loving others. What is my response, this very day?

**Lord, help me to say 'yes' freely to your call to follow you
– each and every day of my life.**

Y ou are not a God who is pleased with wrongdoing;
you allow no evil in your presence.
You cannot stand the sight of the proud;
you hate all wicked people.
You destroy all liars
and despise violent, deceitful people.
But because of your great love
I can come into your house;
I can worship in your holy Temple
and bow down to you in reverence.

Psalm 5: 4-7

"You are not a God
who is pleased with wrongdoing…"

The judge

A friend of mine is a judge. Every day he
hears stories of deceit, betrayal, violence and heartbreak. His job is to
listen carefully, sift through the words and feelings and motivations,
and bring justice to the situation. It is an incredibly delicate and
difficult process. He often feels that the law is not enough to bring
about true healing and transformation, but it is the tool he has been
given to work with.

God is a judge, too, but a judge with a difference. Mixed in with
the doling out of justice are generous helpings of love and mercy,
which temper the judgment and which allow me to make peace with
God, others and myself, and to change my ways.

Lord, thank you for guiding me with a loving hand.

The Lord is my shepherd;
I have everything I need.
He lets me rest in fields of green grass
and leads me to quiet pools of fresh water.
He gives me new strength.
He guides me in the right paths,
as he has promised.
Even if I go through the deepest darkness,
I will not be afraid, Lord,
for you are with me.
Your shepherd's rod and staff protect me....
I know that your goodness and love
will be with me all my life;
and your house will be my home as long as I live.   *Psalm 23: 1-6*

"I have everything I need."

All that I need

We lost the first home we ever bought. Because of the costs of renovating and the poor state of the building, our 'dream home' had to be abandoned. We ended up living in a mobile home on the property – completely disillusioned and demoralized.

My wife and I both agree that in many ways, it was the best thing that ever happened to us because it caused us to re-evaluate our goals and our values.

We are now living in a rented farmhouse, and as we walk through the beautiful fields, it doesn't matter whether we own them or not. The whole world was created for everyone. We have everything we need – in our family, in nature and in God.

Lord, help me to remember that you provide me
with all that I need.

"The kingdom of heaven is like this. Once there was a king who prepared a wedding feast for his son. He sent his servants to tell the invited guests to come to the feast, but they did not want to come. So he sent other servants … but the invited guests paid no attention and went about their business. The king was very angry; he called his servants and said, 'My wedding feast is ready, but the people I invited did not deserve it. Now go to the main streets and invite to the feast as many people as you find.' So the servants went out into the streets and gathered all the people they could find, good and bad alike; and the wedding hall was filled with people."

Matthew 22: 1-14

"Invite to the feast
as many people as you find."

Celebrate life

My friend Helen celebrated her birthday in style. We cooked her favourite food, decorated the house, invited her closest friends, put out lots of flowers and balloons and, of course, a cake with candles. After dinner there was singing, gifts and prayer. It was our way of giving thanks for Helen's life.

Celebration, giving thanks, is at the heart of the Christian life. It is, as Jesus says, a taste of the kingdom of heaven.

Busyness can make me blind and deaf to the invitation to the feast. Am I too busy to give thanks for a friend by phoning her on her birthday? To spend quality time with my family at mealtimes? To hear the gentle invitation of God's love in prayer?

God, how are you inviting me to the wedding feast today?

W hen the Pharisees heard that Jesus had silenced the Sadducees, they came together, and one of them, a teacher of the Law, tried to trap him with a question. "Teacher," he asked, "which is the greatest commandment in the Law?"

Jesus answered, "'Love the Lord your God with all your heart, with all your soul and with all your mind.' This is the greatest and the most important commandment. The second most important commandment is like it: 'Love your neighbour as you love yourself.' The whole Law of Moses and the teachings of the prophets depend on these two commandments."

Matthew 22: 34-40

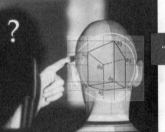

"...which is the greatest commandment?"

Love first

Sometimes the big questions of life seem too complicated to answer. How should I live in order to be environmentally responsible? What can I do to reduce poverty and its twin, violence? What does it mean to be a citizen of the world?

When completely opposing perspectives battle it out in my brain, my head starts to spin. It all seems too overwhelming, and I seem too small. If I'm not careful, a kind of paralysis sets in and I barely know how to get out of bed.

But these words of Jesus cut through my confusion like a hot knife through butter: look right in front of you, and within you, and love what you see.

Lord, help me learn to live your commandment to love.

J esus said: "The teachers of the Law and the Pharisees are the authorized interpreters of Moses' Law. So you must obey and follow everything they tell you to do; do not, however, imitate their actions, because they don't practise what they preach. They tie onto people's backs loads that are heavy and hard to carry, yet they aren't willing even to lift a finger to help them carry those loads. They do everything so that people will see them…. They love to be greeted with respect in the marketplaces and to have people call them 'Teacher.' You must not be called 'Teacher,' because you are all equal and have only one Teacher…. The greatest one among you must be your servant. Whoever makes himself great will be humbled, and whoever humbles himself will be made great."

Matthew 23: 1-12

"…they don't practise what they preach."

Practise what you preach

"Do what I say, not what I do!" my dad would say with a small smile when we caught him in a contradiction between what he taught and his own behaviour.

When I was a trusting boy, I thought he was being funny. When I was a righteous teenager, I thought he was being hypocritical. Now that I'm a father, I realize that he was just being human. Like him, I often don't uphold the high ideals I try to present to my children. I don't live up to the expectations I set for myself.

I understand the importance of the smile that accompanied my father's words. It said that he recognized his failing, and forgave himself for it. It also told me that when my time came for failure, he would forgive me, too.

Lord, my father gave me the gift of forgiveness.
Help me offer it to my own children.

S omeone asked, "Sir, will just a few people be saved?" Jesus answered, "Do your best to go in through the narrow door; because many people will surely try to go in but will not be able. The master of the house will get up and close the door; then when you stand outside and begin to knock on the door and say, 'Open the door for us, sir!' he will answer you, 'I don't know where you come from!' Then you will answer, 'We ate and drank with you; you taught in our town!' But he will say again, 'I don't know where you come from. Get away from me, all you wicked people!' … Then those who are now last will be first, and those who are now first will be last."

Luke 13: 22-30

> "Those who are now last will be first…"

Last in line?

My daughter often lives in a world of her own making, completely unaware of the attitudes or expectations of those around her. While I find her behaviour extremely exasperating, at times I have also learned from her.

My daughter's music teacher periodically brings the children together for a special lesson. This often involves playing a game. One day the teacher asked the children to line up. I hoped my daughter would be close to the front – I want her to get the most out of these "learning opportunities." My heart sank as she happily drifted to the end of the line.

To my surprise she easily followed her teacher's instructions, and played the game completely unaware of the anxious jostling for first place going on at the front. We each learned something that day.

Loving God, I know you are near, whether I am first or last.

"How terrible for you, teachers of the Law and Pharisees! You hypocrites! You lock the door to the kingdom of heaven in people's faces, but you yourselves don't go in, nor do you allow in those who are trying to enter!

"How terrible for you, blind guides! You teach, 'If someone swears by the Temple, he isn't bound by his vow; but if he swears by the gold in the Temple, he is bound.' Blind fools! Which is more important, the gold or the Temple which makes the gold holy? You also teach, 'If someone swears by the altar, he isn't bound by his vow; but if he swears by the gift on the altar, he is bound.' How blind you are! Which is the more important, the gift or the altar which makes the gift holy?"

Matthew 23: 13-22

> "How terrible for you, blind guides!"

Blind parenting

Despairing at how badly my daughter's violin practices were going, I recorded a practice session and gave the cassette to the teacher. I was hoping she would affirm how obstinate my daughter was being, and give her a talking to.

Instead, she pointed out that I had interrupted my daughter continuously and, at one point, I had asked her to correct six different errors at once! I was just like the Pharisees who held the keys to the kingdom but had locked everyone out.

The last thing my child was learning was a love of music and the joy of playing. If anything, she was more likely to hate the violin, and anything to do with it, for the rest of her life.

Lord, help me remember the goal, and not get lost in details.

Philip found Nathanael and told him, "We have found the one whom Moses wrote about in the book of the Law and whom the prophets also wrote about. He is Jesus son of Joseph, from Nazareth."

"Can anything good come from Nazareth?" Nathanael asked. "Come and see," answered Philip.

When Jesus saw Nathanael coming to him, he said about him, "Here is a real Israelite; there is nothing false in him!" Nathanael asked him, "How do you know me?" Jesus answered, "I saw you when you were under the fig tree before Philip called you."

"Teacher," answered Nathanael, "you are the Son of God! You are the King of Israel!"
John 1: 45-51

> "Can anything good come from Nazareth?"

False judgments

As we edge closer to the beginning of another school year, I try not to second-guess our decision to send our children to the local neighbourhood school. It's a small school, without lots of bells and whistles. There are plenty of 'better schools' available – with higher testing scores and state of the art resources.

I sometimes wonder if anything good might come from a place that is often overlooked. Nathaniel's words in today's reading challenge me.

For centuries, it seems that we have been judging others based on where they come from. And, for centuries, we have been wrong.

Lord, teach me to leave my own prejudices at home.

Happy are those who obey the Lord,
who live by his commands.
Your work will provide for your needs;
you will be happy and prosperous.
Your wife will be like a fruitful vine in your home,
and your children will be like young olive trees around your table.
A man who obeys the Lord
will surely be blessed like this.
May the Lord bless you from Zion!
May you see Jerusalem prosper
all the days of your life!

Psalm 128: 1-5

"...you will be happy and prosperous."

Remembering blessings

I'm always amazed that, when I'm not feeling well, I stop doing the very things that help me feel better. During these times I'm unable to see any good in my life; it's almost as if I want to be miserable. I avoid talking to my friends, skip my exercise regime, stay away from my creative work, and resist any form of prayer. Instead, I seek out comfort food and watch mindless television shows.

This doesn't happen often or last too long – just enough for me to appreciate the difficulties imposed by depression. Though I *know* what to do to help myself, at times I simply can't do it.

If I can't move forward, I can still look backward, and recall the blessings that I've already received.

God, help me to see the good in my life when I'm feeling low.

n all our trouble and suffering we have been encouraged about you, friends. It was your faith that encouraged us, because now we really live if you stand firm in your life in union with the Lord. Now we can give thanks to our God for you…. Day and night we ask him with all our heart to let us see you personally and supply what is needed in your faith.

May our God and Father and our Lord Jesus prepare the way for us to come to you! May the Lord make your love for one another and for all people grow more and more and become as great as our love for you. In this way he will strengthen you, and you will be perfect and holy in the presence of our God and Father when our Lord Jesus comes with all who belong to him.

I Thessalonians 3: 7-13

> "It was your faith that encouraged us…"

Love in practice

Until she became too frail to travel, Dorothy Day, co-founder of the Catholic Worker movement, liked to spend a lot of time on the road, visiting small communities that were living the gospel message of love. "Love in practice," Dorothy often quoted from Dostoyevsky, "is a harsh and dreadful thing compared to love in dreams."

As a prelude to her visits, Dorothy would correspond with people in those communities. When she couldn't visit she would ask people to write about their work for her Catholic Worker newspaper. She wanted to encourage people who were taking personal responsibility for peace and justice, and she wanted to inspire others to do the same. Like Paul in today's reading, she was building communities of love in practice.

**Lord, give me the strength to live your love
and the courage to speak about it.**

" **T**he kingdom of heaven will be like this. Once there were ten young women who took their oil lamps and went out to meet the bridegroom. The foolish ones took their lamps but did not take any extra oil with them, while the wise ones took containers full of oil for their lamps. The bridegroom was late in coming, so they began to nod and fall asleep. It was already midnight when the cry rang out, 'Here is the bridegroom! Come and meet him!' The ten young women woke up and trimmed their lamps. Then the foolish ones said to the wise ones, 'Let us have some of your oil, because our lamps are going out....'" Jesus concluded, "Watch out, then, because you do not know the day or the hour."

Matthew 25: 1-13

"...you do not know the day or the hour."

Live in the moment

What can I say? Personally, I've always felt sorry for the foolish women. I'm always forgetting things myself. I need a book for an assignment and forget it at school. I do the assignment and forget it at home. It's not fair to punish someone for forgetting. I can hear my dad, "No, it's not fair. It's life. Fairness is your idea."

And so I try to remember. Because you never know when they'll ask for my work. And you know what else I try to remember? To live each day the best I can: to look at each flower, to smile at each person. Because you never know the moment when you'll be called, like when my dad was called.

No, it's not fair. It's life.

Just for today,
let me live the best I can and revel in your gift of life.

Now remember what you were, my friends, when God called you. From the human point of view few of you were wise or powerful or of high social standing. God purposely chose what the world considers nonsense in order to shame the wise, and he chose what the world considers weak in order to shame the powerful. He chose what the world looks down on and despises and thinks is nothing, in order to destroy what the world thinks is important. This means that no one can boast in God's presence. But God has brought you into union with Christ Jesus, and God has made Christ to be our wisdom. By him, we are put right with God; we become God's holy people and are set free.

1 Corinthians 1:26-31

"...what the world considers weak..."

Strength in weakness

Back in the 1960s, Pauline Vanier thought her son Jean had gone crazy. He chose to leave a promising career in the navy and move in with two mentally challenged men – the start of the international movement called l'Arche. Over time, she came to share her son's conviction that the lowly and despised in the world have much to teach us about God.

After her husband, Governor General Georges Vanier, died, Pauline moved into a small house in the French village where l'Arche originated. Leaving behind years of wining and dining with kings, queens and presidents, Pauline found peace and joy in living with the foolish and weak. Affectionately called 'Mammi,' she was everyone's Great Lady until her death.

**Jesus, give me the courage to meet your greatness
in foolishness and weakness, in myself as well as others.**

One Sabbath Jesus went to eat a meal at the home of one of the leading Pharisees; and people were watching Jesus closely…. Jesus said to his host, "When you give a lunch or a dinner, do not invite your friends or your brothers or your relatives or your rich neighbours – for they will invite you back, and in this way you will be paid for what you did. When you give a feast, invite the poor, the crippled, the lame, and the blind; and you will be blessed, because they are not able to pay you back. God will repay you on the day the good people rise from death."

Luke 14: 7-14

> "…invite the poor, the crippled,
> the lame, and the blind…"

Open to others

When I was a kid, there was one classmate who we'd sometimes avoid or run away from. An immigrant kid: not too cool. Not cool, but a better friend than I was. He was the first one to befriend me when I moved into the neighbourhood. As the song says, "torn by what we've done and can't undo."*

In a way, I'm still running. To my nice suburban home and my happy family and a beer on a Friday night. When my city's streets are full of "the poor, the crippled, the lame and the blind." I can't help them all. Some don't seem to want help. I don't know what to do. Don't know, or don't care?

* Leonard Cohen and Jennifer Warnes, *Song of Bernadette*

Lord, help me to become good.

H ow I love your law!
I think about it all day long.
Your commandment is with me all the time
and makes me wiser than my enemies.
I understand more than all my teachers,
because I meditate on your instructions.
I have greater wisdom than those who are old,
because I obey your commands.
I have avoided all evil conduct,
because I want to obey your word.
I have not neglected your instructions,
because you yourself are my teacher.

Psalm 119: 97-102

"How I love your law! I think about it all day long."

The law of love

Today's reading talks of learning to understand and to obey God's law.
But how do I live according to God's law within our society's rule of
law?

We know that any nation that ignores the rule of law can never
offer justice and freedom to its citizens. If government leaders – the
rich and the powerful – believe they are above the law, their democracy will fail. If religious leaders teach the law, but don't practise it
themselves, their authority is undermined.

Sometimes the laws themselves may be bad – such as the segregation laws that prevented blacks from attending schools, eating in
restaurants and occupying seats on buses. That's when God's law of
love means breaking society's rule of law.

Lord, help me to keep your law in my heart.
Let it shape my words and actions.

J esus went to Capernaum, a town in Galilee, where he taught the people on the Sabbath. They were all amazed at the way he taught, because he spoke with authority. In the synagogue was a man who had the spirit of an evil demon in him; he screamed out in a loud voice, "Ah! What do you want with us, Jesus of Nazareth? Are you here to destroy us? I know who you are: you are God's holy messenger!"

Jesus ordered the spirit, "Be quiet and come out of the man!" The demon threw the man down in front of them and went out of him without doing him any harm.

The people were all amazed and said to one another, "What kind of words are these? With authority and power this man gives orders to the evil spirits, and they come out!"

Luke 4: 31-37

"With authority and power…"

More than the message

The Galileans were amazed at Jesus – not just at his message – but because his message had authority. Then, after the evil demon incident, they were amazed – not just at the message, not just at his authority – but also at his power.

I'm a freelancer, and thanks to e-mail, I have several clients with whom I've worked for years but never met. This reading makes me ask myself whether I'm allowing this era of electronic communications – where message is all – to influence my relationship with Jesus.

Jesus' message is fine, by me. But a message with authority? And power? Do I really believe in the power of his love – could it be even more powerful than modern communications technologies?

Lord, let me not be seduced by any other power but yours.

Simon's mother-in-law was sick with a high fever, and they spoke to Jesus about her. He went and stood at her bedside and ordered the fever to leave her. The fever left her, and she got up at once and began to wait on them.

After sunset all who had friends who were sick with various diseases brought them to Jesus; he placed his hands on every one of them and healed them all. Demons also went out from many people, screaming, "You are the Son of God!" Jesus gave the demons an order and would not let them speak, because they knew he was the Messiah.

The people... tried to keep [Jesus] from leaving. But he said to them, "I must preach the Good News about the kingdom of God in other towns also."

Luke 4: 38-44

> "...and ordered the fever to leave her."

Faith in God

The telephone rang while I was watching the ten o'clock news. "Could you mind the kids for a while?" my neighbour asked. "I need to take my wife to the hospital." Karen had a devastating headache. She was scared. Her sister had almost died of a cerebral haemorrhage. They got back at 3:00 a.m. And Karen still had the headache.

Jesus rebuked a fever, and it went away. It's easy to assume that a fever, like Simon's mother-in-law's – or a headache, like Karen's – is brought on by the person's own state of mind, and therefore easily banished by the power of suggestion.

But I saw Karen's pain with my own eyes. If it vanished at a word, I know I would believe.

Lord, I put my faith in medicine, in science, in business – in anything but you. Forgive my unbelief.

Y ou should not fool yourself. If any of you think that you are wise by this world's standards, you should become a fool, in order to be really wise. For what this world considers to be wisdom is nonsense in God's sight. As the scripture says, "God traps the wise in their cleverness"; and another scripture says, "The Lord knows that the thoughts of the wise are worthless." No one, then, should boast about what human beings can do. Actually everything belongs to you: Paul, Apollos and Peter; this world, life and death, the present and the future – all these are yours, and you belong to Christ, and Christ belongs to God.

I Corinthians 3: 18-23

> "God traps the wise in their cleverness."

True wisdom

Jim wore his learning on his sleeve. He loved to go on about all the books he had read and would draw people into complicated philosophical debates which he would always "win" – usually by intimidating the other person.

At first, we were all very impressed by Jim's intelligence, and we all deferred to him. Over time, however, his attitude began to wear thin and some people began to question his sincerity.

It got to the point where Jim was regularly mocked behind his back. I felt very sorry for Jim, because I knew he just wanted what everyone wants – to be loved and accepted. He confused impressing people with being liked. He confused being smart with being a good friend.

Lord, teach me humility about my intelligence.
Let me always put the heart before the head.

S ome people said, "The disciples of John fast frequently… but your disciples eat and drink." Jesus answered, "Do you think you can make the guests at a wedding party go without food as long as the bridegroom is with them? Of course not! But the day will come when the bridegroom will be taken away from them, and then they will fast.…

"You don't tear a piece off a new coat to patch up an old coat. If you do, you will have torn the new coat, and the piece of new cloth will not match the old. Nor do you pour new wine into used wine-skins, because the new wine will burst the skins, the wine will pour out, and the skins will be ruined. Instead, new wine must be poured into fresh wineskins!"

Luke 5: 33-39

"…new wine must be poured into fresh wineskins!"

Open to new life

A craggy little woman of close to 85 years, Nano is a proud World War II veteran, retired social worker, grandmother and social activist. A role model in our women's group, she teaches me to express myself creatively and to challenge the status quo. Spiritually close to nature, she lives with her husband in a small house in the country. She is a free spirit.

However, there have been dark moments to challenge Nano's life-long faith. Some time ago, her younger daughter took her own life. Since then, Nano has continued to live life with passion, working on a screenplay about her wartime experiences.

Despite crushing loss, she greets each day with an eagerness I admire, opening herself to the new wine each day has to offer.

God, help me to live with joy and with gratitude today.

Jesus was walking through some wheat fields on a Sabbath. His disciples began to pick the heads of wheat, rub them in their hands, and eat the grain. Some Pharisees asked, "Why are you doing what our Law says you cannot do on the Sabbath?"

Jesus answered them, "Haven't you read what David did when he and his men were hungry? He went into the house of God, took the bread offered to God, ate it, and gave it also to his men. Yet it is against our Law for anyone except the priests to eat that bread." And Jesus concluded, "The Son of Man is Lord of the Sabbath."

Luke 6: 1-5

> "Why are you doing what our Law says you cannot do...?"

Rules and regulations

I once taught in a girls' school where the students had to wear a uniform. Regulations decreed that the top button on the blouse had to be fastened at all times. But the blouses came in only one collar-size meant for thin necks. The students with larger necks found the blouses very uncomfortable.

"You can leave the top button undone as long as you're in my class," I told the girls. "But the moment you step outside the room... button up!"

Instead, I should have gone to the school authorities and said, "These uniforms are supposed to be made for the students – not the students made to fit the uniform!" At times, I lose sight of the purpose of rules and regulations.

Lord, teach me to stand up for what is loving and right, even if it means going against the rules.

Before you created the hills
or brought the world into being,
you were eternally God,
and will be God forever.
You tell us to return to what we were;
you change us back to dust....
Seventy years is all we have –
eighty years, if we are strong;
yet all they bring us is trouble and sorrow;
life is soon over, and we are gone....
Fill us each morning with your constant love,
so that we may sing and be glad all our life....
Let us, your servants, see your mighty deeds;
let our descendants see your glorious might.

Psalm 90: 2-16

> "Fill us each morning with your constant love..."

Time to appreciate

For years I've considered including a time for reflection in my morning routine. Usually I hop out of bed and immediately spring into action. After all, there are breakfasts to be made, and children to be clothed and coaxed off to school....

When morning comes, rarely do I stop to recognize the gift of each new day. No wonder life seems to whiz by! Today's psalm reminds me that, if I don't take time to reflect, life can quickly pass me by.

I *am* going to stop for a moment of quiet reflection each morning. The signs of God's love are present all around me. I hope to learn to savour them – before I gulp down my juice and head out the door.

God, I awake each morning to signs of your love.
May I remember to give you thanks.

J esus went into a synagogue and taught. A man was there whose right hand was paralyzed. Some teachers of the Law and some Pharisees wanted a reason to accuse Jesus of doing wrong, so they watched him closely to see if he would heal on the Sabbath. But Jesus knew their thoughts and said to the man, "Stand up and come here to the front." The man got up and stood there. Then Jesus said to them, "I ask you: What does our Law allow us to do on the Sabbath? To help or to harm? To save someone's life or destroy it?" Then he said to the man, "Stretch out your hand." He did so, and his hand became well again.

Luke 6: 6-11

"What does our Law allow us to do...?"

Sabbath shopping

In our province, Sunday shopping is no longer an issue. Everything's open. I don't shop on Sunday if I can avoid it – it's one way of trying to keep the Sabbath holy – but sometimes....

One Sunday we got a call before church that some friends were arriving that afternoon. My wife looked in the refrigerator and announced that we had to stop at the supermarket on the way home. We met eight other church members doing the same thing!

According to the Mosaic laws practised in Jesus' time, we were all doing wrong. But Jesus took a more pragmatic approach. Do what's necessary, he said. As long as it helps, not harms.

Give me the wisdom to know when to make exceptions, and when not to.

J esus went up a hill to pray and spent the whole night there praying to God. When day came, he called his disciples to him and chose twelve of them, whom he named apostles....

When Jesus had come down from the hill with the apostles, he stood on a level place with a large number of his disciples. A large crowd of people was there from all over Judea and from Jerusalem and from the coast cities of Tyre and Sidon; they had come to hear him and to be healed of their diseases. Those who were troubled by evil spirits also came and were healed. All the people tried to touch him, for power was going out from him and healing them all.

Luke 6: 12-19

"Jesus went up a hill to pray..."

A firm foundation

I have been in situations similar to the one in which Jesus finds himself here. Big things are going to happen and a new phase of life is about to begin.

But when I've been faced with taking a major step in life, I usually weigh the likely outcomes of various scenarios, trying to keep my anxiety under control, and wondering what I should do. It's all quite exhausting, and not very helpful or productive.

Instead, I need to follow Jesus' example. As he prepared for a new direction, he found a quiet place to talk with God. This prayerful connection became the foundation of his future.

And that's the solid foundation I need to stand on, too.

**Lord, help me share my fears and doubts with you
so that I may walk with a surer step.**

This is the list of the ancestors of Jesus Christ…. From Abraham to King David: Abraham, Isaac, Jacob, Judah and his brothers; then Perez and Zerah (their mother was Tamar), Hezron, Ram, Amminadab, Nahshon, Salmon, Boaz (his mother was Rahab), Obed (his mother was Ruth), Jesse, and King David.

From David to the time when the people of Israel were taken into exile in Babylon: David, Solomon (his mother was the woman who had been Uriah's wife), Rehoboam, Abijah, Asa, Jehoshaphat, Jehoram, Uzziah, Jotham, Ahaz, Hezekiah, Manasseh, Amon, Josiah, and Jehoiachin and his brothers.

From the time after the exile in Babylon to the birth of Jesus: Jehoiachin, Shealtiel, Zerubbabel, Abiud, Eliakim, Azor, Zadok, Achim, Eliud, Eleazar, Matthan, Jacob, and Joseph, who married Mary, the mother of Jesus, who was called the Messiah.   *Matthew 1: 1-23*

> "…the list of the ancestors of Jesus Christ…"

Rootedness

How deep our roots go! Reaching down, down into the past. There is, it seems, a comfort in having roots. Deep within, unknown to us, lies our strength.

I am not a craftsman. I'm the kind of guy who *pays* someone to fix the door. But my son is becoming a carpenter. What? But wait. One of my grandfathers was a carpenter, the other a sawyer in a sawmill, and a great-grandfather built schooners. It's there. It's in my son.

And what did these ancestors, with the weird names, bequeath to Joseph? What strength did they give this humble man? What wisdom – to raise and understand this strange and wondrous son?

Whatever it was, Joseph had faith and when he needed it, it was there.

Lord, let me accept my inheritance. Let me fulfill it.

"Love your enemies, do good to those who hate you, bless those who curse you, and pray for those who mistreat you. If anyone hits you on one cheek, let him hit the other one too; if someone takes your coat, let him have your shirt as well. Give to everyone who asks you for something, and when someone takes what is yours, do not ask for it back. Do for others just what you want them to do for you.... You will then have a great reward, and you will be children of the Most High God....

"Give to others, and God will give to you. Indeed, you will receive a full measure, a generous helping, poured into your hands – all that you can hold. The measure you use for others is the one that God will use for you."

Luke 6: 27-38

> "...you will be children of the Most High God."

Child of God

It's not easy to see God in the soup kitchens. When gnarled, sore hands stretch out to mine in the cold, grey morning, it's hard to see the hand of God in theirs. Only rot and disease, anger and ingratitude.

One morning, I tiptoed past one of our regulars, fast asleep on the pavement. I peered closer and, for the first time, really *looked* at him. His usually taut, angry face was smoothed out gently with the peace that only sleep can provide. "The face," I thought, "of an angel."

That 'angel' taught me how seldom I see the true beauty in a person. I hope he will inspire me to be a real child of God: to give not only my coat, but my shirt as well.

Lord, when I cannot see your face in the people I meet today, help me to trust that you really are there.

J esus told them this parable: "One blind man cannot lead another one; if he does, both will fall into a ditch. No pupils are greater than their teacher; but all pupils, when they have completed their training, will be like their teacher.

"Why do you look at the speck in your brother's eye, but pay no attention to the log in your own eye? How can you say to your brother, 'Please, brother, let me take that speck out of your eye,' yet cannot even see the log in your own eye? You hypocrite! First take the log out of your own eye, and then you will be able to see clearly to take the speck out of your brother's eye."

Luke 6: 39-42

> "One blind man cannot lead another one."

Distorted views

The side-view mirror on my car displays a warning, "Objects are closer than they appear." Sometimes passing judgment on other people is a little bit like using a side-view mirror.

An example to illustrate my point: There's a woman I often feel like criticizing. One day my sister told me I was just like her. I was flabbergasted! Yet when I took a good, hard look, I saw there was a lot of truth in what my sister said. I hadn't realized my criticism was based on a distortion, that my judgments reflected things much 'closer than they appear.' The very faults I criticize the loudest in others are also alive in me.

This knowledge now makes me pause before I criticize another's behaviour.

Lord, deliver me from the distortions
that lead me to criticize others.

" **A** healthy tree does not bear bad fruit, nor does a poor tree bear good fruit. Every tree is known by the fruit it bears; you do not pick figs from thorn bushes or gather grapes from bramble bushes. A good person brings good out of the treasure of good things in his heart; a bad person brings bad out of his treasure of bad things. For the mouth speaks what the heart is full of."

Luke 6: 43-49

"Every tree is known by the fruit it bears…"

Fruits of the heart

Anyone listening to Jesus would not go looking for figs and grapes among thorns and brambles. They understood Jesus was talking about thorn and bramble bushes that were disguised *to look like* fig trees and grapevines.

Maybe Jesus was talking about the Pharisees – church leaders and hardworking exponents of law and dogma – who had lost the flexibility necessary for compassion, the soul of the law. Or leaders of governments who regularly invoke God's name, but whose fruits show a preference for the rich, and a denial of the poor.

The fruit of human hearts is not so easy to judge as a grape or fig. But compassion, peace and justice do have identifiable shapes that hearts, even more readily than minds, can recognize.

**Lord, help me to bring forth good fruit
from my own imperfect heart.**

"There was once a man who had two sons. The younger one said, 'Father, give me my share of the property....' After a few days the younger son sold his part of the property and left home. He went to a country far away, where he wasted his money in reckless living. Then a severe famine spread over that country, and he was left without a thing. So he went to work for one of the citizens of that country, who sent him out to take care of the pigs.... As last he said, 'I will get up and go to my father and say, "Father, I have sinned against God and against you. I am no longer fit to be called your son; treat me as one of your hired workers."' So he got up and started back."

Luke 15: 1-32

> "So he got up and started back…"

Free to return home

I was going home! The thought filled me with excitement but also with apprehension. Would I still feel the same as when I left home? Would I want, once again, to flee the too familiar?

The morning after my arrival, I went for a walk. The sleeping town, the fields and the mountain seemed to speak to me: telling me who I'd been, showing me who I'd become. I thrilled to see the old, familiar sights. But more, I thrilled to realize they no longer constrained me. The mountain didn't loom quite as large. The fields on the outskirts of town no longer fenced me in.

How fortunate I am to have a place to which I can return… and know that I was, and continue to be, loved.

**Lord, help me return to my past,
to reclaim it and find healing there.**

A Roman officer had a servant who was very dear to him; the man was sick and about to die. When the officer heard about Jesus, he sent some Jewish elders to ask him to come and heal his servant....

[Jesus] was not far from the house when the officer sent friends to tell him, "Sir, don't trouble yourself. I do not deserve to have you come into my house.... Just give the order, and my servant will get well. I, too... have soldiers under me. I order this one, 'Go!' and he goes; I order that one, 'Come!' and he comes...."

Jesus was surprised and said, "I tell you, I have never found faith like this, not even in Israel!" The messengers went back to the officer's house and found his servant well.

Luke 7: 1-10

"I order this one, 'Go!' and he goes..."

True humility

This Roman officer is someone I have met many times – sometimes simply by looking in the mirror.

Our modern world is full of people who say, "Go!" and someone goes, and "Come!" and someone comes. We all seem to have someone above us who tells us what to do, and people below us whom we tell what to do. That's the natural way the world is, we believe. That's reality. Freedom, of course, is having as few people as possible telling us what to do and as many people as possible doing what we tell them.

Now here's the difference. The Roman officer knows his real place in the world and is humble. We are puffed up with the illusion of our importance and are vain.

Lord, the Roman soldier could see clearly who he was.
Give me the wisdom to see myself truly, as I am.

The Israelites left Mount Hor.... On the way the people lost their patience and spoke against God and Moses. They complained, "Why did you bring us out of Egypt to die in this desert, where there is no food or water...?" Then the Lord sent poisonous snakes among the people, and many Israelites were bitten and died. The people came to Moses and said, "We sinned when we spoke against the Lord and against you. Now pray to the Lord to take these snakes away...." Then the Lord told Moses to make a metal snake and put it on a pole, so that anyone who was bitten could look at it and be healed. So Moses made a bronze snake and put it on a pole. Anyone who had been bitten would look at the bronze snake and be healed.

Numbers 21: 4-9

"The people lost their patience and spoke against God..."

Healed and made new

Several years ago I was hired by a small television production house: my dream job, or so I thought.

Because the company was small, all the staff was required to perform technical duties. I had a terrible time; handling buttons and cables does not come naturally to me. I complained bitterly: "What happened to my dream job? Editing suites, program lengths, countdowns, transmission: that wasn't part of the deal!" Surprisingly, I stayed with that job for more than three years.

I've since changed jobs. Now, after more than a year in my new job, I can see how the time spent in that tiny production house helped me overcome many of my old hang-ups, and helped make me into someone very new.

Lord, help me to believe that you are with me in difficult times, shaping me and renewing me.

I n his life on earth Jesus made his prayers and requests with loud cries and tears to God, who could save him from death. Because he was humble and devoted, God heard him. But even though he was God's Son, he learned through his sufferings to be obedient. When he was made perfect, he became the source of eternal salvation for all those who obey him.

Hebrews 5: 7-9

"...he learned through his sufferings..."

Learning the hard way

These days, a close friend of mine is struggling (suffering, even) as she's examining her past, and making decisions about her future. Was Jesus' suffering the result of a similar process – of examining who he was, and learning where his path was leading?

Growing up, we receive messages of how to act and what to think. Messages that come to define us. There was a lot of stress in my friend's childhood – due to illness and a tragic death in her family. As a result, she misinterpreted some of these 'messages' and ended up with a distorted sense of herself.

Examining – and changing – familiar ways of thinking and acting isn't easy. But I see a deep, inner peace in my friend, and a new energy that is nourishing her self and others.

Dear God, give me the courage to listen to that inner voice that reveals who I am and what I am to do.

In that town was a woman who lived a sinful life. She heard that Jesus was eating in the Pharisee's house, so she brought an alabaster jar full of perfume and stood behind Jesus, by his feet, crying and wetting his feet with her tears. Then she dried his feet with her hair, kissed them, and poured the perfume on them. When the Pharisee saw this, he said, "If this man really were a prophet, he would know what kind of sinful life this woman lives!"

Jesus said, "I came into your home, and you gave me no water for my feet, but she has washed my feet with her tears and dried them with her hair.... I tell you, then, the great love she has shown proves that her many sins have been forgiven."

Luke 7: 36-50

> "...a woman who lived a sinful life."

Sin and forgiveness

I am envious of this woman. She can admit she is a sinner and can also grieve over it. Like most modern people, the word 'sin' is not one I feel comfortable using. Words like 'broken' and 'wounded' work better. There's something about them that makes me seem, well, less responsible for my 'sins.' After all, broken or wounded things have usually had things done to them, rather than by them.

Today's reading reminds me of a terrible sin I committed many years ago. A friend needed help and I did not give it. Now that friend has died and I can never give it. Will there be forgiveness for me?

Lord, I am sorry for the good I do not do. Please forgive me.

S ome time later Jesus travelled through towns and villages, preaching the Good News about the kingdom of God. The twelve disciples went with him, and so did some women who had been healed of evil spirits and diseases: Mary (who was called Magdalene), from whom seven demons had been driven out; Joanna, whose husband Chuza was an officer in Herod's court; and Susanna, and many other women who used their own resources to help Jesus and his disciples.

Luke 8: 1-3

"…women who used their own resources to help Jesus…"

Health and healing

In her mid-thirties, Nicole – doctor, mother, wife and friend – was diagnosed with an aggressive breast cancer. Everyone would have understood had she turned her energies inward – to care for her own health and for the needs of her young family.

Instead, Nicole chose, time after time, to place her many talents and resources at the service of the community. Convinced that pesticides were at the root of her cancer, she initiated a movement that resulted in a total ban of pesticides in our community. She travelled far and wide – to other towns and villages, even countries – sharing the results of her research.

Like the women in today's reading, Nicole's action helped bring health and healing to the many lives that she touched.

Loving God,
help me to choose to put my resources at your service.

"Once there was a man who went out to sow grain. As he scattered the seed in the field, some of it fell along the path, where it was stepped on, and the birds ate it up. Some of it fell on rocky ground, and when the plants sprouted, they dried up because the soil had no moisture. Some of the seed fell among thorn bushes, which grew up with the plants and choked them. And some seeds fell in good soil; the plants grew and bore grain, one hundred grains each...."

His disciples asked Jesus what this parable meant, and he answered, "The knowledge of the secrets of the kingdom of God has been given to you, but to the rest it comes by means of parables, so that they may look but not see, and listen but not understand."

Luke 8: 4-15

"Once there was a man who went out to sow grain."

Generous and free

Last spring, when I told Susanna that we would be planting a garden, her eyes filled with delight. She exclaimed, "You know, Daddy, planting a garden is my most favourite thing to do with you."

I smiled at her exuberance, knowing what 'gardening' means to Susanna. She stands in the garden – amid my carefully mapped-out rows – and then scatters seeds everywhere, throwing back her head, and laughing with joy at such sowing.

Now, as I read Jesus' parable, I hear Susanna's joy-filled laughter. What strikes me is not that some of the seeds do not grow, but that the sower, like Susanna, is willing to scatter them everywhere, regardless of how promising the ground looks.

Dear God, help me to scatter my faith
as extravagantly as the sower scattered his seeds.

" So I tell you: make friends for yourselves with worldly wealth, so that when it gives out, you will be welcomed in the eternal home. Whoever is faithful in small matters will be faithful in large ones; whoever is dishonest in small matters will be dishonest in large ones. If, then, you have not been faithful in handling worldly wealth, how can you be trusted with true wealth? And if you have not been faithful with what belongs to someone else, who will give you what belongs to you?

"No servant can be the slave of two masters; such a slave will hate one and love the other or will be loyal to one and despise the other. You cannot serve both God and money."

Luke 16: 1-13

> "...how can you be trusted with true wealth?"

True wealth

Eight months ago, after living in refugee camps for twelve years, my friends Godelìève and David-Louis arrived in Canada with their three small children. They live on welfare in a small basement apartment. They have no car. They have no family here – indeed many family members have been killed. I have family around me. I have work. I have a car.

One day I arrived to find them busy getting a huge meal organized. Some people they knew had just arrived in Canada as refugees and were waiting in a motel for accommodation. Children in tow, Godelìève and David-Louis were taking their feast – by bus – to the motel, to welcome the new arrivals to Canada.

They showed me what Jesus means by 'true wealth.'

Help me see where my genuine riches lie.
May I use them to help others.

"No one lights a lamp and covers it with a bowl or puts it under a bed. Instead, it is put on the lamp stand, so that people will see the light as they come in. Whatever is hidden away will be brought out into the open, and whatever is covered up will be found and brought to light. Be careful, then, how you listen; because those who have something will be given more, but whoever has nothing will have taken away from them even the little they think they have."

Luke 8: 16-18

> "...whatever is covered up
> will be found and brought to light."

Into the light

When my youngest son was little he was afraid of the dark. So, after bedtime stories and goodnights were said, I always left a bright light on in his room. Later when I came upstairs, I always found him sleeping peacefully, but with every light in every room turned on!

The expression on his sleeping face showed that the light had dispelled his fears and, looking at him, I sometimes felt a little envious. Like him I am afraid of things that are hidden away or covered up. But unlike him I am reluctant to turn on the light because it would reveal my weaknesses and failures for what they are.

If I can uncover and acknowledge my fears, perhaps I will find peace, as my son did.

**Lord, help me illuminate the dark corners of my life
with your loving light.**

As Jesus walked along, he saw a tax collector, named Matthew, sitting in his office. He said to him, "Follow me." Matthew got up and followed him.

While Jesus was having a meal in Matthew's house, many tax collectors and other outcasts came and joined Jesus and his disciples at the table. Some Pharisees saw this and asked his disciples, "Why does your teacher eat with such people?"

Jesus heard them and answered, "People who are well do not need a doctor, but only those who are sick. Go and find out what is meant by the scripture that says: 'It is kindness that I want, not animal sacrifices.' I have not come to call respectable people, but outcasts."

Matthew 9: 9-13

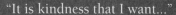

"It is kindness that I want..."

Is this seat taken?

One of my colleagues often sits alone at the staff table. Though she usually arrives at lunch first, few of us are drawn to sit with her. She can be abrasive, and conversation does not flow easily. I feel guilty when I see the empty seat beside her. Sometimes out of obligation, I sit with her. I try to make small talk but I'm sure the strain of duty shows.

I imagine Jesus sitting with the outcasts. I'm sure he didn't sit among them with a pained expression on his face. He brought kindness to the table. Kindness – perhaps this is what is missing in my efforts. A foundation of true kindness surely could warm any conversation.

Lord, may kindness guide my words and actions today.

J esus called the twelve disciples together and gave them power and authority to drive out all demons and to cure diseases. Then he sent them out to preach the kingdom of God and to heal the sick, after saying to them, "Take nothing with you for the trip: no walking stick, no beggar's bag, no food, no money, not even an extra shirt. Wherever you are welcomed, stay in the same house until you leave that town; wherever people don't welcome you, leave that town and shake the dust off your feet as a warning to them."

The disciples left and travelled through all the villages, preaching the Good News and healing people everywhere.

Luke 9: 1-6

> "He sent them out to preach the kingdom of God…"

Sent forth

During my days as a working journalist, I was sent to write about a student minister on the prairies. He landed in the community just like Jesus' disciples, with nothing. The community took him under their wing. They found him a place to live in. They brought him into their homes for meals.

By any professional standards, the student was awful. He had no theological training, no knowledge of liturgy, no pastoral experience. In that way too, he was like the disciples that Jesus sent out.

But the people of that little rural parish taught him all they knew about worship. I wonder what the disciples learned from the homes that took them in.

Help me to trust that you, and your people, will look after me, God.

T each us how short our life is,
 so that we may become wise.
 How much longer will your anger last?
Have pity, O Lord, on your servants!
Fill us each morning with your constant love,
so that we may sing and be glad all our life....
Lord our God, may your blessings be with us.
Give us success in all we do!

Psalm 90: 3-6, 12-14, 17

"Teach us how short our life is…"

The gift of time

Recently, a well-meaning relative gave my four-year-old daughter a clock. "It's time you learned to tell the time!" she claimed. I cringed. This period of life when clocks have no power over us is so short! My daughter wanders through the day oblivious to schedules and deadlines. I delight when she is surprised that the day is coming to an end. (Although I admit this can be frustrating when we are trying to get out the door!)

I know there is a wisdom that comes with understanding that life is short. My daughter will learn this soon enough. For now, I hope to let her enjoy the magic of living in the moment. And I will try to meet her there.

Lord, help me to truly live this moment.

God sets the time for birth and the time for death,
the time for planting and the time for pulling up,
the time for killing and the time for healing,
the time for tearing down and the time for building.
God sets the time for sorrow and the time for joy,
the time for mourning and the time for dancing,
the time for making love and the time for not making love,
the time for kissing and the time for not kissing.
God sets the time for finding and the time for losing,
the time for saving and the time for throwing away,
the time for tearing and the time for mending,
the time for silence and the time for talk.
God sets the time for love and the time for hate,
the time for war and the time for peace....
God has set the right time for everything.

Ecclesiastes 3: 1-11

"God has set the right time for everything."

The right time

The measured poetry of today's reading is a contrast to the pattern of my life. Just to read it slows me down, causing me to pause and reconsider. Its simple rhythm calls me into rare and quiet reflection.

I am known as one of those people who like to 'make things happen.' This, however, has been both a blessing and a curse. Sometimes it's my saving grace; sometimes it gets me into trouble.

In my effort to take charge, at times I've overlooked subtleties, stepped on toes and put my foot in my mouth – which, of course, has led to swallowing a lot of pride. This reading reminds me that the rhythm of God's wisdom is constant – even when I can't hear it.

God, you have given me ears.
May I use them to tune into your rhythm.

All the people were amazed at the mighty power of God.

The people were still marvelling at everything Jesus was doing, when he said to his disciples, "Don't forget what I am about to tell you! The Son of Man is going to be handed over to the power of human beings." But the disciples did not know what this meant. It had been hidden from them so that they could not understand it, and they were afraid to ask him about the matter.

Luke 9: 43-45

"...they were afraid to ask him about the matter."

Avoidance

Author Michael Smith calls it 'the horse on the dining table syndrome.' Writing about grief and loss, he imagines people gathered around a table, unwilling to discuss the one subject that weighs on everyone's mind – as evident as a horse planted among the platters of food.

I've experienced that syndrome. After my father died, my son, my dog, people came to express sympathy. Their faces showed their pain, but they didn't want to talk about it.

But the syndrome is not limited to grief. Shortly before this passage, Jesus had been transfigured in the presence of the three disciples. He had healed a boy stricken with epilepsy. Then he told his disciples he was going to be betrayed and killed.

And they didn't want to talk about it, either.

**You know my inmost thoughts, God.
I cannot hide anything from you. So why do I try?**

H ow terrible it will be for you that have such an easy life in Zion and for you that feel safe in Samaria – you great leaders of this great nation Israel, you to whom the people go for help.

How terrible it will be for you that stretch out on your luxurious couches, feasting on veal and lamb! You like to compose songs, as David did, and play them on harps. You drink wine by the bowlful and use the finest perfumes, but you do not mourn over the ruin of Israel. So you will be the first to go into exile. Your feasts and banquets will come to an end.

Amos 6: 1, 4-7

"Your feasts and banquets will come to an end."

A moral life?

How fast can I turn the page? As I read today's passage, my children are safely sleeping, and I am drinking my imported coffee. Who picked the beans? At what cost? It's cold in the house, so I turn up the heat.

I read the paper: something about Third World debt. I put on my shirt made in Indonesia. Who sewed it? For how much?

I start to make breakfast… what to have? So hard to choose, so many things to eat.

Then I get in my minivan…. But you get my drift. How moral is my life? Really? How can I escape my birth, my inheritance? How fast can I turn the page?

Lord, help me to be conscious of the good life I have, and to share with others who have less.

One day a messenger came running. "We were plowing the fields... and suddenly the Sabeans attacked. They killed every one of your servants...." Another servant came: "Lightning struck the sheep and the shepherds and killed them all...." Another servant came: "Three bands of Chaldean raiders attacked us, took away the camels, and killed all your servants...." Another servant came: "Your children were having a feast at the home of your oldest son, when a storm swept in from the desert. It blew the house down and killed them all...."

Job got up and tore his clothes in grief. He shaved his head and threw himself face downward on the ground. He said, "I was born with nothing, and I will die with nothing. The Lord gave, and now he has taken away. May his name be praised!"

Job 1: 6-22

> "The Lord gave, and now he has taken away."

The value of suffering

Someone has referred to our culture as the 'air bag culture': a culture that will do anything to insulate itself from suffering.

But I have heard many stories of suffering in the Twelve Step Program to which I belong. I see many people who have been to the brink, but who were saved by handing control over to their 'higher power.'

Job, too, is left with only one thing: faith. He simply has to believe that there is a benevolent 'higher power' greater than his own ego.

C. S. Lewis said, "Suffering is God's trumpet blast to a sleeping world." We think we are in control. We think we rule our lives. One thing that keeps our arrogance in check is suffering.

**Lord, help me to accept with humility
your 'higher power' in my life.**

As the time drew near when Jesus would be taken up to heaven, he made up his mind and set out on his way to Jerusalem. He sent messengers ahead of him, who went into a village in Samaria to get everything ready for him. But the people there would not receive him, because it was clear that he was on his way to Jerusalem. When the disciples James and John saw this, they said, "Lord, do you want us to call fire down from heaven to destroy them?"

Jesus turned and rebuked them. Then Jesus and his disciples went on to another village.

Luke 9: 51-56

> "Jesus turned and rebuked them."

Harder to live

The disciples' reaction was pretty natural: "Oh yeah? I'll show them!" The older I get, the more I realize how difficult it is not to respond in kind.

Compared to the disciples' experience, my own seems trivial… but real nonetheless. My son plays hockey. Parents on either side want their kids to win. It's natural: at times tempers flare, words are yelled. Sometimes after a loss, it's hard to walk over to 'the other side' and talk. Easier to keep it 'us' and 'them.' How often would Jesus have to "turn and rebuke" parents in a hockey rink?

A small example, I know, but it shows me how easy it is to say, "Love your neighbour," but how much harder to live it.

**Lord, truly I want to live what I preach.
Please help me to do it!**

When Jesus saw Nathanael coming to him, he said about him, "Here is a real Israelite; there is nothing false in him!"

Nathanael asked him, "How do you know me?" Jesus answered, "I saw you when you were under the fig tree before Philip called you." "Teacher," answered Nathanael, "you are the Son of God! You are the King of Israel!"

Jesus said, "Do you believe just because I told you I saw you when you were under the fig tree? You will see much greater things than this!" And he said to them, "I am telling you the truth: you will see heaven open and God's angels going up and coming down on the Son of Man."

John 1: 47-51

> "...there is nothing false in him!"

False honesty

We all know people who pretend to be honest – who feel 'you need to know the truth.' Unfortunately, their ugly version of reality often spreads destruction and bitterness. On the other hand, what a pleasure it is to meet an honest person with no axe to grind! – someone like Nathaniel who has "nothing false in him."

Truly honest people know that indiscreet remarks and vicious gossip are best left unsaid. They don't need to make themselves look important by digging into the nasty, dark side of human nature.

If I'm going to help build a strong family and a healthy community, I need to tell the truth, but I have to cast aside the desire to score points by using a false kind of honesty.

Lord, stop me when I'm tempted to spread gossip or tell someone an unnecessary truth.

Y ou are my friends! Take pity on me!
The hand of God has struck me down.
Why must you persecute me the way God does?
Haven't you tormented me enough?
How I wish that someone
would remember my words
and record them in a book!
Or with a chisel carve my words in stone
and write them so that they would last forever.
But I know there is someone in heaven
who will come at last to my defence.
Even after my skin is eaten by disease,
while still in this body I will see God.
I will see him with my own eyes,
and he will not be a stranger. *Job 19: 21-27*

> "...and he will not be a stranger."

Secure in God's love

I was deeply hurt the first time she asked, "Who is that man?" She meant me, her son-in-law of 15 years. As her memory disintegrates, names, words, ideas become increasingly difficult to articulate.

At first there were flashes of anger and frustration when she was still aware of the depth of her difficulties. Now her visitors, even her four daughters, must constantly remind her who they are.

Ninety years old and, like Job, weary and broken, she lives in a world she can no longer comprehend. Her stories fragment; today, yesterday and long ago blur. Now we must remember for her. Nevertheless, this painful journey takes her ever closer to the one who will never be a stranger to her.

God, as I become a stranger to those whose memories fade, hold me securely in your love.

"How terrible it will be for you, Chorazin! How terrible for you too, Bethsaida! If the miracles which were performed in you had been performed in Tyre and Sidon, the people there would have long ago sat down, put on sackcloth, and sprinkled ashes on themselves, to show that they had turned from their sins! God will show more mercy on the Judgment Day to Tyre and Sidon than to you. And as for you, Capernaum! Did you want to lift yourself up to heaven? You will be thrown down to hell!"

Jesus said to his disciples, "Whoever listens to you listens to me; whoever rejects you rejects me; and whoever rejects me rejects the one who sent me."

Luke 10: 13-16

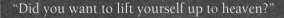

"Did you want to lift yourself up to heaven?"

Living hell

I have a lot in common with the arrogant, indifferent cities Jesus condemned. I often fail to acknowledge the miracle of the beautiful world God has given me. In fact, every day I use up more than my share of the world's resources. I am also frequently indifferent to the plight of others. And yet I like to think of myself as moral and clever.

In my heart I know such arrogance leads to separation from God, which is the definition of hell.

How can I root out my arrogance? If I recognize my own weakness, if I fight for the weakest in my community, if I respect the fragility of the earth, then Jesus will help me hear his word and show me mercy.

**Lord, help me turn from myself to others and to you.
Open my eyes to your gifts.**

T he disciples came to Jesus, asking, "Who is the greatest in the kingdom of heaven?" So Jesus called a child to come and stand in front of them, and said, "I assure you that unless you change and become like children, you will never enter the kingdom of heaven. The greatest in the kingdom of heaven is the one who humbles himself and becomes like this child. And whoever welcomes in my name one such child as this, welcomes me.

"See that you don't despise any of these little ones. Their angels in heaven, I tell you, are always in the presence of my Father in heaven."
Matthew 18: 1-5, 10

> "...unless you change
> and become like children..."

Like a child

There is a little boy who lives next door to me. Every morning he knocks on my door, with a big smile and an eagerness to start the day.

While my children are older than he, they always welcome him. They think he's cute. I, on the other hand, am often annoyed and wish he would go home so I can proceed with my chores and not have responsibility for another child.

Today's reading makes me rethink my attitude. I need to become like my own children who welcome this child and treat him with dignity and respect. I also need to become like this little boy who finds joy in the everyday. I don't need to look very far to find those who are the greatest in the kingdom of heaven.

Lord, help me find joy in the everyday.
Give me patience to welcome the little ones.

T he apostles said, "Make our faith greater." The Lord answered, "If you had faith as big as a mustard seed, you could say to this mulberry tree, 'Pull yourself up by the roots and plant yourself in the sea!' and it would obey you.

"Suppose one of you has a servant.... When he comes in from the field, do you tell him to hurry along and eat his meal? Of course not! Instead, you say to him, 'Get my supper ready and wait on me while I eat and drink; after that you may have your meal.' The servant does not deserve thanks for obeying orders, does he? It is the same with you; when you have done all you have been told to do, say, 'We are ordinary servants; we have only done our duty.'"

Luke 17: 5-10

> "If you had faith as big as a mustard seed…"

Nothing special?

One winter day, Sister Geraldine MacNamara went out the back door of her convent, on her way to work at a legal aid clinic in Winnipeg. She found two adolescents who'd passed out on her doorstep from sniffing glue. That moment planted the seed of a great work.

She uprooted herself from a promising law career to plunge into a sea of kids in her impoverished neighbourhood. They needed a safe place to go, and people to care about them.

'Sister Mac' died young of cancer. She always said she hadn't done anything special. But her little mustard seed of faith and compassion had grown into something extraordinary: a drop-in centre, with its own school and many outreach programs, serving children and youth in the city's core area.

Lord, help me trust that a little mustard seed of faith can accomplish great things.

"There was once a man who was going down from Jerusalem to Jericho when robbers attacked him, stripped him, and beat him up, leaving him half dead. It so happened that a priest was going down that road; but when he saw the man, he walked on by on the other side. In the same way a Levite also came there, went over and looked at the man, and then walked on by on the other side. But a Samaritan came upon the man, and when he saw him, his heart was filled with pity. He went over to him, poured oil and wine on his wounds and bandaged them…."

Jesus concluded, "In your opinion, which one of these three acted like a neighbour toward the man attacked by the robbers?" The teacher of the Law answered, "The one who was kind to him." Jesus replied, "You go, then, and do the same."

Luke 10: 25-37

> "You go, then, and do the same."

With kindness

The past two days have left me somewhat uneasy. As I walk from my hotel to my meetings, I pass some panhandlers. One young woman in shabby black dress kneels – head bowed, eyes closed, holding a cup against her forehead. A cardboard sign in front of her asks for money for her three children.

Around the corner a heavy-set man lies sleeping, sprawled on a sleeping bag on top of the vent for the subway where the warm air heats a whole city block. To his side, a large black dog sits motionless; between them, a paper cup with some coins in it.

The more I look around, the more I realize how I have distanced myself from 'going and doing the same.'

God, I tend to observe life while avoiding full participation in the world around me. Give me a rude awakening.

Tuesday | OCTOBER 5

As Jesus and his disciples went on their way, he came to a village where a woman named Martha welcomed him in her home. She had a sister named Mary, who sat down at the feet of the Lord and listened to his teaching. Martha was upset over all the work she had to do, so she came and said, "Lord, don't you care that my sister has left me to do all the work by myself? Tell her to come and help me!"

The Lord answered her, "Martha, Martha! You are worried and troubled over so many things, but just one is needed. Mary has chosen the right thing, and it will not be taken away from her."

Luke 10: 38-42

"Mary has chosen the right thing..."

Faced with a choice

No matter how many times I hear this passage, I usually find myself sympathizing with the hard-working Martha. I often feel that I do nothing but work: I take care of my child, work at my office, do errands, clean the house.

There doesn't seem to be time to savour the important things: my child's moment of discovery; the co-worker who needs someone to listen; the beauty and abundance that surround me; the five minutes of peace in the morning.

Every once in a while, though, I do have that moment of wisdom that lets me see what is important. Like Mary, I choose the right thing, and I put my daily worries and troubles into perspective.

Lord, there is so much for me to do each day.
Help me choose 'the right thing' more often.

One day Jesus was praying in a certain place. When he had finished, one of his disciples said to him, "Lord, teach us to pray, just as John taught his disciples."

Jesus said to them, "When you pray, say this: 'Father: May your holy name be honoured; may your kingdom come. Give us day by day the food we need. Forgive us our sins, for we forgive everyone who does us wrong. And do not bring us to hard testing.'"

Luke 11: 1-4

"Lord, teach us to pray…"

Simplicity itself

I once spent time with a woman who was a great pray-er. I don't mean that she knew many prayers by heart, or that she was quick to drop to her knees. No, I mean that for her, praying was as much part of her life as checking e-mails, drinking coffee, and reading the newspaper are part of mine. That is to say, it was unremarkably normal.

I was, of course, amazed and envious.

I was *amazed* because prayer is something I've always felt self-conscious about. After all, isn't it something only children or alarmingly holy people do? I was *envious* because I longed for a prayer life, without even knowing what that meant.

And from her I learnt what it meant: just say this….

Lord, the first prayer is silence. Teach me this prayer.

J esus said, "Suppose one of you should go to a friend's house at midnight and say, 'Friend, let me borrow three loaves of bread. A friend of mine who is on a trip has just come to my house, and I don't have any food for him!' And suppose your friend should answer, 'Don't bother me! The door is already locked, and my children and I are in bed. I can't get up and give you anything.' Well, what then? I tell you that even if he will not get up and give you the bread because you are his friend, yet he will get up and give you everything you need because you are not ashamed to keep on asking. And so I say to you: Ask, and you will receive; seek, and you will find; knock, and the door will be opened to you."

Luke 11:5-13

> "Ask, and you will receive…"

Fear and faith

We had spent seven hours in a fully loaded airplane, and crossed two busy international airports. My daughter developed a fever and a cough, and was having trouble breathing. Even though the odds were stacked against it, I was afraid she had caught a deadly form of influenza.

We were many miles from the nearest emergency room. Despite the doctor's reassurances at the clinic, I was sick with terror. I sat in the cold sunshine clutching my daughter, hoping the cool air would help her breathe, taking her temperature every half hour.

Not only did fear banish reason, it seemed to have banished my faith as well. Frantic with worry, I found that I couldn't even turn to God to ask for strength. I barely even prayed, until the crisis had passed.

Lord, deepen my faith and help me to seek your love, in good times and in bad.

Praise the Lord!
With all my heart I will thank the Lord
in the assembly of his people.
How wonderful are the things the Lord does!
All who are delighted with them want to understand them.
All he does is full of honour and majesty;
his righteousness is eternal.
The Lord does not let us forget his wonderful actions;
he is kind and merciful.
He provides food for those who honour him;
he never forgets his covenant.
He has shown his power to his people
by giving them the lands of foreigners. *Psalm 111: 1-6*

"He provides food for those who honour him…"

The gift of giving

He resented being downsized. In spite of the 'golden handshake,' it still felt like being fired. And he missed the guys from work. Sure, now he could go bowling, play some golf and have a few beers; but something was missing.

During their weekly poker game, a friend asked, "Would any of you be interested in volunteering at the Food Bank?" He decided to go along and he's made a few discoveries. While they're making sandwiches, they'll banter about last night's scores, just like they did at work. Also, there are a lot of hungry children in town.

Yesterday, as her mother was waiting in line, a little girl reached up and touched his hand. "Will you be my grandfather? My best friend Tracey is always bragging about her grandfather."

**God, keep me aware that every time I give something away,
I receive a hundred fold.**

When Jesus had said this, a woman spoke up from the crowd and said to him, "How happy is the woman who bore you and nursed you!"

But Jesus answered, "Rather, how happy are those who hear the word of God and obey it!"

Luke 11: 27-28

"Happy is the woman who bore you and nursed you!"

A mother's love

What better image could there be for nourishment and sustenance than a nursing mother?

I remember, when each of my three children were babies, how their mother's breast satisfied them when they were hungry, comforted them when they were troubled, and made them feel secure and loved. And I saw how mother and child delighted in their shared bond. I witnessed this astounding miracle daily for years. The closeness I shared with my children was but a shadow of the closeness they shared with their mother.

Yet, in today's reading, Jesus says that there is something of even greater power than this. For those who truly hear it, God's word surpasses the satisfaction, comfort, security and happiness that a loving mother's breast brings to her nursing child. It's an almost unbelievable promise.

**Lord, help me hear your word
so that my deep hunger can be satisfied.**

J esus was going into a village when he was met by ten men suffering from a dreaded skin disease. They stood at a distance and shouted, "Jesus! Master! Have pity on us!" Jesus saw them and said to them, "Go and let the priests examine you."

On the way they were made clean. When one of them saw that he was healed, he came back, praising God in a loud voice. He threw himself to the ground at Jesus' feet and thanked him. The man was a Samaritan. Jesus spoke up, "There were ten who were healed; where are the other nine? Why is this foreigner the only one who came back to give thanks to God?" And Jesus said to him, "Get up and go; your faith has made you well."

Luke 17: 11-19

> "When one of them saw that he was healed…"

Gratitude for healing

My husband died of cancer at the age of thirty-six and I was left alone to care for our three young children. I was overwhelmed with the experience of our loss, and the effort of trying to bring some order to the chaos we experienced. Grief, anger and loneliness seemed to consume me.

Now several years have passed. Recently, in a phone call with my mum, I was filled with a deep sense of gratitude. "Thank you," I said, "for accepting me when I wasn't the easiest person to be around. Your love brought healing in ways I never thought possible."

God's healing often happens through friends and family. Do I recognize it, and remember to give thanks?

God, heal me so that I can believe again in love.
Help me bring your healing love to others.

"How evil are the people of this day! They ask for a miracle, but none will be given them except the miracle of Jonah. In the same way that the prophet Jonah was a sign for the people of Nineveh, so the Son of Man will be a sign for the people of this day. On the Judgment Day the Queen of Sheba will stand up and accuse the people of today, because she travelled all the way from her country to listen to King Solomon's wise teaching; and there is something here, I tell you, greater than Solomon. On the Judgment Day the people of Nineveh will stand up and accuse you, because they turned from their sins when they heard Jonah preach; and I assure you that there is something here greater than Jonah!"

Luke 11: 29-32

> "There is something here greater than Jonah…"

Close to home

I am fortunate enough to live in the country. When I look out my window, I can see trees and water and hills. Every once in a while, my husband and I go on a trip. We enjoy new vistas spread out before us, but when we come back home, we say, "You know, what we have here is just as beautiful as anything we've seen."

It's much the same with glimpses of spiritual beauty I observe: the parents who lavish love and attention on a severely handicapped child; the teachers who go the extra mile with troubled students; the neighbour who gives dedicated volunteer service in my community.

I don't have to travel far away: there are spiritual beauties to inspire and nourish me close at hand.

Lord, give me the grace to look for the surprising signs of your presence in the familiar places.

When Jesus finished speaking, a Pharisee invited him to eat with him; so he went in and sat down to eat. The Pharisee was surprised when he noticed that Jesus had not washed before eating. So the Lord said to him, "Now then, you Pharisees clean the outside of your cup and plate, but inside you are full of violence and evil. Fools! Did not God, who made the outside, also make the inside? But give what is in your cups and plates to the poor, and everything will be ritually clean for you."

Luke 11: 37-41

"...but inside you are full of violence and evil."

Called to task

It's so easy to bash the Pharisees: their hypocrisy is so thinly veiled! I'm with Jesus when he calls them to task. "Go get 'em," I say!

But, in fact, I've missed the point of today's reading. The Pharisee is *me* and their hypocrisy is *mine*.

I say I care for the homeless, but I give nothing to help provide them with shelter. I say I care for my children, but I offer them so little of my time. I say I love my wife, but I show it so infrequently.

Along with the Pharisees, Jesus is calling *me* to task! I need to get my beliefs and my actions to agree. To be one in word and deed. To be whole.

**God, cleanse my heart.
Give me the courage to live from your source of goodness.**

"How terrible for you Pharisees! You give to God one tenth of the seasoning herbs, such as mint and rue and all the other herbs, but you neglect justice and love for God. These you should practise, without neglecting the others.

"How terrible for you Pharisees! You love the reserved seats in the synagogues and to be greeted with respect in the marketplaces. How terrible for you! You are like unmarked graves which people walk on without knowing it."

One of the teachers of the Law said to him, "Teacher, when you say this, you insult us too!" Jesus answered, "How terrible also for you teachers of the Law! You put onto people's backs loads which are hard to carry, but you yourselves will not stretch out a finger to help them carry those loads."

Luke 11: 42-46

> "...will not stretch out a finger to help..."

People first

When I was a university student, I shared a house with seven other women. We led a structured communal life that was efficient and satisfying. In my youth I thought it was nearly perfect.

However, looking back, I have come to see that while I was superficially committed to the group, I rarely became involved in the lives of my housemates. It's only now, in learning of the personal battles they were then waging (chronic illness, depression, crisis of faith), that I see I neglected the cries and the needs of the women with whom I shared a home.

Yes, I followed all the rules. But how much of a difference could I have made if I'd stretched out a finger to help them carry those loads?

**Today, Lord, help me to put people before things,
and love before obedience.**

S ing a new song to the Lord;
    he has done wonderful things!
    By his own power and holy strength
he has won the victory.
The Lord announced his victory;
he made his saving power known to the nations.
He kept his promise to the people of Israel
with loyalty and constant love for them.
All people everywhere have seen
the victory of our God.
Sing for joy to the Lord, all the earth;
praise him with songs and shouts of joy!

Psalm 98: 1-4

> "…with loyalty and constant love for them."

Unending love

One balmy October evening, as I walked
among the fallen leaves, a splash of colour
caught my eye. Reaching down, I picked up a maple leaf, each yellow-
and red-flecked tip perfectly intact. I marvelled briefly at this wonder
then let it drift back to the ground.

I continued on, absorbing the splendour of the multi-coloured
leaves dancing in the wind, and the sound of dried-up leaves crunch-
ing underfoot.

Suddenly, my eyes were opened to something greater than nature's
beauty. In a moment of insight I realized that I'd held in my hand a
symbol of God's faithfulness. How God, whose loyalty and love crafts
the seasons' remarkable cycles, also promises to stay by me with
unending love.

**Your unfaltering loyalty and love
draws me to sing your praises, my God.**

Jesus said, "Be on guard against the yeast of the Pharisees – I mean their hypocrisy. Whatever is covered up will be uncovered, and every secret will be made known. So then, whatever you have said in the dark will be heard in broad daylight, and whatever you have whispered in private in a closed room will be shouted from the housetops.

"Do not be afraid of those who kill the body but cannot afterward do anything worse. I will show you whom to fear: fear God, who, after killing, has the authority to throw into hell....

"Aren't five sparrows sold for two pennies? Yet not one sparrow is forgotten by God. Even the hairs of your head have all been counted. So do not be afraid; you are worth much more than many sparrows!"

Luke 12: 1-7

> "...every secret will be made known."

Known and loved

Everything covered will be uncovered – what a terrifying thought! Imagine if all the petty arguments I've had with my partner, or the quiet cruelties I've practised when I was angry, were broadcast on the evening news. What if the contempt for certain people that sits secretly in my heart were made visible to all, especially the people I want most to impress! What if everyone could see how casually I have dismissed people I considered unimportant.

But this very threat makes Jesus' words about the sparrows that much more consoling. In spite of all my failings, I am deeply and intimately cherished by God, not just in my thoughts and my feelings, but in my body too – down to the last hair on my head.

**Lord, help me to dig out all that is hidden
and give it over to you, trusting in your love.**

"I assure you that those who declare publicly that they belong to me, the Son of Man will do the same for them before the angels of God. But those who reject me publicly, the Son of Man will also reject them before the angels of God.

"Whoever says a word against the Son of Man can be forgiven; but whoever says evil things against the Holy Spirit will not be forgiven.

"When they bring you to be tried in the synagogues or before governors or rulers, do not be worried about how you will defend yourself or what you will say. For the Holy Spirit will teach you at that time what you should say."

Luke 12: 8-12

> "Do not be worried about how you will defend yourself…"

Much-needed faith

When I was a student, it was fashionable to be a rebel, an atheist, a communist. After all, young people are expected to reject their parents' values! Not much of a rebel, I felt awkward explaining to my friends why I still believed in God. My 'old-fashioned' faith was sometimes an embarrassing burden to me. The Holy Spirit never taught me any wise things to say during those old arguments about the meaning of life.

Now forty years later, I look back and chuckle at our earnest discussions. I still don't know many persuasive, logical proofs for the existence of God. But the experience of living – working, struggling, suffering, loving – has convinced me of the need for faith, the faith that Jesus lived and preached so eloquently.

Lord, help me see that the day-to-day choices I make are the true witnesses to my faith.

J esus told his disciples a parable to teach them that they should always pray and never become discouraged. "In a certain town there was a judge who neither feared God nor respected people. And there was a widow in that same town who kept coming to him and pleading for her rights, saying, 'Help me against my opponent!' For a long time the judge refused to act, but at last he said to himself, 'Even though I don't fear God or respect people, yet because of all the trouble this widow is giving me, I will see to it that she gets her rights. If I don't, she will keep on coming and finally wear me out!'"

Luke 18: 1-8

"...always pray and never become discouraged."

The need to pray

Last summer, at the ocean, I saw something I had never seen before. A strong wind came up along the shore, and the birds, rather than seeking shelter, flew into the wind. There they were, wings flapping, facing forward, and losing ground all the time.

This may be a common phenomenon, but to me it seemed extraordinary. Why would the birds do such a thing? Did they know they were not reaching their destination? Did they care?

I now think of this image when I pray. Like those birds, I must turn my face to God, send forth my best words and thoughts, and not worry about the results. God will look kindly upon my efforts. God will provide.

Dear God, hear my prayer. Bring me your comfort.

After this the Lord chose another seventy-two men and sent them out two by two, to go ahead of him to every town and place where he himself was about to go. He said to them, "Go! I am sending you like lambs among wolves. Don't take a purse or a beggar's bag or shoes; don't stop to greet anyone on the road. Whenever you go into a house, first say, 'Peace be with this house.' If someone who is peace-loving lives there, let your greeting of peace remain on that person; if not, take back your greeting of peace…. Whenever you go into a town and are made welcome, eat what is set before you, heal the sick in that town, and say to the people there, 'The kingdom of God has come near you.'"

Luke 10: 1-9

> "Don't take a purse or a beggar's bag or shoes…"

Tools for the journey

I think Jesus was worried about the disciples as they set off on their own. Worried about their safety, their well-being, the reception they would receive 'out there.'

Although the disciples didn't carry "a purse or a beggar's bag or shoes," they did carry the 'tools' they would need for their journey. They carried, within their hearts, the example of how Jesus had lived among them – aware of the danger that surrounded him, yet always willing to share God's love with others.

Perhaps Jesus' last minute advice is much like the words of caution I give my children as they leave home. Instead of worrying, I need to remind myself that they, too, carry the 'tools' to help them be in this world.

Loving God, when I am fearful, give me the knowledge that you are with me, every step of the way.

"Be ready for whatever comes, dressed for action and with your lamps lit, like servants who are waiting for their master to come back from a wedding feast. When he comes and knocks, they will open the door for him at once. How happy are those servants whose master finds them awake and ready when he returns! I tell you, he will take off his coat, have them sit down, and will wait on them. How happy they are if he finds them ready, even if he should come at midnight or even later!"   *Luke 12: 35-38*

"Be ready for whatever comes…"

Ready for what comes

The table was set, dinner ready in the kitchen. But where were our out-of-town visitors? Their expected arrival time was 6 p.m. The clock ticked away, but no guests arrived. Worried and anxious, we finally ate some of the dinner, but we had little appetite. Then the telephone rang with reassuring news: our friends had been held up by bad weather and would be arriving eventually!

When they finally knocked on the door, at midnight or even later, the weary travellers were comforted to find us awake and eager to greet them.

When we're talking about friends and houseguests, it's easy to be ready for whatever comes. What about the other less welcome visitors – sickness, bad luck, unemployment – that also show up sooner or later on our doorsteps?

O Lord, help me to be ready for whatever is waiting for me.

was made a servant of the gospel by God's special gift, which he gave me through the working of his power. I am less than the least of all God's people; yet God gave me this privilege of taking to the Gentiles the Good News about the infinite riches of Christ… in order that at the present time, by means of the church, the angelic rulers and powers in the heavenly world might learn of his wisdom in all its different forms. God did this according to his eternal purpose, which he achieved through Christ Jesus our Lord. In union with Christ and through our faith in him we have the boldness to go into God's presence with all confidence.

Ephesians 3: 1-12

"I am less than the least of all God's people…"

Doing my best

I was a scrawny kid, small for my age, hiding behind thick spectacles. When the other kids picked teams for baseball or soccer, they usually picked me near the last. It hurt.

But I still remember my rush of pride and gratitude when George, an acknowledged leader of our grade, picked me first for a game of tag.

So I can sympathize with Paul. Before his conversion, he wasn't on the team at all – he was on the other side. And then God picked him to be a messenger of the good news of Jesus Christ.

I did my best for George. I didn't want to let him down. Perhaps Paul felt the same about God.

On my own, I am nothing.
Thank you, God, for you make me worthwhile.

ask God from the wealth of his glory to give you power through his Spirit to be strong in your inner selves, and I pray that Christ will make his home in your hearts through faith. I pray that you may have your roots and foundation in love, so that you, together with all God's people, may have the power to understand how broad and long, how high and deep, is Christ's love. Yes, may you come to know his love – although it can never be fully known – and so be completely filled with the very nature of God.

To him who by means of his power working in us is able to do so much more than we can ever ask for, or even think of: to God be the glory... forever and ever! Amen.

Ephesians 3: 13-21

> "Christ will make his home in your hearts..."

Awake to life

Adam was a man who couldn't speak and who had very little movement in his limbs. Yet his eyes were engaging: following you around the room, reflecting sometimes interest, sometimes fear, but most often a simple peace. Being with Adam helped me to slow down and be more in touch with my own inner self. I experienced God's peace through him.

After Adam died, a bench in his memory was placed beside our pond. The other night as I sat there, gazing out over the water, I gradually became more aware of the birds singing, the frogs croaking, the silence of the evening. It was as if my inner self was being awakened.

I am grateful to Adam for helping my inner self grow stronger.

O God, may your Spirit live in me
and strengthen my inner self.

J esus said, "When you see a cloud coming up in the west, at once you say that it is going to rain – and it does. And when you feel the south wind blowing, you say that it is going to get hot – and it does. Hypocrites! You can look at the earth and the sky and predict the weather; why, then, don't you know the meaning of this present time?

"Why do you not judge for yourselves the right thing to do? If someone brings a lawsuit against you and takes you to court, do your best to settle the dispute before you get to court. If you don't, you will be dragged before the judge, who will hand you over to the police, and you will be put in jail... until you pay the last penny of your fine."

Luke 12:54-59

> "You can look at the earth and the sky…"

Signs of the times

When I was growing up on the Pacific coast, we knew how to predict the weather. "If you can see the mountains," we said, "it's going to rain. If you can't see the mountains, it *is* raining."

Jesus cites similar sayings from his own time. But then he challenges his listeners: "Why do you read weather signs, but not the signs of the times?" Perhaps they were in denial – to use a psychological term invented 20 centuries later!

People in denial refuse to recognize signs. When my mother was dying, the signs were clear: increasing shortness of breath, lapses into unconsciousness, loss of lucidity. But my father and I couldn't accept them – until the telephone call came, in the middle of the night.

I wonder what I may be in denial about, these days.

**If I don't hear you speaking, Lord,
is it because I don't want to hear your message?**

Jesus told this parable: "There was once a man who had a fig tree growing in his vineyard. He went looking for figs on it but found none. So he said to his gardener, 'Look, for three years I have been coming here looking for figs on this fig tree, and I haven't found any. Cut it down! Why should it go on using up the soil?' But the gardener answered, 'Leave it alone, sir, just one more year; I will dig around it and put in some fertilizer. Then if the tree bears figs next year, so much the better; if not, then you can have it cut down.'"

Luke 13: 1-9

"Leave it alone just one more year… "

Loving patience

I tend to be impulsive about some things. I throw stuff out or give it away as soon as I'm finished with it. I make decisions without carefully weighing all the pros and cons. I offer opinions without thinking them through. Leaving things alone just one more year is hard for me.

But, as a parent, I'm forced to leave things alone sometimes, because children, like fig trees, can always use a little more time and care. I never know where this year's difficulty will lead us, but I remain hopeful that patience, love and generosity will go a long way toward helping the tree bear fruit – if not this year, then next year.

**Lord, when I feel like giving up,
help me remember that patience always bears good fruit.**

"Once there were two men who went up to the Temple to pray…. The Pharisee stood apart by himself and prayed, 'I thank you, God, that I am not greedy, dishonest, or an adulterer…. I thank you that I am not like that tax collector over there. I fast two days a week, and I give you one tenth of all my income.' The tax collector stood at a distance and would not even raise his face to heaven, but beat on his breast and said, 'God, have pity on me, a sinner!' I tell you," said Jesus, "the tax collector, and not the Pharisee, was in the right with God when he went home. For those who make themselves great will be humbled, and those who humble themselves will be made great."

Luke 18: 9-14

> "…those who humble themselves will be made great."

Honest with myself

This story has become so familiar that I'm almost immune to its powerful message.

Jesus asks me to be like the tax collector, standing open and vulnerable before God. My kind gestures and my charitable donations mean little if they merely serve to deny or disguise my need for God's love and mercy.

Sometimes it seems easier to *do* for others. I would rather say to my co-worker, "Take a break and I'll cover for you," than sit with her over coffee and listen to her worries. Being attentive to another person's concerns seems much too demanding. But how am I any different from the Pharisee if I let my self-satisfied busyness keep me from a genuine relationship?

**God, help me turn to you
instead of distracting myself in the busyness of 'doing.'**

One Sabbath Jesus was teaching in a synagogue. A woman there had an evil spirit that had kept her sick for eighteen years.... When Jesus saw her, he called out to her, "Woman, you are free from your sickness!" He placed his hands on her, and at once she straightened herself up and praised God.

The official of the synagogue was angry that Jesus had healed on the Sabbath, so he said to the people, "There are six days in which we should work; so come during those days and be healed, but not on the Sabbath!"

The Lord answered him, "You hypocrites! Any one of you would untie your ox or your donkey from the stall and take it out to give it water on the Sabbath.... Should [this woman] not be released on the Sabbath?"   *Luke 13: 10-17*

> "Should she not be released on the Sabbath?"

To rest and be renewed

To work or not to work...? According to Jesus, that is *not* the question!

Respecting Sabbath time is more than a question of whether or not I should do productive work. In some way, the answer to this contentious issue lies in Jesus' very act of healing!

I find it difficult to 'waste' time. When I read a book, it's to become a better parent or to update myself professionally. When I go for a walk, it's usually part of an exercise regime I've set for myself. Sabbath time reminds me to stop pushing myself. To learn to simply 'be.' To stop rushing around and, in the stillness, to discover healing in my body, mind and spirit. To recognize that all of creation, including myself, is good.

Lord, help me stop amidst my daily chores,
and to know that it is good to rest and refresh myself.

J esus asked, "What is the kingdom of God like? What shall I compare it with? It is like this. A man takes a mustard seed and plants it in his field. The plant grows and becomes a tree, and the birds make their nests in its branches."

Again Jesus asked, "What shall I compare the kingdom of God with? It is like this. A woman takes some yeast and mixes it with a bushel of flour until the whole batch of dough rises."

Luke 13: 18-21

"...until the whole batch of dough rises."

The patience of a baker

For my mother, baking bread was a labour of love. What a wonderful ritual! Greasing pans, mixing, kneading, laying dough aside for the rising. Every Saturday, we grew to expect the heavenly smell of freshly baked bread as we burst through the doors. Bread, blessed and broken for the family by a mother's love. No wonder Jesus chooses to compare the kingdom to baking bread!

But how often do I go about my tasks with the patience and care of a baker? Usually the burden of time weighs so heavily on me that I demand immediate results.

How I wish I could trust that God's grace will leaven my small efforts and transform them into something greater, the way yeast turns dough into bread.

Lord, help me trust that my small acts of kindness will rise with the leaven of your love.

All your creatures, Lord, will praise you,
and all your people will give you thanks.
They will speak of the glory of your royal power
and tell of your might,
so that everyone will know your mighty deeds
and the glorious majesty of your kingdom.
Your rule is eternal,
and you are king forever.
The Lord is faithful to his promises;
he is merciful in all his acts.
He helps those who are in trouble;
he lifts those who have fallen.
All living things look hopefully to you,
and you give them food when they need it.   *Psalm 145: 10-14*

> "…all your people will give you thanks."

Gratitude and joy

Each night my husband or I try to take time for a bedtime prayer with our two-year-old. I usually ask her, "Who are you thankful for today?" And after she names a few people, we ask God to bless whoever is on her list.

One night, after an exhausting day at the zoo, there was a long silence before she replied, "apples" and then, after another pause, "and monkeys too."

I smiled and thought to myself: when was the last time I've been deeply thankful for something as basic as apples or part of God's creation like monkeys? In my own prayers I often overlook simple pleasures and forget to thank God for them. I'm thankful for my daughter's reminder.

**Thank you, God,
for all the small things that bring me joy today.**

Jesus went up a hill to pray and spent the whole night there praying to God. When day came, he called his disciples to him and chose twelve of them, whom he named apostles....

When Jesus had come down from the hill, he stood on a level place with a large number of his disciples. A large crowd of people was there from all over Judea and from Jerusalem and from the coast cities of Tyre and Sidon; they had come to hear him and to be healed of their diseases. Those who were troubled by evil spirits also came and were healed. All the people tried to touch him, for power was going out from him and healing them all.

Luke 6: 12-19

"...to be healed of their diseases."

Prayer and healing

Martha was born with cerebral palsy. She doesn't speak and she must use a wheelchair to get around. Her mother is constantly trying to figure out how Martha can live an integrated life in the community, have friends and interesting work, and realize some of her dreams.

Today Martha's life is amazingly rich. She has a circle of friends who meet regularly at her home to encourage and support her. Martha's mother, a woman of prayer, has been a source of love and healing in Martha's life.

Prayer, community, healing: Jesus, too, lived this pattern. Before choosing his twelve disciples, he spent the whole night in prayer. Then, together they came down from the hill to the people who were longing to be healed.

**Lord, may prayer and community give me strength
to be a healing presence.**

One Sabbath Jesus went to eat a meal at the home of one of the leading Pharisees; and people were watching Jesus closely. A man whose legs and arms were swollen came to Jesus, and Jesus spoke up and asked the teachers of the Law and the Pharisees, "Does our Law allow healing on the Sabbath or not?"

But they would not say a thing. Jesus took the man, healed him, and sent him away. Then he said to them, "If any one of you had a child or an ox that happened to fall in a well on a Sabbath, would you not pull it out at once on the Sabbath itself?"

But they were not able to answer him about this.

Luke 14: 1-6

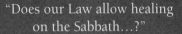

"Does our Law allow healing on the Sabbath…?"

Priorities

How often I have tried to focus on the work at hand, trying to 'get it done right,' while forgetting to take the time to pay attention to the people around me.

A few months ago, I was so focused on making my quota of telephone calls, that I did not take time to talk to the other volunteers working beside me. One of them, a single mother who has shown great courage under difficult circumstances, could have used some moral support at the time.

Jesus reminds me that concern for people is always more important than obeying the letter of the law. 'Getting it right' is less about deadlines and more about seeing the needs of others. People before process – now is the time to act!

Compassionate God,
may I serve others with your spirit of love.

Jesus noticed how some of the guests were choosing the best places, so he told this parable: "When someone invites you to a wedding feast, do not sit down in the best place. It could happen that someone more important than you has been invited, and your host, who invited both of you, would have to come and say to you, 'Let him have this place.' Then you would be embarrassed and have to sit in the lowest place. Instead, when you are invited, go and sit in the lowest place, so that your host will come to you and say, 'Come on up, my friend, to a better place.' This will bring you honour in the presence of all the other guests. For those who make themselves great will be humbled, and those who humble themselves will be made great."

Luke 14: 1, 7-11

> "...those who humble themselves will be made great."

Gifts to be shared

He was the most important person in his department. And he made sure everyone knew it. He chaired all the 'best' committees, and his name was on everyone's Rolodex. And why not? He'd worked hard and deserved recognition. So what if he stepped on a few toes and made more enemies than friends along the way?

And yet, the satisfaction of seeing his name in print didn't last as long as it once had. At the end of the day, he was alone – with nothing but a file full of newspaper clippings for company. Everyone knew him, but he didn't know anyone.

For someone in his position to admit he needed companionship was unthinkable. He hadn't expected success to feel so hollow. Where had he gone wrong?

God, may I remember that my abilities
were given to me to be shared with others.

There was a chief tax collector there named Zacchaeus, who was rich.… He was a little man and could not see Jesus because of the crowd. So he ran ahead and climbed a sycamore tree to see Jesus.… [Jesus] looked up and said, "Hurry down, Zacchaeus, because I must stay in your house today." Zacchaeus hurried down and welcomed him with great joy. All the people who saw it started grumbling, "This man has gone as a guest to the home of a sinner!" Zacchaeus stood up and said to the Lord, "Listen, sir! I will give half my belongings to the poor, and if I have cheated anyone, I will pay back four times as much." Jesus said, "Salvation has come to this house today.… The Son of Man came to seek and to save the lost."

Luke 19: 1-10

> "The Son of Man came to seek and to save the lost."

Down from my perch

As a short person, I've always been fond of Zacchaeus and his approach to problems. Can't see? Climb a tree!

But when Zacchaeus climbs a tree to see Jesus more clearly, he ends up giving half of his goods to the poor and instituting a four-for-one repayment scheme for some shady transactions in his past. Wait a minute! Solving one problem created a more demanding challenge!

I prefer the safety of a detached spirituality, straddling a tree limb high above the crowds. But Jesus wants more. He invites me down from my 'tree,' to place my feet on solid ground. Like Zacchaeus, I'm called to do something concrete about the poor, to make restitution for the wrongs I've done. Sometimes staying in the tree is easier!

Jesus, I can't turn my life around overnight.
Help me to take one concrete step toward you each day.

See how much the Father has loved us! His love is so great that we are called God's children – and so, in fact, we are. This is why the world does not know us: it has not known God. My dear friends, we are now God's children, but it is not yet clear what we shall become. But we know that when Christ appears, we shall be like him, because we shall see him as he really is. Everyone who has this hope in Christ keeps himself pure, just as Christ is pure.

1 John 3: 1-3

> "…it is not yet clear what we shall become."

God's children

My four-year-old daughter changes her mind about her future career on a daily (if not hourly) basis. This week she has made plans to become a veterinarian, figure skater, astronaut, archaeologist and/or entomologist.

Today she asks me what I would like to be 'when I grow up.' I laugh. I figure that since I've moved into my fourth decade, the answer to that question is pretty well a done deal. She reminds me to think again.

It seems the writer of today's reading agrees. I am reminded that defining myself in terms of what I *do* or what I might *be* is really of little consequence. What really matters is who I am: a member of God's family.

Jesus, teach me to live with the openness of knowing that I am part of your family.

Jesus answered them, "The hour has now come for the Son of Man to receive great glory. I am telling you the truth: a grain of wheat remains no more than a single grain unless it is dropped into the ground and dies. If it does die, then it produces many grains. Those who love their own life will lose it; those who hate their own life in this world will keep it for life eternal. Whoever wants to serve me must follow me, so that my servant will be with me where I am. And my Father will honour anyone who serves me."

John 12: 23-26

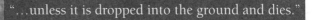

"…unless it is dropped into the ground and dies."

Cycles of life

Childhood memories of a year on the family farm: I remember winter-white fields, asleep under the snow. Then spring and the first signs of new life: tender green stalks of wheat. The golden ripening as summer passed. New anxieties as autumn drew near: would the weather stay fine? At last, the excitement of the harvest! Then, already thinking about next year, winter wheat to plant. "Get a head start on spring by sowing in the fall." So the cycle continued, season after season.

Life eternal? As I try to imagine the ultimate 'tomorrow,' I am comforted by these memories. Jesus, in his wisdom, uses the easy rhythm of nature to teach a hard truth – a simple grain of wheat, symbolizing the universal cycle of death and life.

**Lord, help me to trust your promise of eternal life,
just as I trust in the rhythm of the seasons.**

"If one of you is planning to build a tower, you sit down first and figure out what it will cost.... If you don't, you will not be able to finish the tower after laying the foundation; and all who see what happened will make fun of you. 'You began to build but can't finish the job!' they will say. If a king goes out with ten thousand men to fight another king who comes against him with twenty thousand men, he will sit down first and decide if he is strong enough to face that other king. If he isn't, he will send messengers to meet the other king to ask for terms of peace while he is still a long way off. In the same way," concluded Jesus, "none of you can be my disciple unless you give up everything you have."

Luke 14: 25-33

> "...all who see what happened will make fun of you."

Accepting limits

It is always difficult for me to accept that I have limits – that there are some things I simply cannot do; that there are places I cannot go and challenges that are beyond my abilities; that I do not know everything.

Accepting those limits often feels like admitting defeat. Sometimes the only thing that keeps me from overestimating my time, talents and resources is the sheer terror of losing face!

It generally takes an honest reckoning of my assets and liabilities before I acknowledge that losing face is better than losing my head. No one ever dies of shame... but, when I have to back off, it sure feels like I could. Learning to live with limits – planning instead of bluffing – is a painful but necessary truth.

**God, help me to acknowledge my limits honestly
and to accept them gracefully.**

When many tax collectors and other outcasts came to listen to Jesus, the Pharisees and the teachers of the Law started grumbling, "This man welcomes outcasts and even eats with them!" So Jesus told them this parable: "Suppose one of you has a hundred sheep and loses one of them – what do you do? You leave the other ninety-nine sheep in the pasture and go looking for the one that got lost until you find it. When you find it, you are so happy that you put it on your shoulders and carry it back home. Then you call your friends and neighbours together and say to them, 'I am so happy I found my lost sheep. Let us celebrate!' In the same way, I tell you, there will be more joy in heaven over one sinner who repents than over ninety-nine respectable people who do not need to repent."

Luke 15: 1-10

"I am so happy I found my lost sheep."

Lost and found

Did anyone ever come looking for me, their 'lost sheep'? Perhaps they did, and I just never knew it. Lost sheep, by definition, aren't very aware of what's going on around them.

While I don't remember any dramatic rescues, I know there have been people who went out of their way for me, when they didn't have to. There were people whose time and attention made such a difference at crucial moments in my life. Was I their 'lost sheep'?

I like to think of myself as the 'heroic rescuer.' Maybe I learned to be a rescuer by first being the one rescued. I've never thought of myself as a lost-sheep-found. But maybe that's what we all are – found-sheep who go on to be lost-sheep-finders.

Thank you, God, for the people who have looked out for me, whether I was aware of it or not.

"A rich man was told that the manager was wasting his master's money, so he called him in and said, 'Turn in a complete account of your handling of my property....' The servant said to himself, 'My master is going to dismiss me from my job. What shall I do...?' So he called in all the people who were in debt to his master. He asked the first one, 'How much do you owe my master?' 'One hundred barrels of olive oil,' he answered. 'Here is your account,' the manager told him; 'sit down and write fifty.' Then he asked another one, 'And you – how much do you owe...?' As a result the master of this dishonest manager praised him for doing such a shrewd thing; because the people of this world are much more shrewd in handling their affairs than the people who belong to the light."

Luke 16: 1-8

> "...the master of this dishonest manager praised him..."

A story with a twist

Jesus can't really be saying what I thing he's saying, can he? Perhaps the disciples felt the same way I do: first curiosity, slowly changing to surprise, then doubt, and finally incredulity. "Is he really praising this dishonest crook? No. Couldn't be... or could it?"

I think of my teenagers when I listen to this reading. They can look me straight in the eye and tell a preposterous story that just might be true. I'm always looking for clues that reveal whether what I'm hearing is true or whether they're just pulling my leg.

Maybe Jesus had the same mischievous sense of humour. By telling this story, he shocks me into thinking about how much shrewd intelligence is required to live by his values.

Lord, thank you for the gift of the unexpected.
Help me remember that my search for you is full of surprises.

"Whoever is faithful in small matters will be faithful in large ones; whoever is dishonest in small matters will be dishonest in large ones. If, then, you have not been faithful in handling worldly wealth, how can you be trusted with true wealth? And if you have not been faithful with what belongs to someone else, who will give you what belongs to you?

"No servant can be the slave of two masters; such a slave will hate one and love the other or will be loyal to one and despise the other. You cannot serve both God and money."

Then Jesus said to the Pharisees, "You are the ones who make yourselves look right in other people's sight, but God knows your hearts. For the things that are considered of great value by people are worth nothing in God's sight."   *Luke 16: 9-15*

> "Whoever is faithful in small matters…"

Small matters

Every Wednesday for the last 25 years, John, a man with Down's syndrome, has been taking out the garbage at L'Arche Daybreak. His faithfulness is something you can count on. Neighbours along the street check John's curb to see if it is a recycling day or not.

What inspires me is the wonderful spirit with which John does his job. As he drives the tractor, picking up garbage from several locations, he greets people with a ready wave and a cheery smile. "It's Mary!" he shouts, pointing at me. "Are you home tonight?"

John's worldly job is putting out the garbage, but his real vocation is being an ambassador of goodwill and a builder of community. Just knowing John gives me a clue of what Jesus means when he talks about 'small matters' and 'large ones.'

**Dear God, as I go about my daily tasks,
keep my heart centred on what really matters.**

S ome Sadducees, who say that people will not rise from death, came to Jesus [with a question.] … Jesus answered them, "The men and women of this age marry, but the men and women who are worthy to rise from death and live in the age to come will not then marry. They will be like angels and cannot die. They are the children of God, because they have risen from death. And Moses clearly proves that the dead are raised to life. In the passage about the burning bush he speaks of the Lord as 'the God of Abraham, the God of Isaac, and the God of Jacob.' He is the God of the living, not of the dead, for to him all are alive."

Luke 20: 27-40

"…to him all are alive."

All are alive

Several times each week I drive by the little cemetery located between the highway and St. Camilus Church in Farrellton, Quebec. At night, sometimes the more polished headstones reflect my car's headlights, and the light flickers back eerily. Other times, because the cemetery is also close to the river, there's a thick fog that doesn't burn off until mid-morning, and the headstones and the tops of the crosses poke out of the mist.

But the most notable thing about the cemetery is how it reminds me of the extraordinary meaning of the words, "to him all are alive." The more I think about this, the more extraordinary – and wonderful – it seems. In God's eyes, the dead live as much as I do.

Lord, I know that all people must die.
You teach me that all may live.

J esus said, "Things that make people fall into sin are bound to happen, but how terrible for the one who makes them happen! It would be better for him if a large millstone were tied around his neck and he were thrown into the sea than for him to cause one of these little ones to sin....

"If your brother sins, rebuke him, and if he repents, forgive him. If he sins against you seven times in one day, and each time he comes to you saying, 'I repent,' you must forgive him."

The apostles said, "Make our faith greater." The Lord answered, "If you had faith as big as a mustard seed, you could say to this mulberry tree, 'Pull yourself up by the roots and plant yourself in the sea!' and it would obey you."

Luke 17: 1-6

> "...and if he repents, forgive him."

Forgive me

Last week, I was having one of those days. The last straw came when one of my boys knocked over a lamp while jumping in the living room.

I lost my temper and sent him outside so I could cool off and assess the damage. A few minutes later he appeared at the door and said, "I'm sorry, Mom. But remember that Jesus says we must forgive seven times in one day? So will you forgive me, Mommy?"

His words made me stop dead in my tracks. Not only was he able to integrate Jesus' teaching into his life, but he forced me to take it seriously, too. We hugged and I said those magic words, "I forgive you." The rest of the day went much better!

**Lord, when I am slow to forgive,
help me to remember your words and deeds.**

I n the Temple Jesus found people selling cattle, sheep, and pigeons, and also the moneychangers sitting at their tables. So he made a whip from cords and drove all the animals out, both the sheep and the cattle; he overturned the tables of the moneychangers and scattered their coins; and he ordered those who sold the pigeons, "Take them out of here! Stop making my Father's house a marketplace!" His disciples remembered that the scripture says, "My devotion to your house, O God, burns in me like a fire."

The Jewish authorities asked, "What miracle can you perform to show us that you have the right to do this?" Jesus answered, "Tear down this Temple, and in three days I will build it again...." But the temple Jesus was speaking about was his body.

John 2: 13-22

> "My devotion... burns in me like a fire."

Today's temple

Recalling childhood pictures of 'Jesus, meek and mild,' I try to make sense of today's reading. Jesus must have been walking for days; maybe he was dusty and sweaty. And, faced with merchants in the Temple, he started a riot. If I'd been there, in that Temple, how would I have reacted? I don't know. But I wonder.

Today, what would Jesus think of our modern temples of consumerism? The ads telling us how designer clothes will make us happy, and that designer bodies make us lovable? Our working – day and night – to buy ever bigger houses that we fill with more things... while our children starve for meaning in their lives?

What would this angry, sweating prophet do in an upscale shopping centre during the Christmas rush? I don't know. But I wonder.

God, give me strength to cleanse the temples in my life.

Jesus was met by ten men suffering from a dreaded skin disease. They stood at a distance and shouted, "Jesus! Master! Have pity on us!" Jesus saw them and said to them, "Go and let the priests examine you."

On the way they were made clean. When one of them saw that he was healed, he came back, praising God in a loud voice. He threw himself to the ground at Jesus' feet and thanked him. The man was a Samaritan. Jesus spoke up, "There were ten who were healed; where are the other nine? Why is this foreigner the only one who came back to give thanks to God?" And Jesus said, "Get up and go; your faith has made you well."

Luke 17: 11-19

"Where are the other nine?"

Voices of praise

No one takes greater joy in or shows deeper reverence for the natural wonder of the earth than my friend, Max. His summer garden is an exuberant celebration of fruit and vegetables, flowers and herbs.

Not a day goes by without Max praising God for the sheer gift of creation. But Max is an agnostic philosopher. Like the Samaritan leper, he offers his gratitude as a 'foreigner.'

Some might question whether his praise even counts if he doesn't knowingly offer it to God. But I think God is pleased with whatever gratitude human beings offer. Perhaps we, who do believe, could learn something about gratitude from Max.

**God, thank you for all voices,
including those that are 'foreign,' that sing your praises.**

make a request to you on behalf of Onesimus, who is my own son in Christ....

I am sending him back to you now, and with him goes my heart. I would like to keep him here with me, while I am in prison for the gospel's sake, so that he could help me in your place. However, I do not want to force you to help me; rather, I would like for you to do it of your own free will. So I will not do anything unless you agree....

So, if you think of me as your partner, welcome him back just as you would welcome me. If he has done you any wrong or owes you anything, charge it to my account. Here, I will write this with my own hand: I, Paul, will pay you back.

Philemon 7-20

> "...welcome him back just as you would welcome me."

An open door

For about twenty years, strangers kept arriving on my aunt's doorstep in Northern Ireland. They were friends of my mother, travelling to Britain for holidays, graduate studies or various personal crises.

They had only one thing in common: they all came with my mother's recommendation. She had learned that they were going to a strange place. They needed some place to stay while they got themselves organized. So my mother sent them to her sister. And my aunt welcomed them as if they were family.

Like my mother, Paul was a letter writer. And he made a similar request of Philemon: to welcome an escaped slave, not as a criminal deserving punishment, but as a friend, a brother, a member of the family.

Forgive me, God, when I judge people by society's standards. Encourage me to value people just because you do.

"As it was in the time of Noah so shall it be in the days of the Son of Man....

"On that day someone who is on the roof of a house must not go down into the house to get any belongings; in the same way anyone who is out in the field must not go back to the house. Remember Lot's wife! Those who try to save their own life will lose it; those who lose their life will save it. On that night, there will be two people sleeping in the same bed: one will be taken away, the other will be left behind. Two women will be grinding meal together: one will be taken away, the other will be left behind."

Luke 17: 26-37

> "Those who lose their life will save it."

Faced with the choice

My old hockey coach used to say, "There's a million ways to lose a hockey game, and you've tried most of them." So many things happen so quickly that it's easy to lose focus: to forget that, in essence, hockey is a simple game.

In my life, I find myself running: to make meetings, phone calls and deadlines. How many ways there are to lose my focus – to lose my life trying to save it – only to wake up some morning and ask, "Where did my life go?"I know that these things must be done. But I have a choice. I can let go and realize what is important: my God, my family, my friends, the ones I tell myself I'm working for.

**Today, in the midst of my busyness,
I will try to remember who and what are important in my life.**

J esus told his disciples a parable: "In a certain town there was a judge who neither feared God nor respected people. And there was a widow who kept coming to him and pleading for her rights saying, 'Help me against my opponent!' For a long time the judge refused to act, but at last he said to himself, 'Even though I don't fear God or respect people, yet because of all the trouble this widow is giving me, I will see to it that she gets her rights. If I don't, she will keep on coming and finally wear me out!'"

And the Lord continued, "Now, will God not judge in favour of his own people who cry to him day and night for help…? But will the Son of Man find faith on earth when he comes?"

Luke 18: 1-8

> "…who kept coming to him and pleading for her rights…"

Beyond pride

I am certainly not like the woman in today's parable. I would feel embarrassed and humiliated to repeatedly ask someone for help when that person was both corrupt and not interested in helping me. I would rather do without than pay the price she was willing to pay.

But maybe there's something for me to learn here. After all, it's my pride that would be offended, and pride is not always a good guide for behaviour. Over the years I have learned that pride is often a hindrance in my relationship with God. I regularly struggle with acknowledging my own weakness, and my need for God's help.

Perhaps the lesson for me is not to focus on the woman's self-abasement, but to see her powerful determination.

**Lord, help me learn to be simple and direct
in expressing my need for you.**

Some of the disciples were talking about the Temple, how beautiful it looked with its fine stones. Jesus said, "All this you see – the time will come when not a single stone here will be left in its place; every one will be thrown down."

"Teacher," they asked, "when will this be?"

Jesus said, "Watch out; don't be fooled. Many men, claiming to speak for me, will come and say, 'I am he!' and, 'The time has come!' But don't follow them. Don't be afraid when you hear of wars and revolutions; such things must happen first, but they do not mean that the end is near…. Countries will fight each other; kingdoms will attack one another. There will be terrible earthquakes, famines and plagues everywhere; there will be strange and terrifying things coming from the sky."

Luke 21:5-11

"When will this be?"

Misery loves company

Sometimes I feel surrounded by misery. Human suffering is rampant: war, cruelty, loneliness, addiction, brokenness. Natural disasters are commonplace: earthquakes, famines, tornadoes, tsunamis, droughts. When I read the newspaper, I despair: Where is God in all this chaos? Who's minding the store? Where will it all end? When will it all work out?

Like the disciples, I get anxious. And like them, I hear Jesus' words of comfort: "Do not be afraid." Just as a young child finds refuge with her parents during a thunderstorm, I find refuge with Jesus in the midst of the world's sorrow. He sees the bigger picture; he knows where things are going. He keeps me company during the dark days.

**Lord, I don't know how to fix the problems I see in the world.
Help me have faith that all will be well.**

There was a blind man sitting by the road. When he heard the crowd passing by, he asked, "What is this?"

"Jesus of Nazareth is passing by," they told him. He cried out, "Jesus! Son of David! Have mercy on me!" The people in front scolded him and told him to be quiet. But he shouted even more loudly, "Son of David! Have mercy on me!" So Jesus stopped and ordered the blind man to be brought to him. When he came near, Jesus asked him, "What do you want me to do for you?"

"Sir," he answered, "I want to see again." Jesus said, "Then see! Your faith has made you well." At once he was able to see, and he followed Jesus, giving thanks to God.

Luke 18: 35-43

"I want to see again."

Faced with a choice

The busy pace of raising young children – while keeping up with the demands of work – can be overwhelming. There are days when I look at my to-do list and only see what is lacking. I'm blind to the small wonders and real accomplishments that are occurring every day. Is this really what I want from life?

The blind man's determination reminds me that I don't have to live this way. He could have easily let the crowd prevent him from crying out to Jesus. But he chose to speak up. And he knew what he wanted.

I can choose to continue to live in my self-imposed blindness, or I can do something to change how I see and live in my world.

Loving God, heal my blindness. I want to see.

Jesus went on into Jericho and was passing through. There was a chief tax collector there named Zacchaeus, who was rich. He was trying to see who Jesus was, but he was a little man and could not see Jesus because of the crowd. So he ran ahead of the crowd and climbed a sycamore tree to see Jesus, who was going to pass that way. When Jesus came to that place, he looked up and said to Zacchaeus, "Hurry down, Zacchaeus, because I must stay in your house today."

Zacchaeus hurried down and welcomed him with great joy. All the people who saw it started grumbling, "This man has gone as a guest to the home of a sinner…!" Zacchaeus stood up and said to the Lord, "Listen, sir! I will give half my belongings to the poor."

Luke 19: 1-10

> "…but he was a little man and could not see…"

No limits

As a young woman, Joyce contracted polio. She survived, but was told that she would never walk again. Yet walk she did… with three young children in her care, she says that she had no choice!

In the years that followed, with a weakened leg and caring for six children, Joyce signed up for a correspondence course. Years later, her children watched proudly as she received her Master's degree in Judaism and Christianity. Now retired, Joyce continues to lead prayer and scripture reflection groups in her community.

Zacchaeus' limitation – being little – meant that he had to be creative in order to reach his objective. Like Zacchaeus, Joyce went out on a limb to meet her goals. Like Zacchaeus, she continues to welcome Jesus in her home.

**Lord, when I feel discouraged and defeated,
help me find ways to move beyond my limitations.**

"There was once a man of high rank who was going to a country far away.... Before he left, he called his servants and gave them each a gold coin and told them, 'See what you can earn with this while I am gone....'

"The man came back... and ordered his servants to appear before him, in order to find out how much they had earned. The first one said, 'Sir, I have earned ten gold coins with the one you gave me.' 'Well done,' he said; 'you are a good servant!' ... Another servant said, 'Sir, here is your gold coin; I kept it hidden in a handkerchief. I was afraid of you, because you are a hard man....' He said to him, 'You bad servant! I will use your own words to condemn you!'"

Luke 19: 11-28

> "I kept it hidden in a handkerchief..."

No excuses

At first glance this story sounds like an endorsement for capitalism. It could even pass as an editorial from *The Economist*.

But when I look more closely, I see Jesus telling me to stop making excuses for not using the talents God has handed out so generously. The third servant said, "I was afraid of you, so I hid it." The excuses I come up with are: "No one really values what I have to offer"; or "I'm a humble person; I don't like to push myself and my abilities forward"; or "I don't think I'll try; I might fail."

God has given me everything I need to play a part in making this a better world. When will I stop making excuses?

Lord, help me to realize the gifts you have given me, and to share them with others.

Jesus came closer to [Jerusalem], and when he saw it, he wept over it, saying, "If you only knew today what is needed for peace! But now you cannot see it! The time will come when your enemies will surround you with barricades, blockade you, and close in on you from every side. They will completely destroy you and the people within your walls; not a single stone will they leave in its place, because you did not recognize the time when God came to save you!"

Luke 19: 41-44

"If you only knew today
what is needed for peace!"

Tears of compassion

I find it hard to watch Jesus cry over Jerusalem. The city has rejected his message of peace, and I can feel his pain.

I listen to his lament over Jerusalem. At first it sounds as though Jesus is condemning the city's inhabitants to unimaginable torment. But if I listen carefully, I hear not judgment, but compassion that suffers with the city's people.

Do I recognize that God weeps over us, too? We, who have rejected his message of peace by depleting the world's resources, developing nuclear weapons, and tolerating a widening gap between rich and poor nations? Can we open our hearts to feel the tears and compassion of a God who offers us, once again, the way to peace?

**Compassionate God, help me choose things
that make for peace rather than destruction.**

J esus went into the Temple and began to drive out the merchants, saying to them, "It is written in the Scriptures that God said, 'My Temple will be a house of prayer.' But you have turned it into a hideout for thieves!"

Every day Jesus taught in the Temple. The chief priests, the teachers of the Law, and the leaders of the people wanted to kill him, but they could not find a way to do it, because all the people kept listening to him, not wanting to miss a single word.

Luke 19: 45-48

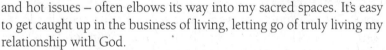

"My Temple will be a house of prayer."

Restoring the temple

I can see how things at the Temple got off the rails. These days, the world – with its pressures and crises, its new technologies and hot issues – often elbows its way into my sacred spaces. It's easy to get caught up in the business of living, letting go of truly living my relationship with God.

Once in a while, I have to take myself in hand and sort myself out, like Jesus sorted out the merchants. That's when I relegate my business to the place that it belongs. And I restore my house of prayer so that I can be there with God – and God alone.

Lord, help me remember to clean out my house of prayer when it gets cluttered.

S ome Sadducees said, "Teacher, Moses wrote this law for us: 'If a man dies and leaves a wife but no children, that man's brother must marry the widow....' Once there were seven brothers; the oldest got married and died without having children. Then the second one married the woman, and then the third. The same thing happened to all seven – they died without having children.... Now, on the day when the dead rise to life, whose wife will she be?"

Jesus answered, "The men and women of this age marry, but the men and women who are worthy to rise from death and live in the age to come will not then marry. They will be like angels and cannot die. They are the children of God, because they have risen from death.... He is the God of the living, not of the dead, for to him all are alive."   *Luke 20: 27-40*

> "…because they have risen from death."

Alive to God

Not long ago I took a ham casserole and some homemade pies to Marie's house. Her family was gathering from Britain and from Cape Breton to grieve the death of her husband.

For nine years Marie lovingly nursed David at home as he wasted away from early-onset Alzheimer's disease and cancer. She watched the brilliant scholar become a shadow of his former self. Her children forgot about normal social lives as they supported Marie in caring for their father. The daily strain of the family's struggle was intense. When David finally slipped away in his sleep, they were numb and bewildered.

Now, not only David is among the angels, but Marie and her children have also triumphed over death by their love and selfless care.

Compassionate God, help me to support those who grieve.

was glad when they said to me,
"Let us go to the Lord's house."
And now we are here,
standing inside the gates of Jerusalem!
Jerusalem is a city restored
in beautiful order and harmony.
This is where the tribes come,
the tribes of Israel,
to give thanks to the Lord
according to his command.
Here the kings of Israel
sat to judge their people.

Psalm 122: 1-5

> "...in beautiful order and harmony."

God's house

"Time to get ready for church," I said, as we chatted together in our garden. "Why do we have to go to church?" asked my then five-year-old son. "Well, it's where we get together to say thank you to God," I explained. "But we can say thank you to God here!" he promptly responded.

Now that my children are teenagers, I struggle even more to get them to go to church. How I wish they were "glad... to go to the Lord's house." At times I, too, struggle with going to church. Where I seek "beautiful order and harmony," often I experience ugly squabbles and division.

These days we're trying to strike a balance between giving thanks to God in our daily lives *and* in the house of the Lord.

**Lord, I often seek order and harmony. Help me to recognize
your presence in the messiness of everyday life.**

Jesus looked around and saw rich people dropping their gifts in the Temple treasury, and he also saw a very poor widow dropping in two little copper coins. He said, "I tell you that this poor widow put in more than all the others. For the others offered their gifts from what they had to spare of their riches; but she, poor as she is, gave all she had to live on."

Luke 21: 1-4

"...two little copper coins."

A challenge

Christmas is just over a month away. I've tried to trim down my gift-list to a reasonable length, but still it is long. And, as I do every year, I wonder: is all this really necessary? I never manage to avoid the last minute rush of obligatory gift-giving. Why do I fall into keeping watch on who gave what to whom and at what price?

At the heart of today's reading is the image of the widow's gift: 'two little copper coins.' I see her cradling them: humbly, secretly, in the palm of her hand. I hear them dropping: clink, clink. Small notes of graced giving amid the cacophony of commercialism. Those two coins challenge me to look at my attitude toward gift-giving this Christmas.

**Lord, help to give simply and sincerely,
straight from my heart.**

"**D**on't be afraid when you hear of wars and revolutions; such things must happen first, but they do not mean that the end is near."

[Jesus] went on to say, "Countries will fight each other; kingdoms will attack one another. There will be terrible earthquakes, famines and plagues everywhere; there will be strange and terrifying things coming from the sky. Before all these things take place, however, you will be arrested and persecuted; you will be handed over to be tried in synagogues and be put in prison; you will be brought before kings and rulers for my sake. This will be your chance to tell the Good News."

Luke 21:5-19

"…earthquakes, famines and plagues everywhere."

Not the end

The news, almost any evening, sounds like the fulfillment of today's reading. Earthquakes feel like a welcome break from the standard fare of wars, famines, plagues, and the worst pestilence of all, politics.

I wish my parents were still alive. They survived two world wars. During the second, Japanese forces came within 40 miles of their home. As missionaries, they survived epidemics of cholera, typhoid, smallpox, malaria….

I'd like to ask my parents if they think things are getting worse. I could use a reminder that today's wars, famines and plagues are not necessarily a harbinger of Armageddon. They've been around for a long time.

**Lord, when doubt and pessimism cloud my perspective,
send me a ray of light.**

Sing a new song to the Lord;
he has done wonderful things!
By his own power and holy strength
he has won the victory.
The Lord announced his victory;
he made his saving power known to the nations.
He kept his promise to the people of Israel
with loyalty and constant love for them.
All people everywhere have seen the victory of our God....
Roar, sea, and every creature in you;
sing, earth, and all who live on you!
Clap your hands, you rivers;
you hills, sing together with joy before the Lord,
because he comes to rule the earth.

Psalm 98: 1-3, 7-9

"Clap your hands, you rivers…"

Stewards of the earth

Every day the news is filled with terrible stories about our planet. The air and water are bad and getting worse. Animals and plants are dying off at unprecedented rates. The depleted land groans with exhaustion and the wind and rain show us their anger in devastating ways. Even the sun, source of light and warmth, has become dangerous to us.

We have done a terrible job at being God's stewards and the world is suffering.

I can imagine all Creation longing for God to take charge, and fire the selfish incompetents who have run things into the ground. As the psalmist says, even the rivers and hills would sing and clap with joy!

**Lord, give me the strength
to serve your world as a good steward.**

"**W**hen you see Jerusalem surrounded by armies, then you will know that it will soon be destroyed. Then those who are in Judea must run away to the hills; those who are in the city must leave, and those who are out in the country must not go into the city. For those will be 'The Days of Punishment....' How terrible it will be in those days for women who are pregnant and for mothers with little babies.... Some will be killed by the sword, and others will be taken as prisoners to all countries; and the heathen will trample over Jerusalem until their time is up....

"Then the Son of Man will appear.... When these things begin to happen, stand up and raise your heads, because your salvation is near."

Luke 21: 20-28

> "How terrible it will be in those days…"

Time of salvation

Janet dropped by to visit and we talked easily until I turned on the TV with news of the latest horrors. Suddenly she gave a startled cry. Her eyes glazed over and I knew that her soul had left the room.

Later she said, "I've spent a lot of time in therapy, talking about what happened to me when I was a child. But when I hear about women and young girls being raped, I go right back into that awful place with my grandfather."

Likely those men will never be held accountable. They may forget, but the women never will. I can only hope that, for those women and for Janet, the time of salvation will bring healing.

Lord, be with the victims of the 'days of punishment.'
Be their salvation.

J esus told this parable: "Think of the fig tree and all the other trees. When you see their leaves beginning to appear, you know that summer is near. In the same way, when you see these things happening, you will know that the kingdom of God is about to come.

"Remember that all these things will take place before the people now living have all died. Heaven and earth will pass away, but my words will never pass away."

Luke 21: 29-33

"…my words will never pass away."

Steadfast love

After watching the nightly news, reading the daily newspaper, and listening to radio updates on world events, I often feel disheartened. At every turn I am faced with wars and civil unrest, famines, pestilence and disease, economic downturns and rising unemployment. I wonder how much more suffering we – both at home and around the world – can handle before we reach our breaking point.

Today's reading reminds me that in the midst of the trials we experience in our lives, God promises to be with us. I don't face these challenges on my own. God invites me to place my burdens – whatever I may be carrying – in his hands.

Now, when I feel the worries of the day piling up inside of me, I turn to God and seek comfort in his steadfast love.

**Lord, help me to remember that your love,
like your words, will last forever.**

"**B**e careful not to let yourselves become occupied with too much feasting and drinking and with the worries of this life, or that Day may suddenly catch you like a trap. For it will come upon all people everywhere on earth. Be on watch and pray always that you will have the strength to go safely through all those things that will happen and to stand before the Son of Man." Jesus spent those days teaching in the Temple, and when evening came, he would go out and spend the night on the Mount of Olives. Early each morning all the people went to the Temple to listen to him.

Luke 21: 34-36

> "Be on watch and pray always…"

Prayerful support

When friends ask, "Would you like another drink?" I find it hard to say, "No." As the adult child of an alcoholic, I have struggled with alcohol all my life. Beer commercials, peer pressure and my own family history make it very difficult to resist the temptation to consume too much. And yet Jesus warns me that all excess is like a trap.

I would like to recover a healthy attitude toward both food and drink, to put them in their proper place, to see their essential goodness.

Once again, prayer and the cultivation of an inner life seem the best defence against being consumed by a culture of consumption. Jesus went away to spend the night praying on the Mount of Olives. I must pray, too.

**Lord, give me the strength to resist destructive influences
and to focus on what is life-giving.**

"The coming of the Son of Man will be like what happened in the time of Noah. In the days before the flood people ate and drank, men and women married, up to the very day Noah went into the boat; yet they did not realize what was happening until the flood came and swept them all away. That is how it will be when the Son of Man comes…. Watch out, then, because you do not know what day your Lord will come. If the owner of a house knew the time when the thief would come, you can be sure that he would stay awake and not let the thief break into his house. So then, you also must always be ready, because the Son of Man will come at an hour when you are not expecting him."

Matthew 24: 37-44

"…you also must always be ready…"

Always ready

I have a friend who always has her Christmas fruitcake made by Hallowe'en, allowing it to soak in brandy for weeks. Her readiness sends me into a panic: will I ever be ready for Christmas?

Is that what it means to 'be ready'? To have everything under control? To be ahead of the countdown of shopping days left until Christmas?

The material preparations for Christmas can be all-consuming. I'm told that if I plan well I'll be able to create an almost perfect Christmas. Yet Jesus is talking about being ready for something that comes unexpectedly, "like a thief in the night." For that I need an interior readiness; I need to be present in the moment – my heart and mind open to see and respond to the needs of others.

**Lord, in these days leading up to Christmas,
help me prepare my heart to welcome the unexpected.**

W hen Jesus entered Capernaum, a Roman officer met him and begged for help: "Sir, my servant is sick in bed at home, unable to move and suffering terribly."

"I will go and make him well," Jesus said.

"Oh no, sir," answered the officer. "I do not deserve to have you come into my house. Just give the order, and my servant will get well…."

When Jesus heard this, he was surprised and said to the people following him, "I tell you, I have never found anyone in Israel with faith like this…." Then Jesus said to the officer, "Go home, and what you believe will be done for you."

And the officer's servant was healed that very moment.

Matthew 8: 5-13

"…a Roman officer met him…"

Beyond 'us and them'

We like to think of ourselves as part of the 'in-crowd,' to believe we are the 'chosen ones.' And here, Jesus is approached by the outsider. And what an outsider! The Roman centurion: agent of the force of occupation. What easier target?

Yet Jesus responds to the person he meets. And he points out that membership is not enough. Faith is about the individual.

As our world becomes smaller, as we live in communities rife with an 'us/them' attitude, I need to follow Jesus' path of reaching out to the person in front of me… not the 'club' to which they belong. Jesus shows me how to respond with compassion – breaking free from the endless circle of self-interest and violence.

**God, help me to see people for who they are,
and to focus on our sameness and not our differences.**

A s Jesus walked along the shore of Lake Galilee, he saw two brothers who were fishermen, Simon (called Peter) and his brother Andrew, catching fish in the lake with a net. Jesus said to them, "Come with me, and I will teach you to catch people." At once they left their nets and went with him. He went on and saw two other brothers, James and John, the sons of Zebedee. They were in their boat with their father Zebedee, getting their nets ready. Jesus called them, and at once they left the boat and their father, and went with him.

Matthew 4: 18-22

"...they left their nets and went with him."

Open to the call

How did the father of James and John feel? Did he take comfort in knowing his boys were following the call they heard in their hearts? Was he worried about what it might cost them? The rejection, the lack of security, the possibility of death?

Zebedee must have raised his sons to be open to God's call, to be faithful to whatever God asked. In the end, he let them go.

I, too, watch as my children struggle to find their way. I encourage them to ask the deeper questions, to be compassionate, to speak up for those who can't defend themselves. I know that they'll be hurt along the way. And I try to prepare myself for the day they leave to follow their dreams.

**Lord, guide me as I help my children
to live with a heart open to your call.**

L arge crowds came to Jesus, bringing with them the lame, the blind, the crippled, the dumb, and many other sick people, whom they placed at Jesus' feet; and he healed them…. Jesus said to his disciples, "I feel sorry for these people, because they have been with me for three days and now have nothing to eat. I don't want to send them away without feeding them." The disciples asked, "Where will we find enough food in this desert to feed this crowd?"

"How much bread do you have?" Jesus asked. "Seven loaves," they answered, "and a few small fish…." Then Jesus took the seven loaves and the fish, gave thanks to God, broke them, and gave them to the disciples; and the disciples gave them to the people. They all ate and had enough.

Matthew 15: 29-37

> "Jesus took the seven loaves and the fish…"

A shared miracle

Cooking in a l'Arche household, I'm often faced with the unpredictability of how many people to expect for dinner and what food will be on hand. Recently, I helped an assistant who was cooking for the first time. "This is what we call 'creative cooking,'" I explained, while scrounging in the fridge for something that could feed twelve people. As we examined the eight chicken legs, two bunches of broccoli and an assortment of leftovers, I added, "It also takes a miracle!" She thought I was joking.

As we began serving the plates, I cut a few slices off some of the drumsticks to make the meat go farther. "The miracle starts with people sharing," I said with a laugh. Much to our surprise, as the plates were passed around, everybody had enough to eat.

Jesus, help me to trust that what you have given me to work with is enough.

A day is coming when the people
will sing this song in the land of Judah:
Our city is strong!
God himself defends its walls!
Open the city gates and let the faithful nation enter,
the nation whose people do what is right.
You, Lord, give perfect peace
to those who keep their purpose firm
and put their trust in you....
He has humbled those who were proud;
he destroyed the strong city they lived in,
and sent its walls crashing into the dust.
Those who were oppressed walk over it now
and trample it under their feet.

Isaiah 26: 1-6

> "...whose people do what is right."

On behalf of the poor

I do, in fact, live on the steep banks of a 'strong city': the citadel
in Quebec City. These days, the poor are being squeezed out of my
neighbourhood. A rich couple bought a house to use as a ski chalet
for two weeks each year; the tenants were all evicted.

Another neighbour was evicted because the landlord decided
he no longer wanted dogs in his building. A fragile person, she was
pushed to the limit. She got into a fight with him and was taken off
to prison yesterday.

My friend, who knows this neighbour, sent a message to her in
prison and went to court to testify on her behalf. Perhaps through her
action, people will "do what is right," and God's peace will reign.

**Give me the courage to speak on behalf of your people,
the poorest among us.**

A s Jesus walked along, two blind men started following him. "Have mercy on us, Son of David!" they shouted.

When Jesus had gone indoors, the two blind men came to him, and he asked them, "Do you believe that I can heal you?"

"Yes, sir!" they answered.

Then Jesus touched their eyes and said, "Let it happen, then, just as you believe!"– and their sight was restored. Jesus spoke sternly to them, "Don't tell this to anyone!"

But they left and spread the news about Jesus all over that part of the country.

Matthew 9: 27-31

> "Let it happen, then, just as you believe!"

Enthusiastic disobedience

Today's reading reminds me of when my children were very young and wanted something – really badly. Like the two blind men, they would shout for what they wanted, totally oblivious to the public nature of their surroundings. They didn't care about that; all they knew was what they wanted.

When Jesus finally reached his destination, the blind men rushed up and stood expectantly in front of him. Jesus gave them what they wanted and then told them – sternly, mind you – not to tell anyone. They agreed, but as soon as they left, promptly went and told, not just their family or friends, but everyone they met!

I'm sure Jesus wasn't angry. After all, what parent hasn't smiled at the enthusiastic disobedience of their children, and loved them anyway.

Lord, you give me what I need and overlook my weaknesses.
Help me do the same for others.

As Jesus saw the crowds, his heart was filled with pity…. "The harvest is large, but there are few workers to gather it in. Pray to the owner that he will send out workers to gather in his harvest."

Jesus called his twelve disciples together and gave them authority to drive out evil spirits and to heal every disease and every sickness. They were sent out with the following instructions: "Do not go to any Gentile territory or any Samaritan towns. Instead, you are to go to the lost sheep of the people of Israel. Go and preach, 'The Kingdom of heaven is near!' Heal the sick, bring the dead back to life, heal those who suffer from dreaded skin diseases, and drive out demons. You have received without paying, so give without being paid."

Matthew 9: 35 – 10: 8

"You have received without paying…"

Christmas giving

For several weeks now, I've seen and heard the advertisements. If my family and I are to have the merriest Christmas ever, then I'd better get out there and shop! How our commercial culture has turned the Christmas feast into a beguiling celebration of what money can buy!

Matthew's story releases the Christmas story from its commercial captivity. We hear Jesus reminding the disciples to reach out to others: by sharing of themselves.

In the midst of this Christmas-buying bonanza, what is my gift that I can share with others? A fun day spent with my children, with no distracting errands to run; a couple of hours babysitting for the couple next door; a smile of reassurance to a worried student I pass in the hallway.

God, help me to appreciate your generosity. Grant me the courage and the creativity to share my gifts with others.

Whenjohn saw many Pharisees and Sadducees coming to him to be baptized, he said to them, "You snakes – who told you that you could escape from the punishment God is about to send? Do those things that will show that you have turned from your sins. And don't think you can escape punishment by saying that Abraham is your ancestor. I tell you that God can take these rocks and make descendants for Abraham! The axe is ready to cut down the trees at the roots; every tree that does not bear good fruit will be cut down and thrown in the fire. I baptize you with water to show that you have repented, but the one who will come after me will baptize you with the Holy Spirit and fire. He is much greater than I am."

Matthew 3: 1-12

"He is much greater than I am."

Prophet on the edges

John the Baptist is one of my favourite characters in the Bible: the hairy prophet who eats health food and lives on the fringes. We might sugar-coat Jesus, but John the Baptist always stays smelly and real!

Outside my local high school there is a stretch of sidewalk the students call Smokers' Corner – a real little community! There are a lot of hairy, unkempt teenagers there, some John the Baptists, I'm sure.

These kids are a good antidote for the Pharisee and the Sadducee in me: the one who wants to judge by appearances, the one who pushes the letter of the law. I fear that in my self-righteousness, I miss a lot of the prophets who live near me, but on the fringes.

**Lord, give me loving eyes and ears
to see and hear your presence in my world.**

S ome men came carrying a paralyzed man on a bed, and they tried to carry him into the house and put him in front of Jesus. Because of the crowd, however, they could find no way to take him in. So they carried him up on the roof, made an opening in the tiles, and let him down on his bed into the middle of the group in front of Jesus. When Jesus saw how much faith they had, he said to the man, "Your sins are forgiven, my friend…. I tell you, get up, pick up your bed, and go home!"

At once the man got up in front of them all, took the bed he had been lying on, and went home, praising God. They were all completely amazed! "What marvellous things we have seen today!"

Luke 5: 17-26

> "Some men came carrying a paralyzed man…"

A helping hand

Who carried the paralyzed man to Jesus for healing? Relatives? Neighbours? People from the old workplace? Did the man or woman who came up with the idea have to rope the others in? Whoever they were, it would have been easy to give up when they ran into the crowd blocking their way into the house. If they had, the sick person would never have reached Jesus.

When someone I know is paralyzed with grief, misfortune or fear, I realize that, with persistence and inventiveness, I can help in their healing process. It's sobering to realize that both the Lord, and the person in need, may depend on me to find a way around the practical and emotional obstacles that stand in the way of healing.

**Lord, give me the courage and imagination
to carry those who lack the power to help themselves.**

"What do you think a man does who has one hundred sheep and one of them gets lost? He will leave the other ninety-nine grazing on the hillside and go and look for the lost sheep. When he finds it, I tell you, he feels far happier over this one sheep than over the ninety-nine that did not get lost. In just the same way your Father in heaven does not want any of these little ones to be lost."

Matthew 18: 12-14

"...go and look for the lost sheep."

A God who cares

We're so used to the somewhat sentimental image of the Good Shepherd that it's easy to overlook the passionate nature of God's love for us. We may trust God's love, but this parable tells us of God's commitment to us – a commitment that is ever active and ever faithful.

There is a sense of relief and joy when the shepherd finds the sheep that has wandered away. Also, there's the knowledge that the lost sheep will be cared for tenderly, not blamed and scolded. God's love accepts us, cherishes us, cares for all our needs. It rejoices when we return to his friendship.

Knowing this God of love, we in turn are asked to seek out those who hunger and thirst, and care for them in like manner.

Lord, help me to stay near to you, but if I stray from you, look for me quickly.

The angel came to Mary.... Mary was deeply troubled by the angel's message, and she wondered what his words meant. The angel said to her, "Don't be afraid, Mary; God has been gracious to you. You will become pregnant and give birth to a son, and you will name him Jesus...."

Mary said to the angel, "I am a virgin. How, then, can this be?" The angel answered, "The Holy Spirit will come on you, and God's power will rest upon you. For this reason the holy child will be called the Son of God.... Remember your relative Elizabeth. It is said that she cannot have children, but she herself is now six months pregnant.... There is nothing that God cannot do."

"I am the Lord's servant," said Mary; "may it happen to me as you have said."

Luke 1: 26-38

> "...may it happen to me as you have said."

Love made real

I always knew my mother shared something special with Mary. She, too, went into labour on Christmas Eve, and gave birth to a baby boy during the middle of the night – me! Sometimes I've wondered, when the doctor told her she was pregnant, and due around Christmas, did she whisper, "May it happen to me as you have said"?

Later I learned that this mystery was not unique to Mary and my mother. In the fourteenth century, Meister Eckhart wrote, "What matters *now* is not that Christ was born of Mary, but that Christ longs to be born in you – and is born with each compassionate deed." So, with today's reading, I whisper to myself, "May it happen to me as you have said."

**Gracious God, as Christmas approaches,
make my own life a womb in which your love may become flesh.**

" I assure you that John the Baptist is greater than anyone who has ever lived. But the one who is least in the kingdom of heaven is greater than John. From the time John preached his message until this very day the kingdom of heaven has suffered violent attacks, and violent men try to seize it. Until the time of John all the prophets and the Law of Moses spoke about the kingdom; and if you are willing to believe their message, John is Elijah, whose coming was predicted. Listen, then, if you have ears!"

Matthew 11: 11-15

> "Listen, then, if you have ears!"

Prepared to listen

My young nephews and nieces have a remarkable capacity to actually switch their ears on and off. Their mother's voice, combined with, "Could I ask you…" seem to trigger the 'off' switch, while any words related to food appear to work, albeit slowly, the 'on' switch.

They are not alone. Over the years, I too have mastered the technique, with somewhat different triggers. Of course, I find it more rewarding to point out this weakness in others.

I often interrupt people with a "Yes, but…" long before they have even finished a thought. My arrogance convinces me that I know what they are going to say, so why should I wait? Jesus, as ever, confounds this selfish arrogance with words that comfort as much as they challenge.

**God, help me to slow down
and really reflect on what I hear today.**

The holy God of Israel,
the Lord who saves you, says:
"I am the Lord your God,
the one who wants to teach you for your own good
and direct you in the way you should go.
If only you had listened to my commands!
Then blessings would have flowed for you
like a stream that never goes dry.
Victory would have come to you
like the waves that roll on the shore.
Your descendants would be as numerous as grains of sand,
and I would have made sure they were never destroyed."

Isaiah 48: 17-19

"If only you had listened…"

A wake-up call

"If you're too tired to drive home after the party, sleep over there, okay?" Jeremy rolled his eyes. "Sure, Dad," he said. But after the party, Jeremy decided he was fine to drive. Five minutes from home, he must have dozed off. He hit a pole and totalled the car, but he walked away with just a few scratches.

Upon arriving at the scene, his dad hugged him fiercely. He was thinking, "If only he had listened to me!" Aloud he said, "I'm so glad you're okay."

More things were shattered that early morning than the family car. Jeremy and his dad were jolted into a new, deeper relationship – one where "I'm sorry" and "I love you" became the cornerstones of mutual respect and caring.

Lord, my mistakes can bring me closer to you. Help me learn from them as I keep trying to listen to your commands.

The disciples asked Jesus, "Why do the teachers of the Law say that Elijah has to come first?"

"Elijah is indeed coming first," answered Jesus, "and he will get everything ready. But I tell you that Elijah has already come and people did not recognize him, but treated him just as they pleased. In the same way they will also mistreat the Son of Man."

Then the disciples understood that he was talking to them about John the Baptist.

Matthew 17: 10-13

"…and people did not recognize him…"

Recognizing God

Stuck in snarled, snow-bound traffic, I couldn't understand why the driver behind kept beeping at me in the dark. I was already late for the Christmas festivities at home, so his persistent honking was the last straw. I rolled down my window, let him have it and ploughed on.

Later that evening, one of our guests arrived at our door. "So much for goodwill toward all!" he laughed. "I tried beeping at you to say hello and you practically took my head off!" The darkness had obscured his face but it had revealed my nastiness. Thankfully he was more forgiving than I was.

Why do I easily unleash my anger on a stranger, instead of taking the time to recognize the humanity of each person I meet?

God, help me to treat all those I meet today with respect.

W hen John the Baptist heard about the things that Christ was doing, he sent some of his disciples to him. "Tell us," they asked Jesus, "are you the one John said was going to come, or should we expect someone else?"

Jesus answered, "Go back and tell John what you are hearing and seeing: the blind can see, the lame can walk, those who suffer from dreaded skin diseases are made clean, the deaf hear, the dead are brought back to life, and the Good News is preached to the poor. How happy are those who have no doubts about me!"

Matthew 11: 2-11

"…should we expect someone else?"

First-hand witness

What a wonderful opportunity John's disciples had! They had witnessed, first-hand, the wonders of Jesus, yet they still doubted that Jesus was the messiah that John had described.

If I were in the shoes of one of John's disciples, how would I react? How do I react today when I see the wonders of God in my own life – for example, when a friend with a debilitating injury defies all odds and lives? Do I put the miraculous down to coincidence, or as the result of technology or logical reasoning?

Most of the time, like John's disciples, I do not recognize or give credit to God's awesome power even when the evidence of its existence is right in front of me.

Lord, help me to see your hand at work in my world, and to give thanks for your great love.

The chief priests and the elders asked, "What right do you have to do these things? Who gave you such right?"

Jesus answered, "I will ask you just one question, and if you give me an answer, I will tell you what right I have to do these things. Where did John's right to baptize come from: was it from God or from human beings?"

They started to argue among themselves, "What shall we say? If we answer, 'From God,' he will say to us, 'Why, then, did you not believe John?' But if we say, 'From human beings,' we are afraid of what the people might do, because they are all convinced that John was a prophet." So they answered Jesus, "We don't know."

Matthew 21: 23-27

> "What right do you have to do these things?"

Living the questions

The 'I don't know' answer, when used to evade an issue, really angers me. I imagine Jesus must feel some of that same frustration in dealing with the elders. They choose to argue, to second-guess and finally to turn their backs on the opportunity his question presents to them.

Often I have demanded that Jesus provide quick answers to difficult questions in my own life. But he usually declines to do the work for me! Instead he challenges me to struggle honestly with the questions – and my own feelings, thoughts, motivations and actions. In the struggle I find life and growth. God forbid that I should simply give up rather than try to discover an answer – always *for* myself, but never *by* myself.

**I have so many questions, Lord. Stay with me
as I try to live the questions and grow into the answers.**

"There was once a man who had two sons. He went to the older one and said, 'Son, go and work in the vineyard today.' 'I don't want to,' he answered, but later he changed his mind and went. Then the father went to the other son and said the same thing. 'Yes, sir,' he answered, but he did not go. Which one of the two did what his father wanted...?

"I tell you: the tax collectors and the prostitutes are going into the kingdom of God ahead of you. For John the Baptist came... showing you the right path to take, and you would not believe him; but the tax collectors and the prostitutes believed him. Even when you saw this, you did not later change your minds and believe him."

Matthew 21: 28-32

> "I don't want to..."

Good choices

As a parent of five children, including three teens, I can relate to how the father in today's reading must have felt. There have been many times when my own children have answered, "I don't want to," or have not completed assigned chores.

But then they do something that makes up for it all. The other day, my husband and I left two of our children home alone, watching TV. While we were gone, they cleaned the house from top to bottom: tidying, vacuuming and even scrubbing the toilets!

As a parent I try to encourage the good in my children rather than focus on the bad. I pray that they continue on the right path to the kingdom of God.

**O Lord, grant that my children follow you,
and give me strength to pick them up when they fall.**

I am listening to what the Lord God is saying;
he promises peace to us, his own people....
Love and faithfulness will meet;
righteousness and peace will embrace.
Human loyalty will reach up from the earth,
and God's righteousness will look down from heaven.
The Lord will make us prosperous,
and our land will produce rich harvests.
Righteousness will go before the Lord
and prepare the path for him.

Psalm 85: 8-14

"...righteousness and peace will embrace."

Love and faithfulness

I have a notebook in which I record various quotes and comments. It's an eclectic, wide-ranging collection of sayings from novelists, playwrights, composers, theologians and the occasional poet. When this leather-bound notebook is full, I replace the pages and keep the written sheets in a box.

Leafing through my notebook, I come across a biblical quotation – from today's psalm. I have always been mesmerized by the idea that when God and humankind reach toward one another – when loyalty and righteousness combine – we will meet.

I guess I have some justice work to do!

**O God, I long for the moment
when love and faithfulness will meet.**

J esus began to speak to the crowds: "When you went out to John in the desert, what did you expect to see? A blade of grass bending in the wind? A man dressed up in fancy clothes? ... A prophet? Yes indeed, but you saw much more than a prophet.... John is greater than anyone who has ever lived. But the one who is least in the kingdom of God is greater than John."

All the people heard him; they and especially the tax collectors were the ones who had obeyed God's righteous demands and had been baptized by John. But the Pharisees and the teachers of the Law rejected God's purpose for themselves and refused to be baptized by John.

Luke 7: 24-30

"All the people heard him..."

Faced with a choice

The people who listened to John all heard the same message. Why did some respond to his challenge, while others rejected it and turned away?

These days, we all hear the same news reports: thousands of people dying from disease, from hunger, from tribal violence. And closer to home: the reports of thousands of hungry, homeless and lonely in our towns and cities. Why do some people respond and help, and some turn away?

In today's reading, I'm struck by the fact that baptism *follows* the choice to obey "God's righteous demands." I was baptized as a baby; I now must choose – every day – to respond to God's call to help those who are in need. Only then will my baptism mean anything.

God, may I hear your call to help others, and respond.

This is the list of the ancestors of Jesus Christ…. From Abraham to King David: Abraham, Isaac, Jacob, Judah and his brothers; then Perez and Zerah (their mother was Tamar), Hezron, Ram, Amminadab, Nahshon, Salmon, Boaz (his mother was Rahab), Obed (his mother was Ruth), Jesse, and King David.

From David to the exile in Babylon: David, Solomon (his mother was the woman who had been Uriah's wife), Rehoboam, Abijah, Asa, Jehoshaphat, Jehoram, Uzziah, Jotham, Ahaz, Hezekiah, Manasseh, Amon, Josiah, and Jehoiachin and his brothers.

From the time after the exile in Babylon to the birth of Jesus: Jehoiachin, Shealtiel, Zerubbabel, Abiud, Eliakim, Azor, Zadok, Achim, Eliud, Eleazar, Matthan, Jacob, and Joseph, who married Mary, the mother of Jesus, who was called the Messiah.

So then, there were fourteen generations from Abraham to David, and fourteen from David to the exile in Babylon, and fourteen from then to the birth of the Messiah.   *Matthew 1: 1-17*

> "This is the list of the ancestors of Jesus Christ…"

Playing with numbers

In Douglas Adams' series, *The Hitchhiker's Guide to the Galaxy*, a super-computer spent 7.5 million years discovering the ultimate answer to life, the universe, and everything. It came up with 42 – by some coincidence, the number of generations Matthew cited between Abraham and Jesus.

Amazingly, in a culture where only the male parent mattered, Matthew specifically named five women. Just as amazingly, in a culture dedicated to racial purity, three of those women were not Jewish.

When I read the Nativity story, I tend to skip over the genealogy. I shouldn't. It still can surprise me.

**God, even in the most familiar things,
you unveil unexpected insights. Thank you.**

The Lord says, "The time is coming when I will choose as king a righteous descendant of David. That king will rule wisely and do what is right and just throughout the land. When he is king, the people of Judah will be safe, and the people of Israel will live in peace. He will be called 'The Lord Our Salvation.'

"The time is coming," says the Lord, "when people will no longer swear by me as the living God who brought the people of Israel out of the land of Egypt. Instead, they will swear by me as the living God who brought the people of Israel... out of all the other countries where I had scattered them. Then they will live in their own land."

Jeremiah 23: 5-8

> "That king will rule wisely..."

Wise leadership

We live in unsettled and worrying times. The consequences of our decisions over the last 50 years are affecting us more powerfully all the time. The air is bad, and so is the water. The poor are getting poorer, and the world seems an angrier and more dangerous place.

Like many people, I often feel paralyzed by the size of the problems we face. How can we clean up this mess we've made? Who will give us the wise leadership we need? Our leaders seem small and lacking in vision, focusing only on their own self-interest, while ignoring the truly important.

This must be how the Israelites felt, and why God's promise to them was so inspiring. Will we find the same reassurance? Where is the righteous 'king' we need?

**Lord, give your people wisdom
so that we can make this world a good home for all.**

Mary was engaged to Joseph, but before they were married, she found out that she was going to have a baby by the Holy Spirit. Joseph was a man who always did what was right, but he did not want to disgrace Mary publicly; so he made plans to break the engagement privately.... An angel of the Lord appeared to him in a dream and said, "Joseph, descendant of David, do not be afraid to take Mary to be your wife. For it is by the Holy Spirit that she has conceived. She will have a son, and you will name him Jesus – because he will save his people from their sins...."

So when Joseph woke up, he married Mary, as the angel of the Lord had told him to.

Matthew 1: 18-24

"Joseph was a man who always did what was right..."

Doing what is right

During the war, my mother had a friend whose husband was over-sees. Let's call him 'Henry.'

Henry was gone five years. Five long years. His wife was pregnant when he left, and had their child while he was away. And, in his absence, another. She waited in fear on the day Henry returned.

The taxi pulled up, the soldier emerged and saw, for the first time, his son. As he embraced his wife, a second, younger child, who had been shown pictures of Henry, rushed forward crying, "Daddy!" Henry picked the child up, embraced his wife and never said a word. Never. No recriminations. No "How could you?" Just love.

I think Joseph would have liked Henry.

**God of love, give me the wisdom to do what is right,
and to do it with love.**

The Lord sent another message to Ahaz: "Ask the Lord your God to give you a sign. It can be from deep in the world of the dead or from high up in heaven."

Ahaz answered, "I will not ask for a sign. I refuse to put the Lord to the test."

To that Isaiah replied, "Listen, now, descendants of King David. It's bad enough for you to wear out the patience of people – do you have to wear out God's patience too? Well then, the Lord himself will give you a sign: a young woman who is pregnant will have a son and will name him 'Immanuel.'"

Isaiah 7: 10-14

"...to give you a sign."

Trust in God

Enemies were preparing to attack and King Ahaz was terrified. "Trust me," God said. "If you find trust hard, just ask me for a sign of my power and I'll give it to you." But Ahaz was like me: afraid that trusting in God would call for heroism, and heaven knows he was no hero, and neither am I.

But that's the point. God can carry me to heroic heights of courage and depths of compassion. It seems to me that this is the sign of Immanuel: that God's power and love are with me whenever I ask for them.

Over these last hectic days before Christmas, I will trust that God will help me to be courageous or compassionate when I am needed to be.

Lord, teach me to trust in your power.
Today I ask for a sign of your power and love.

M y lover speaks to me.
　 Come then, my love;
　 my darling, come with me.
The winter is over; the rains have stopped;
in the countryside the flowers are in bloom.
This is the time for singing;
the song of doves is heard in the fields....
The air is fragrant with blossoming vines.
Come then, my love;
my darling, come with me.
You are like a dove that hides
in the crevice of a rock.
Let me see your lovely face
and hear your enchanting voice.

Song of Songs 2: 8-14

"Come then, my love…"

Blessed by love

Last summer, my wife and I marked our twenty-fifth wedding anniversary. And I have to admit the inescapable: my days as a gazelle are long over, and my days of running over the mountains are also behind me. I don't think my knees could take it!

But, together we have seen more than twenty-five winters come and go. We have marked blooming flowers sending their fragrance into the air, and birds singing their songs of renewal. Children have been born, grown into young adulthood, and even begun their own days as gazelles.

But the twenty-five years seem like twenty-five minutes. And, in our lives, this is still the time for singing, the time to whisper, "Come then, my love."

Lord, thank you for the blessings of love you have given me.

Mary said, "My heart praises the Lord; my soul is glad because of God my Saviour, for he has remembered me, his lowly servant! From now on all people will call me happy, because of the great things the Mighty God has done for me. His name is holy; from one generation to another he shows mercy to those who honour him. He has stretched out his mighty arm and scattered the proud with all their plans. He has brought down mighty kings from their thrones, and lifted up the lowly. He has filled the hungry with good things, and sent the rich away with empty hands. He has kept the promise he made to our ancestors, and has come to the help of his servant Israel."

Luke 1: 46-56

"My soul is glad because of God my Saviour…"

A gift to the world

How hard it must have been for Mary to believe that she was the one. A woman of low estate, she has reason to cry, "My heart praises the Lord." Sometimes it is difficult to believe that what we have to offer – who we are – is special. That we bring something to the world, to other people. That it is through me, who I am and what I do that the light of God shines, the love of God touches and heals others. That I bring something special… me!

In the dark times of life, we all need someone to whom we can turn. I must remember that my soul, too, can praise the Lord; that I can be that someone who brings God into another person's life.

**Dear God, let me always be aware of
what I have to offer and give it.**

The time came for Elizabeth to have her baby, and she gave birth to a son. Her neighbours and relatives heard how wonderfully good the Lord had been to her, and they all rejoiced with her.

When the baby was a week old, they came to circumcise him, and they were going to name him Zechariah, after his father. But his mother said, "No! His name is to be John."

They said to her, "But you don't have any relative with that name!" Then they made signs to his father, asking him what name he would like the boy to have.

Zechariah asked for a writing pad and wrote, "His name is John." How surprised they all were! At that moment Zechariah was able to speak again, and he started praising God.

Luke 1: 57-66

"Zechariah was able to speak again..."

Continuous love

An elderly lady once told me that the most important thing she learned from raising her children was the meaning of continuity. "I used to think continuity meant doing everything the way we did when I was growing up. I grew up in a different language, culture and era. I was blind to the fact that continuity means continuing to love and to trust who your child is becoming." At some point, this woman was able to 'see' clearly – to love and accept her children for who they are.

Zechariah, deeply entrenched in his family and religious traditions, wasn't able to accept God's plans. Zechariah was literally speechless until he made the decision to break with tradition and trust God's plans for his son.

**Lord, take down the barriers of my fear and pride
so that you can continue to shape my life.**

J ohn's father Zechariah was filled with the Holy Spirit, and he spoke God's message: "Let us praise the Lord, the God of Israel! He has come to the help of his people and has set them free. He has provided for us a mighty Saviour....

"You, my child, will be called a prophet of the Most High God. You will go ahead of the Lord to prepare his road for him, to tell his people that they will be saved by having their sins forgiven. Our God is merciful and tender. He will cause the bright dawn of salvation to rise on us and to shine from heaven on all those who live in the dark

shadow of death, to guide our steps into the path of peace."

Luke 1: 67-79

"He will cause
the bright dawn of salvation to rise..."

A new world vision

My thoughts of Christmas are deeply linked with candles and the flickering light of a fire... sitting quietly in a room decorated with a Christmas tree, being with family and friends. Outside it may be snowing and cold but inside there is warmth and light.

Zechariah had a vision of a world where God would give light to all who lived in darkness. We too dream of a different kind of world. But our present world is such a wilderness – there are so many who have no family, who have no food on the table. How can I reach out to share the love and light that I enjoy? Zechariah's words give us the courage to see things in a new way, to hope, to see that change is possible.

**Lord, let my hands, my thoughts and my prayers
help others to enjoy your light and peace.**

A t that time Emperor Augustus ordered a census to be taken throughout the Roman Empire…. Joseph went to the town of Bethlehem in Judea….

There were some shepherds who were spending the night in the fields, taking care of their flocks. An angel of the Lord appeared to them…. They were terribly afraid, but the angel said to them, "Don't be afraid! I am here with good news for you, which will bring great joy to all the people. This very day in David's town your Saviour was born – Christ the Lord! And this is what will prove it to you: you will find a baby wrapped in cloths and lying in a manger."

When the angels went away, the shepherds said to one another, "Let's go to Bethlehem and see this thing that has happened."

Luke 2: 1-16

> "…taking care of their flocks."

Found in the details

There it is: a night like any night, full of details. Who is the emperor? Where must we go to register? For the shepherds too: details, details. Who will take the first watch? The momentous event arrives but… there are all these details. It seems so… commonplace.

On this Christmas Day, so full of details: who will baste the turkey? Who will mash the potatoes? Let me remember this day's tremendous event and be aware of the momentous presence of others in my life and the miracle of each person. Let me sift through the details and see that, in this moment, in this place, we see God's presence in the love we show to one another.

Dear God, help me see you in each person I meet today and treat them with the care they deserve.

An angel of the Lord appeared in a dream to Joseph and said, "Herod will be looking for the child in order to kill him. So get up, take the child and his mother and escape to Egypt, and stay there until I tell you to leave." Joseph got up, took the child and his mother, and left during the night for Egypt....

After Herod died, an angel of the Lord appeared in a dream to Joseph in Egypt and said, "Get up, take the child and his mother, and go back to the land of Israel...." So Joseph got up, took the child and his mother, and went back to Israel....

He was given more instructions in a dream, so he went to the province of Galilee and made his home in a town named Nazareth.

Matthew 2: 13-15, 19-23

"An angel of the Lord appeared in a dream to Joseph..."

Just do it

Am I as obedient as Joseph? Get up, take the infant and his mother and go back! In the face of all that uncertainty, Joseph certainly possessed an awesome faith in God.

Me? I'm paralyzed in the face of the slightest diversion from my daily routine. "But where will we stay? For how long? How much will the trip cost?" I'd have talked to that angel until I was blue in the face before moving an inch!

I seem to be haggling with God these days. Sometimes I need to 'Just do it.' Just say 'Yes' to the voice I know has my best interests at heart. No questions asked, no consequences weighed. Just the free response.

God, give me the grace to hear and heed your will for my life.

We write to you about the Word of life, which has existed from the very beginning. We have heard it, and we have seen it with our eyes; yes, we have seen it, and our hands have touched it. When this life became visible, we saw it; so we speak of it and tell you about the eternal life which was with the Father and was made known to us. What we have seen and heard we announce to you also, so that you will join with us in the fellowship that we have with the Father and with his Son Jesus Christ. We write this in order that our joy may be complete.

I John 1: 1-4

> "When this life became visible, we saw it…"

Word of life

I was thrilled when my brother and his wife asked me to help during the delivery of their first child. Yet it's hard to pinpoint what was so remarkable about being present "when this life became visible."

Was it the tenderness of my brother as he supported his wife in her labour, or was it the calm confidence of the midwives as they coaxed life forward? Was it my sister-in-law's intense concentration, or her exhilaration as she finally held her baby? Indeed, there is a powerful mystery that surrounds the beginning of life.

Jesus' birth is an opportunity to be attentive to the birth of joy in our midst. When I drift into post-Christmas letdown, I will try to remember what it was like to welcome this new child.

Jesus, as I celebrate your birth, I am filled with joy.

After they had left, an angel of the Lord appeared in a dream to Joseph and said, "Herod will be looking for the child in order to kill him. So get up, take the child and his mother and escape to Egypt, and stay there until I tell you to leave." Joseph got up, took the child and his mother, and left during the night for Egypt, where he stayed until Herod died. This was done to make come true what the Lord had said through the prophet, "I called my Son out of Egypt."

When Herod realized that the visitors from the East had tricked him, he was furious. He gave orders to kill all the boys in Bethlehem and its neighbourhood who were two years old and younger.

Matthew 2: 13-18

> "Joseph got up… and left during the night…"

A call in the night

I remember as a small boy occasionally waking up in what seemed to me to be the middle of the night and hearing my Dad downstairs in the kitchen, quietly making his breakfast before leaving for work. I would hear the kettle boiling, drawers opening and closing, soft footsteps.

Sometimes I would peek through my bedroom curtains and wait until I heard the car start and the headlights go on, and I would follow the red lights down the street and out of sight. Then I would get back into bed *feeling strangely peaceful.*

I didn't know it, of course, but, like the quiet and uncomplaining Joseph, my father was also obeying an angel that had told him to get up in the night for his family's sake.

**Lord, help me hear your angel's voice
telling me what I must do to care for others.**

I f we say that we know God, but do not obey his commands, we are liars and there is no truth in us. But if we obey his word, we are the ones whose love for God has really been made perfect. This is how we can be sure that we are in union with God: if we say that we remain in union with God, we should live just as Jesus Christ did....

If we say that we are in the light, yet hate others, we are in the darkness to this very hour. If we love others, we live in the light, and so there is nothing in us that will cause someone else to sin. But if we hate others, we are in the darkness; we walk in it and do not know where we are going, because the darkness has made us blind.

1 John 2: 3-11

> "...the darkness has made us blind."

Let it go

We'd stop for gas at a place in the country. It was owned by an old man, and operated by a young couple. I don't know, maybe they were relatives. The couple worked seven days a week. Gradually, the place changed. They added a café, and seemed to be working well.

One day, the couple was gone. They had, the old man said, wanted more money, a bigger share. He adamantly refused, and they left. He was very angry. Bitter. That'd be the day. He'd show them.

Years later, the place is closed and still for sale. Weeds have grown up around the pumps and café. An old house and an old, bitter man. Blinded by his anger and stubbornness. He showed them.

Let it go.

God, help me let go of my grudges.

There was a very old prophet, a widow named Anna, daughter of Phanuel of the tribe of Asher. She had been married for only seven years and was now eighty-four years old. She never left the Temple; day and night she worshipped God, fasting and praying. That very same hour she arrived and gave thanks to God and spoke about the child to all who were waiting for God to set Jerusalem free.

When Joseph and Mary had finished doing all that was required by the Law of the Lord, they returned to their hometown of Nazareth in Galilee. The child grew and became strong; he was full of wisdom, and God's blessings were upon him.

Luke 2: 36-40

"...and God's blessings were upon him."

The young and the elderly

Anna: a crazy old woman with nothing left but the Temple and pointless rituals? Or a woman filled with the wisdom and insight of God's Spirit? Only the attentiveness developed through a long lifetime of waiting on and listening for God could have led her to this place, and to this moment... to recognize this child as God's Chosen One.

The young Jesus, too, was full of wisdom. Not yet the human wisdom of age and experience, but certainly divine wisdom born of his Oneness with the Spirit.

As I seek to recognize and experience God's love, I too must be attentive to the ways God shares wisdom with me. I must look for wisdom's face in the people around me, particularly the elderly and young children.

God, when I recognize your wisdom in those around me, help me respond like Anna – with praise and thanksgiving.

I n the beginning the Word already existed; the Word was with God, and the Word was God. From the very beginning the Word was with God. Through him God made all things; not one thing in all creation was made without him. The Word was the source of life, and this life brought light to people. The light shines in the darkness, and the darkness has never put it out.

God sent his messenger, a man named John, who came to tell people about the light, so that all should hear the message and believe. He himself was not the light; he came to tell about the light. This was the real light – the light that comes into the world and shines on all people.

John 1: 1-18

"...to tell people about the light..."

God's Word

Like John, I too am called to "tell about the light." But how? First, I must respond to the question: How does my faith make my life different? Second, I must live the *answer.*

Today we experience so many pressures to see as important what really is not – to worship false gods. If I truly live what I believe, I can be, in a concrete way, a point of light, and expose the lies we are told… that the right house, the right basketball shoes, the right clothes are what give meaning to life. God's Word turns our world upside down and challenges the status quo. He shows us there is more to life.

Dear God, help me to be aware of what is really important.

List of Contributors

Tony Adams: 17, 31, 53, 97, 130, 202, 307, 368
Dale C. Balkovec: 88, 148, 186, 206, 355, 372
Mary Bastedo: 29, 54, 75, 92, 167, 185, 232, 239, 302, 309, 318, 340, 343
Rosalee Bender: 158
Rick Benson: 134
Louisa Blair: 49, 99, 100, 117, 133, 152, 160, 217, 228, 243, 251, 270, 282, 288, 296, 329, 344, 365
Kevin Burns: 40, 42, 55, 72, 106, 108, 166, 173, 222, 229, 281, 285, 312, 351, 357
Mike Cooke: 34, 38, 44, 47, 51, 61, 62, 64, 65, 78, 81, 95, 110, 115, 120, 123, 132, 140, 143, 151, 154, 161, 162, 181, 182, 184, 187, 189, 213, 216, 219, 220, 233, 234, 247, 249, 259, 277, 279, 321, 324, 341, 361, 364, 367, 371, 373
Regina Coupar: 22
Jim Creskey: 68, 91, 111, 114, 163, 171, 246, 250, 262, 319
Rebecca Cunningham: 26, 45, 48, 103, 121, 126, 135, 141, 168, 180, 215, 218, 225, 242, 244, 245, 256, 272, 274, 275, 308, 313, 327, 334, 353, 369
Claudette Derdaele: 20
Helga Doermer: 295
Karen Fee: 80, 156
Patrick Gallagher: 21, 23, 33, 41, 43, 52, 63, 93, 112, 139, 145, 150, 175, 196, 204, 209, 210, 224, 240, 241, 258, 264, 267, 271, 287, 290, 317, 325, 336, 345, 360, 363, 370
George Gilliland: 36, 96 .
Barbara Green: 128, 211, 349, 366
Caryl Green: 12, 74, 79, 11, 124, 137, 144, 165, 170, 174, 183, 190, 201, 214, 236, 266, 268, 291, 299, 306, 328, 333, 342, 358
Calvin Halley: 293
Maryanne Hannan: 66, 104, 164, 298
Krystyna Higgins: 198
Michele Howe: 338
Karen Johnson: 261
Phil Kelly: 27, 50, 60, 67, 102, 119, 194, 203, 231, 289, 315, 337
Nancy Keyes: 193, 294
Bertha Madott: 10, 18, 73, 83, 94, 297, 300, 314
Anne Louise Mahoney: 46, 69, 76, 98, 107, 146, 155, 237, 286, 303, 326, 331, 352

Don McClellan: 84

Marguerite McDonald: 16, 59, 109, 122, 129, 179, 208, 255, 280, 284, 292, 348, 362

Jim McSheffrey: 199

RoseMarie Morris: 32, 77, 254, 310, 332

Rosemary O'Hearn: 11, 30, 153, 283, 320, 356

LauraAnn Phillips: 260, 265

Brian Primeau: 14, 37, 39, 70, 90, 127

Michael Reist: 13, 25, 89, 169, 178, 191, 200, 212, 238, 253, 278, 316, 339, 347

Tawny Sinasac: 354

Kathy Shaidle: 311

Jim Taylor: 9, 19, 56, 58, 82, 86, 101, 105, 125, 136, 138, 142, 149, 159, 188, 197, 235, 252, 257, 273, 276, 301, 303, 323, 335, 359

Marie-Louise Ternier-Gommers: 248

Donald Walker: 85, 176, 195, 207, 230, 305, 346

David Weiss: 15, 24, 57, 87, 113, 131, 147, 157, 221, 269, 322, 350

Susie Whelehan: 35, 71, 172, 177, 192, 205, 223, 226

Geoffrey Whitney-Brown: 330

List of Photographers